OUR
MINDS,
OUR
SELVES

OUR MINDS, OUR SELVES

A Brief History of Psychology

Keith Oatley

Princeton University Press

Princeton & Oxford

Published by Princeton University Press,
41 William Street, Princeton, New Jersey 08540

In the United Kingdom: Princeton University Press,
6 Oxford Street, Woodstock, Oxfordshire OX20 1TR

press.princeton.edu

Jacket design by Faceout Studio, Lindy Martin.

Library of Congress Cataloging-in-Publication Data

Names: Oatley, Keith, author.

Title: Our minds, our selves : a brief history of psychology /
Keith Oatley.

Description: Princeton : Princeton University Press, [2018] |
Includes bibliographical references and index.

Identifiers: LCCN 2017033203 | ISBN 9780691175089 (alk. paper)

Subjects: LCSH: Psychology—History.

Classification: LCC BF81 .O24 2018 | DDC 150.9—dc23
LC record available at https://lccn.loc.gov/2017033203

British Library Cataloging-in-Publication Data is available

This book has been composed in Sabon Next LT Pro

Printed on acid-free paper. ∞

Printed in the United States of America

1 3 5 7 9 10 8 6 4 2

TO DAISY, AMBER, EWAN, KAYA,
AND NANCY

CONTENTS

ACKNOWLEDGMENTS

Very many thanks to Jennifer Jenkins, my partner, who has read this book and made wonderfully helpful suggestions that have prompted amendments.

The book started with an invitation from Silvia Langford of Elwin Street. Among others who made suggestions at that stage were Mark Frary, Pippa Crane, Jeremy Stangroom, and Oliver Salzmann. Next, I took over management of the book myself, and Princeton University Press took it on. During this phase, Oliver Salzmann continued to be helpful. I am grateful to the book's editor, Sarah Caro; to her assistant editor, Hannah Paul, of Princeton University Press in Oxford, UK; to Sara Lerner, the book's production editor in Princeton; to Karen Verde, of Green Pelican Editorial Services, who copyedited the manuscript; to two helpful anonymous reviewers; and to my literary agent, Andrew Gordon. I thank, as well, the many others who have taught me, influenced me, and enabled me to think and write about the issues of this book.

PROLOGUE

What is this person thinking? Can we see from her
eyes, or would it take longer to get to know her?

Are there principles of understanding others and ourselves,
principles of how the mind works in our everyday lives, on
which we can reflect?

What is going on in the mind of the person pictured above?
Questions like this are central to psychology. We cannot look
into someone's eyes and see the soul. Instead, we wonder what
kind of person this may be, imagine what she may be thinking
and feeling.[1] If we were to meet her, we might come to understand her more as we enter into conversation with her.

At the end of the twentieth century, Seiji Ogawa discovered the
method of functional Magnetic Brain Imaging (fMRI), which
enables activations in people's brains to be monitored as they
think, perceive, remember, experience emotions. It has been said
that this method began a revolution comparable to that started
by astronomer Nicolaus Copernicus when he proposed that the
Earth revolves around the Sun.[2] On this view, the revolution is

of enabling us to understand some of the brain's bases of experience. In this book we will discuss findings made by brain imaging. But the aim is to go further: to suggest that the revolution is deeper, not just dependent on a new method.

A revolution is taking place in our understanding how the mind works to know the physical and social world. We are beginning now to understand some principles of the mind, not just to know which parts of the brain are active when we do this, or feel that, not just to know how behavior is affected by events, by social processes such as conversation, and by learning, but to reach inner understandings of the minds of others and ourselves.

You may have seen advertisements for ways to improve your memory or powers of thought. Such methods depend on exercises and practice; they are like working out in a gym. Practice is important, and we come to it in chapter 19. But are there principles that enable us to think more deeply about human psychology? The answer is that some principles of this kind have been discovered, though others are only now being glimpsed. Each chapter of *Our Minds, Our Selves* concerns at least one significant principle in our understanding of who we are: not categorical statements, but to reflect upon.

PART ONE

Significant Ideas

1

Conscious and Unconscious

A shadow on a wall, of the kind Plato described in his parable of people in a cave who see such shadows rather than reality.

Though the mind is usually thought of as conscious, there are three kinds of unconscious knowledge. One, proposed by Plato, is that in this world, we are unconscious of eternal truths. Another, proposed by Sigmund Freud, is that aspects of ourselves that are unacceptable have become unconscious but can still affect our perceptions of others and our actions toward them. A third, proposed by Hermann Helmholtz, is probably the most important. It is the principle of unconscious inference: we project inner understandings, implicit theories, to infer what goes on in the physical world, and in the social world of our interactions with others.

Plato's Cave

It is tempting to think that what we see is real. But what if the mind doesn't work by taking in reality? What if our minds depend in part on movements of which we are not conscious? What if some of these movements are not entirely about what's out there, but come from inner processes, in a way that affects what we see and know?

To invite us to think about this, Plato asked us to imagine that we are prisoners chained to a bench in a cave where we have been since childhood. Our necks are fastened so that we can look only straight ahead. In front of us, on a wall, we see people passing back and forth. This, said Plato, is the human condition. We can't turn around to see that behind us is a large fire that is casting shadows of people onto the wall. We think the shadows are reality.

Now suppose that we are freed. We turn around and look at the fire. Now we see actual people as they walk past, and see other prisoners still shackled. Imagine being taken up a steep ascent, out of the cave and into the light. At first we are dazzled, unable to distinguish much, but then we start to see the world as it is.

The Republic, published nearly 2,400 years ago, in which Plato wrote about the cave, was a significant moment in the history of psychology. Are shadows in a cave what we experience of the world?

With his metaphor of the cave, Plato reached a turning point.[1] He suggested that although, in the world, we seem to experience truth in what we see, and seem to know what we are doing, other processes are at work. Plato was suggesting that we don't know some of the most profound things about the world. They can't be seen in the ordinary way.

Plato thought that before we were born we lived on an-other plane, as souls in the realm of ideals. Although—as Plato thought—in our souls we once knew unchanging truths, in our embodied lives we have forgotten them. Now we see only appearances, shadows onto which we project our beliefs, which are sometimes false. Ideals can, however, be drawn out from us by insightful teachers: the word "education" means to "bring out" or "lead forth." In the history of education, the path out of the cave has come to include philosophy and mathematics, and the acquisition of skills of constructing theories and drawing inferences.

Other questions are not about the physical world but, because we humans are social beings, about our understanding of the social world. How do we know what other people are thinking and feeling? We can wonder to what extent other people are similar to us, to what extent they are different. What if we ask them what they think and feel? Might our impression of them derive in part from what they say, and in part from passing shadows on their faces as they make emotional expressions and speak in certain tones of voice? And what about ourselves? We think we know our own thoughts and memories. But do we really know ourselves?

Plato thought the question of how one can know one's own self was even more difficult than ascending from the cave into the light of the physical world. In his time, an injunction was written at the shrine of the Oracle in Delphi: "Know yourself."[2] Plato offers a thought about this in a story of how Socrates was one day walking by a river with his friend, Protagoras, discussing the myths that had been told about the beautiful place where they were. Socrates said it would take a lot of work to understand myths, and that he didn't have time for it, because he said: "I've not yet succeeded in obeying the Delphic injunction to 'know myself.'"

Alfred Whitehead wrote that Western philosophy is "a series of footnotes to Plato."[3] But not everyone agrees. The innovative philosopher Karl Popper rejected some of Plato's main arguments, saying Plato was an enemy of open society. In *The Republic*, Plato's account of the ideal society, he has organized people into three classes: guardians (rulers), auxiliaries (warriors), and artisans (producers). Only the guardians are free.

Although the form in which Plato wrote his philosophy was the dialogue—a fictional mode in which he imagines the long-dead Socrates discussing issues with acquaintances—he wants to ban writers of fiction from society entirely. Is it an oversight that he didn't point out that his idea of shadows in a cave is neither philosophy nor mathematics? It's a story based on a metaphor, the kind of story a fiction writer might offer. In chapter 17 we come to modern findings of how fiction can enable us to deepen our understandings.

How can we know other people? How can we know ourselves? The modern approach to understanding the mind is cognitive science: understanding mind as the making of meaning. "Cognitive" means having to do with knowledge. The mind makes meaning by organizing and working with knowledge, by making inferences, conscious and unconscious, to see, to remember, to converse, to know others and ourselves. In this quest, cognitive psychology and cognitive neuroscience come together with linguistics, cultural anthropology, philosophy, and other areas of research (see Ulric Neisser's *Cognition and Reality*, Howard Gardner's *The Mind's New Science*, Michael Eysenck's *Dictionary of Cognitive Psychology*, Robert Wilson and Frank Keil's *Encyclopedia of the Cognitive Sciences*, and Morton Hunt's *The Story of Psychology*).

Not all our knowledge can be accessed consciously; some of it is unconscious. It's of three kinds, and three methods are involved in reaching it. For Plato, the methods were philosophy and education. In the next section, the means are those of psychotherapy. In the sections following that, they are of psychological research and theory.

The Freudian Unconscious

The most famous kind of unconscious is psychoanalytic, as proposed by Sigmund Freud. The method he chose now seems obvious, but before his time it was not. Then, most often, doctors would observe people who were mentally ill, see that they would often seem strange, and infer that this signified their insanity. The way Freud worked was different. He listened to what people said as they talked about themselves. He called this listening with "evenly suspended attention."

Freud was not the only one in his time to be thinking about the unconscious in relation to mental illness, but he was a detective of the mind who asked: Who are we? At the center of his ideas is the suggestion that we humans are not always conscious of our reasons for doing what we do. His research affected the very texture of thinking about the self. It became, as W. H. Auden said in a poem to commemorate Freud, "a whole climate of opinion." Concepts such as the unconscious, neurosis, inner conflicts, anxiety states, and psychotherapy acquired the meanings they now have largely through his influence.[4]

Sigmund Freud was born in 1856 in a small town called Příbor, which is now in the Czech Republic.[5] A few years later his family moved to Vienna, where Freud spent most of his life. He attended the University of Vienna and qualified as a doctor in 1881. Soon after this he met Martha Bernays, with whom he fell deeply in love. The frustration of the couple's four-year engagement may have contributed to Freud's emphasis on sexuality as a central aspect of mental life. Sigmund and Martha had six children, the youngest of whom, Anna, also became a famous psychoanalyst. In May 1938, Freud, with his family, fled from the Nazis to London, where he lived until his death in September 1939.

Dora's Case

Freud made the case study central to our understanding of human emotional disorders. In his hands it took the form of a detective story; the culprit being sought was a set of intentions that had gone missing from the patients' conscious experience.[6] The most important of Freud's cases was that of Dora. Her real name was Ida Bauer.[7]

It's 1899. Dora is aged eighteen. She is depressed, and has other nervous complaints. Her parents have found a suicide note in her writing desk. Freud describes her as: "in the first bloom of youth, a girl of intelligent and engaging looks." Freud is aged forty-four, hoping at last to make a name for himself. He sees Dora for an hour every weekday.

Freud says that he began treatment by asking Dora "to give [him] the whole story of [her] life and illness." Then he writes, "As a matter of fact the patients are incapable of giving such reports about themselves . . . their communications run dry, leaving gaps unfilled, riddles unanswered." What is left out—the very matters that the psychological detective is seeking—are the patients' desires and intentions. Some of them are unknown to the patients. They are unconscious. It would be their discovery, to fill gaps in their stories, which would free the patients from disabling disorders.

Freud points out that although Dora is vague about herself, she gives a detailed account of an affair her father was having with a family friend, Frau K. At the same time Dora said that her father had encouraged Herr K to take an interest in herself, when she was only fourteen. This enabled Dora's father to pursue his affair with Frau K. Without denying anything she says, Freud asks Dora whether she may also be reproaching herself in the same way that she is reproaching her father. What is her involvement?

This is a psychoanalytic interpretation, a tentative filling-in of a gap left by the patient. For Dora, Freud's interpretation introduces a new development. She admits that Herr K had sent her flowers every day for a year, spent much of his spare time in her company, and that she felt enlivened by the relationship. She had looked after the Ks' children so that her father and Frau K could carry on their affair. She says Herr K even made her a proposal of marriage. Dora utters a crescendo of reproaches against her father. She has ended things with Herr K, and she tells Freud that she had demanded that her father end his affair with Frau K. Nothing enrages her more than her father's insistence that Herr K's proposal was just her imagination.

Then, one day, after three months of therapy, Dora tells Freud that this would be the last time she would see him. Freud asks her how long ago she had decided this. She tells him that it was two weeks. "That sounds just like a maidservant or governess—a fortnight's notice," says Freud.[8] In this leap of intuition, Freud the mind-detective had found the right clue. This interpretation— for that is what it is—would clear up the case.

In response to this interpretation, Dora tells Freud that, on a holiday with the K family, the Ks had a governess who gave a fortnight's notice of leaving. She had confided in Dora that Herr K had made advances and had sex with her. He'd said to the governess that he got nothing out of his wife. Freud says: "These are the very words he used afterwards when he made his proposal to you." He suggests to Dora that the reason she was so incensed was that Herr K was treating her as he had treated the governess, as someone with whom he could have casual sex.

Freud explains to Dora that she had been hoping that Herr K would divorce his wife and marry her. At the same time, her father would be able to marry Frau K. That is why Dora had been outraged at her father thinking the proposal from Herr K had been just her imagination. She had been caught up in her idea of marriage to Herr K. But when the proposal came it was horribly transformed by what the governess had told her.

Freud added that, as he explained this, Dora had "listened to [him] without her usual contradictions.[9] She seemed to be moved." We might reflect that for Dora what had been at issue was not just her sexual desire, but her whole life. Dora felt moved, perhaps because for the first time she felt understood by another person.

With the two weeks' notice that Dora gave to Freud, he inferred that she was both treating him like a governess or maidservant and dumping him in the way she had dumped Herr K. He called this process, of patients feeling and acting toward him in ways they had felt and acted toward people in their day-to-day lives, "transference," attention to which is another distinctive feature of psychoanalytic therapy.

Controversy and Advance

When Freud's theories were mentioned at a congress on neurology and psychiatry in 1910, one professor who was attending it banged "his fist on the table" and said: "This is not a topic for discussion at a scientific meeting; it is a matter for the police."[10] A minor industry has grown up to show how wrong Freud was. Although Freud said that Dora's problems arose from driving her sexuality underground because it was unacceptable to her, Adolf Grünbaum has argued that Freud was never able to show that patients became psychologically ill because they had buried painful events in their unconscious. Some painful events may be lost to us, said Grünbaum, but others stay for decades sharply in our memories, and Freud was never able to say which would be which.

Why is there such antipathy toward Freud? Is it because Freud was merely wrong about certain things?[11] Or is it because he became famous, and even popular? Or is it because his proposals about our inner selves are unacceptable?

Freud had his own anxieties about his approach, and wrote: "it still strikes me myself as strange that the case histories I write should read like short stories and that, as one might say, they lack the serious stamp of science."[12] Freud is teasing us. "No," we're supposed to say. "It really is science, but because we are human beings it has to be different from chemistry or physics."

It's usually easier to see what is wrong with a piece of research or a line of thinking, such as Freud's, than to do it better. Among those who made new advances from Freud's beginnings were Carl Jung with his idea of archetypes and the collective unconscious, which affect everybody and underlie mythologies, and Melanie Klein, who was among the first to observe and analyze young children. Important, too, was Karen Horney. In 1930, she and her three daughters emigrated from Berlin to the United States, and lived in Brooklyn. Rather than accepting Freud's views of the critical function of the sex drive, Horney proposed that among our most pressing aspirations are the need to feel loved and to feel approved of. She developed the idea, too, of reaching understandings that enable us to practice therapy on ourselves.

In *Self-Analysis*, she invites us to imagine we work for a boss, a woman who is attractive and complacently self-admiring, who is arbitrary, who favors others unfairly, who becomes hostile when she senses any critical attitude toward her. Imagine we need the job. More or less consciously we are careful never to criticize, we make sure any good ideas we have are put in a way that enables her to think they're her own. Privately we would resent having to bootlick. With a different boss, we would be different.

Now imagine this person is our mother. Horney describes a patient, Clare, whose mother was like this boss. Clare had a brother who was treated far more affectionately than she was.[13] Her father was no help to her because he admired his wife and focused his attention on her although she openly despised him. Clare was unable to develop self-confidence. She felt she was unlikable, and that everything that went wrong was her fault. It was safer to join the ranks of admirers. She hoped in this way to receive at least a little affection. Because she started this when she was young, unlike what one might do with a boss, she did so more or less unconsciously. In *Self-analysis*, Horney focuses on how Clare dealt with her mother. She takes up the idea of the case history, but appeals to us to develop our own self-awareness and ask whether anything of this kind is recognizable to us. What do we know of the personalities of our parents, and how have we dealt with them? Do we need to feel loved and approved of?

Here, in a modern translation by Daniel Ladinsky, is how the Persian Sufi poet Hafiz put it some 650 years ago, in a poem called "With that moon language."[14]

Admit something:
Everyone you see, you say to them,
    "Love me."

Of course you do not do this out loud,
   otherwise someone would call the cops.
Still, though, think about this,
   this great pull in us to connect.

Psychological Experiments

The case history remains at the center of research on psychother-apy, but when Freud started to write up his cases toward the end of the nineteenth century, other pioneers had been doing psycho-logical research of a different kind, and these would lead to a dif-ferent kind of understanding of the unconscious: an understand-ing that our minds depend on many millions of processes, which enable us to be who we are, but of which in our day-to-day lives we are unaware.

The new kind of psychology is said to have begun in Leipzig where, in 1879, an experiment was conducted in the first psycho-logical laboratory by Wilhelm Wundt. It was to measure reaction time, the interval between an event and a person's response to it. Wundt wrote that, "by varying . . . external influences we arrive at the laws to which the psychic life is subject."[15] Experimental psy-chology came to be founded on two principles: that any psycho-logical measurement must have validity (it must be of something real), and that it must have reliability (it must be observable, and replicable, in a range of people). Comparisons were critical, for instance between people given one kind of external influence (in an experimental group), and others of a different influence (in a control group). Wundt insisted that in this way psychology was a science, like chemistry.

At least from the time of René Descartes, nearly four hundred years ago, the body has been thought of as a kind of machine, of which the brain is a part. Descartes knew the brain had chambers called ventricles that contain fluid. The way the nervous system works, said Descartes, is that when one's foot is burned by a fire,

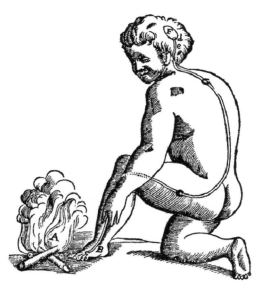

Figure 1. René Descartes's illustration of reflex withdrawal from a painful stimulus. *Source*: Redrawn from Descartes' *Traité de l'homme* and uploaded to WikiMedia Commons: https://commons.wikimedia.org/wiki/File:Descartes-reflex.JPG.

as you may see in figure 1, the nerve cells in the foot pull invisible strings inside the nerves. The other ends of these strings are in the brain, where they open valves to let vital fluids into the nerves that run to the muscles, and inflate these muscles in such a way as to withdraw the foot. This is a reflex. It's still the mechanism that neurophysiologists accept today: a stimulus is picked up by receptors that send a message to the brain where, by a series of switches which are composed of neurons, an appropriate response is selected and produced: stimulus and response. The difference is that we now know the system works not by strings and hydraulics, but by electricity and chemical transmitter substances.

So how fast does a nerve impulse travel? Being electrical, does it travel at something near the speed of light? The answer, discovered by Hermann Helmholtz, was "No." It travels at about 30 meters per second, slower than the speed of sound. Wundt had worked as an assistant to Helmholtz and under the influence of Helmholtz's measurement of the speed of nerve signals, it seems likely that Wundt conceived his experiment on measuring how long it takes to react to an event.

Hermann Helmholtz was born in 1821, in Potsdam, near Berlin.[16] As a child he was sickly and spent a lot of time playing with a large set of children's building blocks, an activity that perhaps helped him develop his imagination. At the age of seventeen, he wanted to study physics. But his father was a high school teacher and not well-off. The young Hermann won a scholarship that paid for him to train at a medical-surgical institute in Berlin in return for working in the army. He went on to serve as an army surgeon for seven years. Somehow during this time he contrived to enjoy a vigorous academic life in Berlin, meeting and working with some of the foremost physicists and physiologists of his day. He published his medical thesis on how nerve cells are connected, and the conceptions he outlined are still those of our modern understanding of brain and mind.[17]

In the late 1850s, Helmholtz underwent a period of personal distress when his father died and not long afterward his wife, Olga, passed as well. This left him with two small children to look after. In 1861, he married Anna von Mohl, who did much to contribute to his life, and with whom he had three more children. Although Helmholtz's contributions to physics, physiology, and psychology were large and far-reaching, he was a modest person. In photographs he looks a bit formal, but people found him kind and trustworthy. His death may have been hastened by injuries to his brain, sustained when he fell down a ship's stairway. The accident happened in 1893, on his return from a visit to the Chicago World's Fair held on the 400th anniversary of Columbus's arrival in the New World. He complained of a lack of energy, and his mind would wander. In the following year he died of a cerebral hemorrhage.

Unconscious Inference

In the third volume of his *Handbook of Physiological Optics*, Helmholtz lays out his proposal of how we see the world. The eyes don't just pick up reality and relay it up the optic nerve into the mind. Helmholtz showed that input to the visual system occurs via an array of receptors in the two-dimensional sheets that are the retinae of our eyes. The task of the mind-brain is to take these two-dimensional arrays of neural excitations, and from them infer three-dimensional visual scenes of people to meet, objects to use, places to go.

Here is one of Helmholtz's verbal images:

A person in a familiar room which is brightly lighted by the sun gets [a perception] that is abundantly accompanied by very vivid sensations. In the same room in the evening twilight he will not be able to recognize any objects except the brighter ones, especially the windows. But what he does actually recognize will be so intermingled with his recollections of the furniture that he can still move about in the room with safety and locate articles he is trying to find, even when they are dimly visible. These images would be utterly insufficient to enable him to recognize the objects without some previous acquaintance with them.[18]

The mind's way of creating visual experience depends on what we now call cues—images or patterns on the retinae—which connect with conscious and unconscious knowledge and expectations, which we then project onto the world.[19] The patterns on our retinae have been focused by the lenses of our eyes onto arrays of receptors that are specialized for being activated by changes of light. They transmit neural impulses to the brain.

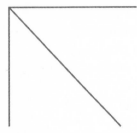

Figure 2. Three lines in a two-dimensional pattern that are a cue to a three-dimensional interpretation of a corner of a boxlike structure. *Source*: Drawn by Keith Oatley.

Look at the two-dimensional pattern shown in figure 2. The pattern of this figure on the retina can be thought of as a cue that connects with what we know innately or from learning. From this inner knowledge, we draw a conclusion from it about a box-like structure that might be there, and project this conclusion onto the world.

A modern version of Plato's shadows in the cave is film.[20] *The Great Train Robbery*, first shown in 1903, is regarded as the earliest film to use modern editing techniques. Its first scene shows two masked robbers with guns forcing a telegrapher to send a message to stop a train. The second scene shows the robbers hiding behind a water tower as the train stops. In the third scene, the robbers kill the train's mail messenger. The scenes were shot separately, in a studio and on location. We see a sequence of enacted scenes edited together and onto them we project events of a story. When we watch the film, there are no robbers and no train: all that happens is that light flickers on a screen. Films and videos depend on the same kinds of processes by which patterns on the retinae enable us to see the world, because some of these processes in life and in movies are the same.

Hippolyte Taine, a French sociologist and art critic, wrote in 1882: "So our ordinary perception is an inward dream, which happens to correspond to things outside; and, instead of saying that a hallucination is a perception that is false, we must say that perception is *a hallucination that is of the truth.*"²¹ Had Taine written this forty years later, he might have added, "*and in film a hallucination that is of the story.*"

One kind of cue, in the ordinary world and in a movie, occurs when, at a spot on the retina, a sudden change of light intensity is registered by the receptors. This change is a cue that there's been a movement. It also draws attention, and directs our eyes toward that place. The eyes move to fixate on it so that the image of the moving object is at the center of our vision.

Figure 3. A cartoon which, despite its simplicity, is recognizable as a human face. *Source*: Drawn by Keith Oatley.

For a different kind of cue, consider an image of the kind you see in figure 3, which contains two dots that are not too far apart, with small semi-circles above each, and below them another small semi-circle, with this pattern surrounded by a circular line. It's a cue to a human face: eyes, mouth, shape of a head. The fact that a cartoon can be so simple implies this pattern is significant for us. We project on to the pattern our knowledge of human faces.

Have a look, too, at figure 4, the Fraser Spiral, to see the effect of cues other than those that suggest a box or a human face. In each case a two-dimensional pattern, or cue, is picked up. In the mind-brain, each cue selects some inner knowledge of what might have given rise to it in the world: something significant, perhaps important.

Figure 4. Frazser Spiral. Hermann Helmholtz proposed that a visual illusion shows us that the way in which we see the ordinary world and the way in which we see an illusion must share a common mechanism, and the illusion points us toward it. In this illusion, invented by James Fraser in 1908, we see a set of spirals. But if you trace each one around with the tip of a pencil, you discover the curved lines are not spirals but circles. The reason we see spirals is that the cues are line segments at an angle to the circumference of the circles. It is these line segments that invite us to project onto the image an understanding of spirals. *Source*: Fraser, J. (1908). A new visual illusion of direction. *British Journal of Psychology*, 2, 307–320. Image author, Mysid https://commons.wikimedia.org/wiki/File:Fraser_spiral.svg.

From Patterns and Cues to Perception

The brain uses visual cues to select mental structures that are then adjusted for size and orientation and manipulated in other ways, and then projected onto the world as conclusions: spatial layouts of things that we see. One could even say that Plato had it almost right with his metaphor of shadows in the cave. It's not quite shadows that we receive on the receptors of our retinae, but it's something like shadows, flickering two-dimensional patterns.

Here's how the whole process works. If you hold a coin the size of an American quarter or a euro at arm's length, the size of that coin is about the area of the visual scene that can be seen in any detail. About 50 percent of the optic nerve and 50 percent of the visual cortex (the part of the brain that is devoted to analyzing visual input) is devoted to information from that small two-dimensional patch. The whole of the rest of the visual field is available only very vaguely. What happens is that we move our eyes to fixate on a patch of this size in the visual field, and during the fraction of a second when the eyes are steady—a fixation—a neural pattern from receptors in the retinae at the fixation point travels up the optic nerve: a small sample. Then the eyes move to pick up another small sample. If you look carefully you can see other people's eyes flicking from place to place. These movements occur two to four times a second; in each waking day we make some 200,000 of them.[22] If, during an eye movement, a new event happens a bit off to one side, we can't notice it. Our eyes don't receive input during eye movements.

How different, then, is this detailed process of picking up visual information in these tiny samples from the seamless and steady sense of the world out there that we experience. If Plato's image of the people in the cave seemed far-fetched, what actually happens is even more remarkable.

We don't consciously experience our eye movements. We don't consciously experience the eye-brain's sampling of the visual field. We make constructions, by what Helmholtz called "unconscious inferences." We are conscious only of the conclusions of such inferences. The brain-mind takes small samples, is sensitive to patterns we call *cues*, and connects them with our inner knowledge, to construct three-dimensional visual scenes that we see.

The psychological principle is that we don't see directly, but rather by picking up cues that guide our understandings, which we then project onto the world. We see our world in terms of how we can act in it. It's useful to us to see it as laid out in space so that we can move in it, and to see it as containing objects we can use, and people to meet. Our species is very social, and we are particularly good at seeing and recognizing other people. So it's in these terms that our visual conclusions are presented to us in our minds: the world as we find it.

Not everyone has been convinced of Helmholtz's theory of unconscious inference. For some, perception involves a more or less direct mapping of the kind Descartes described. A pattern in the world, a stimulus, elicits a pattern of motor action, a response. For instance, in 1960, Eleanor Gibson and Richard Walk found that human infants crawling toward a visual cliff—a visually salient drop in the ground in front of them, as occurs for instance at the top of a set of stairs—would stop and draw back from it. The pattern of the cliff was what Eleanor's husband, James, called an "affordance": a visual stimulus for a response of a certain kind.[23] In chapter 5 we explore whether the mind-brain may work by this kind of direct stimulus-to-response mapping.

The kind of explanation of how we see, offered by Helmholtz and by Gibson, can be thought of in terms of process, of how visual perception derives from ongoing activities in our minds and brains. Another kind of explanation, that we come to in chapter 3 on evolution, is principally in terms of structure; in this case of how genes derived from our evolution give structure to our brains. As we go along in this book, you will see that process and structure interact. Often for a particular issue the one is taken as primary and the other as secondary.

In general, the path out of the cave isn't by way of philosophy and mathematics. The path of psychology suggests that the important kind of unconscious is less about unchanging truths of the physical world, more about truths we can discover, and reflect upon, of the worlds we know as human beings.

Since we humans are so social, one of our most fundamental kinds of knowledge is that of others, and of ourselves with others. To know what another person is feeling and intending, we may have intuitions. To sense the effect we may have on another person, again we may have intuitions. If we follow Helmholtz, our intuitions derive from unconscious inferences and, of course, we may also make inferences consciously: "She said this, which implies that." Inferences can be uncertain. One way forward is to discuss things with the other person, in conversation, which we address in chapters 6 and 14.

2

The Sad Case of Phineas Gage

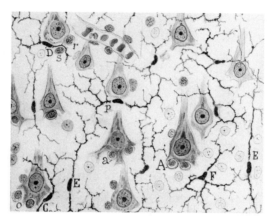

Santiago Ramón y Cajal's drawing of cells in the cerebral cortex. The smaller cells with long extensions, for instance labeled "E" and "F," are neurons, and the larger cells, for instance labeled "A," are glial cells which support the neurons metabolically and help brain function.

The largest part of the human brain is the outer area, the cortex. In 1848, Phineas Gage suffered an injury that changed his life. Part of his cortex was destroyed. Hanna Damasio made a computer reconstruction of Gage's skull, to find that damage was mostly to his frontal lobes. Her husband, Antonio Damasio, found that modern people with the same damage were impaired in their interactions with others. Among newer technologies of brain research is functional Magnetic Resonance Imaging (fMRI), which enables activities of brain areas to be monitored as people have different kinds of experience.

Parts and Connections in the Brain

Of all the subjects of scientific research—the subatomic structure of the universe, the evolution of plant and animal species, the biochemical processes of the body's cells—understanding the mind seems the most challenging. Mind can be thought of as the functioning of the human brain. The figure at the opening of this chapter shows some shapes of the brain's neurons (nerve cells) and glia, which are cells that support them. This image was drawn in 1920 by Santiago Ramón y Cajal.

In an interview for the *Guardian* newspaper, Suzana Herculano-Houzel said that although 100 billion had been assumed to be the number of neurons in the human brain, a recent count has shown that the number is about 86 billion.[1] Herculano-Houzel and her colleagues looked hard in four brains, but just couldn't find the other 14 billion. Even so, 86 billion are a lot: twelve times as many as the number of people in the world. Herculano-Houzel has argued that the brain can have so many neurons, more than any other primate, because neurons use a great deal of energy, and were able to become numerous by means of the invention, 1.5 million years ago, of . . . cooking. This allowed humans to eat foods with more calories than were available to our primate cousins.

In terms of the organization of the brain, three levels of structure are recognized. The level of smallest detail is that of the interiors and membranes of neurons, which transmit signals along their extended parts, called axons, by electrical properties of their membranes. Then, when a message is passed from one neuron to another, this happens not electrically but chemically. Small quantities of chemicals called transmitter substances are released. They cross the tiny gap, called a synapse, to affect the receiving neuron.

At the next level of brain organization are neurons themselves, and connections among them. At these connections a neuron can tend to be activated or to be inhibited, so the synaptic connections are switches of a kind. It's thought that each human brain-neuron's average number of connections with other neurons is about 7,000. So that makes the potential number of switches in the brain something of the order of 86 billion multiplied by 7,000. It is perhaps not surprising therefore that many scientists have made the analogy between the brain and a supercomputer. The brain uses many chemicals that affect neural activations, and they are unevenly distributed among the brain's systems. Nearly all drugs that affect the brain—from alcohol, which has long been used to decrease anxiety, to the newest sleeping pills—work by changing the effects of particular chemicals, or groups of chemicals, on receiving neurons, that is to say they work on the connections.

At the level of anatomy that one can see without a microscope, the human brain has three main regions. The inmost region includes the brain stem and cerebellum. The brain stem is joined to the spinal cord. It receives signals from receptors and sends signals to activate muscles. It's responsible for automatic functions such as breathing, and alertness. The cerebellum is concerned with the orchestration of movement. A middle region consists of areas that include the thalamus, thought to be a relay station for sensory signals; the amygdala, which is concerned with emotions; and the hippocampus, which has functions that include memory and understanding spatial layouts. By far the largest part of the human brain is the outer layer of the brain's hemispheres: the cortex. At the rear of the cortex are areas concerned with vision. Above the ears are areas concerned with bodily sensation and the making of movements. At the front, above the eyes, are areas that are especially well developed in humans, the frontal lobes.

To find out how it all works may seem impossible, but there has been progress. How has it happened? Through a combination of psychology and neuroscience. An important step occurred in the middle of the nineteenth century when our understanding of neurology was given a jolt by effects of an accident that destroyed part of a person's brain. The part was the front region of the cortex. The person was Phineas Gage.

A Railway Accident

The nineteenth century saw the coming of steam engines and trains. Rail construction was intense. Near the town of Cavendish, in Vermont, a group of men worked on a stretch of the Rutland and Burlington Railroad. The men were led by their capable and likeable foreman, Phineas Gage.

To make way for train tracks, rocky outcrops had to be cleared, and this was done by blasting them with gunpowder. A hole would be drilled in a rock and filled with gunpowder. Then a fuse would be inserted. The workers would retreat to a safe distance and an explosion would be set off. At about half past four in the afternoon of September 13, 1848, a rock had been drilled, and Gage had poured gunpowder into it. He rammed it in tight with an iron tamping rod which was three feet, seven inches long, and an inch-and-a-quarter in diameter. As he rammed in the powder, the rod must have set off a spark, because there was an explosion. The tamping rod entered Gage's left cheek, pointed end first, and left through the top of his head. It landed a fair distance away, smeared with brain and blood.

Gage was thrown to the ground. His men, "with whom he was a great favorite," said his limbs convulsed a bit, but a few minutes later he was able to speak. They took him by oxcart to a hotel in Cavendish, where a local doctor, John Harlow, was summoned. Harlow helped Gage to an upstairs room, laid him on a bed, dressed his wounds, and subsequently wrote up Gage's case.

John Harlow provides us with a turning point in our understanding of ourselves.[2] He came from a farming family in upstate New York, near the border with Vermont. He trained in medicine at Jefferson Medical College in Philadelphia. He was twenty-six years old in 1846, when he started his practice in Cavendish, a community of some 1,300 people. His treatment of Gage, two years later, included the draining of an abscess, and also the letting of 16 ounces of blood, as he believed this would reduce inflammation. Other than that, his treatment was conservative. He wrote: "little if anything was done to retard the progress of the case, or to interfere with the natural recuperative powers. Nature is certainly greater than art," and, he said, on the fifty-sixth day after his accident Gage was walking the streets again.[3]

Gage's injury was terrible, and in those days before antibiotics, the wound became infected. But Gage recovered. That is to say his body recovered, but something strange had happened to his mind. Whereas previously he had been even-tempered and friendly, he was now impatient and easily angered. People who knew him said he was "no longer Gage." In his account of the case, Harlow wrote:

> He is fitful, irreverent . . . manifesting but little deference for his fellows, impatient of restraint or advice when it conflicts with his desires, at times pertinaciously obstinate, yet capricious and vacillating, devising many plans of future operation, which are no sooner arranged than they are abandoned.[4]

In the sentences that follow Harlow wrote, "he has the animal passions of a strong man," and "[t]he equilibrium or balance, so to speak, between his intellectual faculties and his animal propensities, seems to have been destroyed."

Although Phineas Gage had previously been the railway construction company's "most efficient and capable foreman," he was no longer capable of doing his former job. He kept the iron tamping rod, and he exhibited himself along with this rod at Barnum's Circus. Later, he worked with horses for eight years in Chile, and then in 1860, with his health failing, he returned to the United States, to San Francisco where his mother and sister

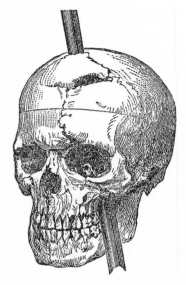

Figure 5. Image from John Harlow's paper showing Phineas Gage's skull, and the tamping iron that had passed through it. *Source*: Harlow, J. (1869). Recovery from the passage of an iron bar through the head. Boston: David Clapp and Son, p. 21, figure 2.

lived. He tried several jobs there, but found something wrong with all of them. In 1861, he died, after suffering several days of convulsions.

Five years later, John Harlow heard about Gage's death, and persuaded the family to allow his body to be exhumed. Harlow read his paper to the Massachusetts Medical Society on June 3, 1868. He said that Gage's family "waiving all claims of personal and private affection ... have cheerfully placed this skull (which I now show you) in my hands, for the benefit of science." In figure 5 you can a see a picture of Gage's skull, with the tamping iron that passed through it.

Our knowledge of Gage comes from Harlow's published account. Although Harlow described himself as "an obscure country physician," this was undue self-deprecation.[5] His skill helped Gage survive. His paper on the brain injury and its psychological effects came at an important moment. Word of it spread, and it became critical to our understanding of the brain's effects on the mind, on emotions, and on personality.

If the brain is damaged, serious consequences occur. Many people will have observed sudden changes of personality that have occurred to a friend or relative who has had a stroke. Sometimes such changes come about slowly, as happens with Alzheimer's disease. The case of Phineas Gage was distinctive in that both the brain damage and its effects were sudden and well-marked. A change occurred to the emotional structure of Gage's way of being in himself and with others as a result of damage to a specific part of the brain.

Modern Phineas Gages

When Gage died, no autopsy was performed. It had been thought from the position of the holes in Gage's skull that the main damage to his brain would have been in the region behind the forehead: the frontal lobes. In 1994, Gage's fame was renewed when Hanna Damasio and colleagues made a computer reconstruction of the damage. In the same year Damasio's husband, Antonio, wrote a best-selling book, *Descartes' Error*, about the personality changes that occurred in some of his patients who had suffered damage to these same areas of the brain. He called these people "modern Phineas Gages."

Harlow had discerned some of the changes that had occurred to the original Gage. By making comparisons with people whose brains were undamaged, Antonio Damasio was able to crystallize what had gone wrong for his modern Phineas Gages. He found that they had not lost their intelligence but that they showed two problems that were connected. They had difficulties in making everyday plans and, in conjunction with this, they suffered from disorders of their emotional lives. This was surprising. We tend to think that making plans requires mere logic: if we want to do this, we must first do this, then that, then something else.

Damasio suggested that planning in everyday life is not pure logic, but is centered on the emotions.

Damasio called one of his patients Eliot, and wrote a case history. Eliot had previously been happily married and had worked professionally in a business. He had lost parts of the frontal region of his brain when a tumor had to be operated on. The operation was a success, but Eliot was no longer able to work properly. He couldn't carry out everyday plans. He needed to be prompted to go to work, his attention was easily distracted by matters that were irrelevant to what he was supposed to be doing, and he lost sight of important goals. He would spend huge amounts of time vacillating about matters of no importance. He was fired from his position. He pursued several new business schemes. One was with a person whom his friends warned him against; it ended in failure. Eliot lost all his money and went bankrupt. His wife divorced him. He married again, someone of whom his family and friends disapproved. He divorced again.

Here is a way to imagine this. Suppose you are on the subway in a big city. A man sits next to you. Before a couple of subway stops have passed, this conversation starts:

"Are your life savings important to you?" he says.
"Of course," you say.
"Have you got fifty thousand dollars?'
"I'm not sure."
"I can double it for you."
"How do you mean?"
"I've started a new business, on the Internet. In six months I can turn your fifty thousand into a hundred thousand."
"What sort of business?"
"You need not worry about that. You can trust me."

Although it would be a nuisance to wait for the next train, many of us might say: "Sorry, this is my stop. Nice to meet you."

We would not trust someone we did not know who made such promises. We might worry that this man could suddenly become threatening. We might have an immediate intuition that we had better avoid this person.

Damasio's Eliot, and other modern Phineas Gages, no longer had this kind of intuition. They did not know whom to trust. Damasio devised a task in which he found that people who had damage to their frontal lobes took large risks that normal people avoid. Because their emotions did not work properly, they were unable to make sensible plans.

Damasio suggests that the main explanation for this effect is that ordinarily in our interactions with others we are affected by what have come to be called conditioned emotional responses, in which, when there is a signal of danger, or when we sense that something in the world isn't right, we become anxious and take avoiding action. This is part of our emotional guidance system. For Eliot and other modern Phineas Gages this was no longer working.

Damasio recounts how this was not the only thing that had gone wrong with Eliot. Although his intelligence and memory were good, other aspects of his emotions seemed no longer to function normally. He seemed to have no conception of the tragedy that had overtaken him. If he talked about his operation, or about losing his job, or his wife divorcing him, he would recount the events without expressing any hurt, sadness, or disappointment. When Damasio showed him pictures of burning buildings or of people injured in accidents, he had no reaction. He felt neither positively nor negatively toward them. He told Damasio that since his operation, he was no longer moved by events that previously would have caused strong emotions. It's clear that different kinds of emotional effect can occur from brain damage. Whereas Phineas Gage had been irritable, Eliot was calm. For both, however, emotional relationships stopped working properly. An older way of thinking about this was that emotions arise in lower parts of the brain and are inhibited by higher parts such as the cortex.[6] More likely to be correct is a modern view, of the kind for which Damasio is arguing. It is that emotions are to be thought of as the center of who we are and of how we relate to each other.

In describing an interaction with another patient with frontal lobe damage, Damasio recounts how he had suggested two possible dates for the patient's next visit. Then, he writes: "For the better part of half an hour the patient enumerated reasons for and against each of the two dates." Damasio says he found it difficult to avoid pounding on the table and telling him to stop. In the end he told the patient quietly that he should come on the second of the dates. "That's fine," said the patient. When those of us whose emotional systems are working properly have to make decisions of this kind we can say, "It's all the same to me, let's say the Tuesday." It's unimportant. But without properly functioning emotions, one may not know what is important and what is not.

Tim Shallice and Paul Burgess studied patients who suffered brain damage, and they have done research on how the carrying-out of plans is affected. To three such patients whose intellectual capacities were normal, they gave shopping lists and some money and asked them to go to a shopping center near their hospital, to buy the things on this list, and to find out some information. As compared with eleven people who did not have brain damage who undertook the same task, the three patients made four times more errors and two of the three got into social problems. One had a shopkeeper run after him when he took a copy of the previous day's newspaper without paying for it. He thought that if it were yesterday's, it was free. The other got into a heated argument with a shop assistant.

The patients we've discussed in this chapter are unusual. They suffered damage to discrete areas of their brains. What about changes of a far more common kind that occur to people who, perhaps toward the ends of their lives, become demented from widespread vascular damage, from Alzheimer's disease, or from Parkinsonism?

Studies of the Brain

It's more than a century-and-a-half since John Harlow published his paper on how the damage to the brain of Phineas Gage affected his emotions and personality. We no longer rely on effects of accidents to understand the brain's contribution to the mind.

The anatomy of the brain at different levels has been studied, as have the effects of lesions such as that sustained by Phineas Gage. To this evidence has been added the effects of stimulating the brain electrically or with chemicals, as well as of electrical recording of nerve impulses from single neurons, and of summed neural activity in whole brain areas. Among recent methods of recording are computerized brain scans, the most popular of which is functional Magnetic Resonance Imaging (fMRI). It depends on monitoring the rate at which oxygen from the blood is absorbed into brain tissues in particular regions; it shows when neurons in these regions are active. By means of computer reconstructions, detailed images of the brain show areas that are activated during some particular task, or in certain circumstances, in contrast with those that are inactive. We discuss studies of such brain activations in chapter 11.

Studies that use neuro-imaging, and other brain-based methods, are appealing in psychology because they can seem to have more substance than the usual kinds of psychological measurement, which rely on people's reports on their experience, or mere observations of behavior.[7] Some people think, therefore, that it's to brain science rather than to psychology that we should look to understand the mind. But imagine that you are a member of a technologically advanced alien species and have managed to acquire a consignment of one hundred mobile phones from planet Earth. You know nothing about humans. You only have these objects, and you can study them in the four ways in which researchers study the brain: anatomy, lesions, stimulation, recording. What would you be able to discover about these objects? You might find that the devices work by electricity, perhaps even that they could send and receive radio waves. But without knowing what such objects were used for in society, or what concepts of a functional kind were relevant, would not your task, perhaps, be hopeless? In an equivalent way, would not brain science be empty without psychological understandings of the mind and of how the mind makes meaning?

Descartes said, "I think therefore I am." Damasio says he was in error, that it's not in our ability to think, but in our emotions and our connections with other people that we are ourselves. Jaak Panksepp continued this line of thought and has written that what Descartes should have said is, "I feel therefore I am."[8] It was in their emotions and ability to make interpersonal arrangements that Phineas Gage and modern Phineas Gages had lost themselves.

We depend on friends and acquaintances being predictable to themselves and to others, on them being sensible. And despite the influence of unconscious processes, we depend on them being essentially capable of choosing their actions and interactions. What happens when damage or deterioration occurs in the brain? Are these people still the same as those we knew, the same as those on whom we once perhaps depended? Are they still themselves?

Stephanie Preston, with Hanna and Antonio Damasio, and other colleagues, used brain imaging in a study of people when they thought about stories of others.[9] When participants could relate to the circumstances of another person they exhibited, in themselves, patterns of brain activation and physiological states that were equivalent to those that occurred when they imagined themselves to be in that situation. As they sought to understand the person, they experienced empathy. When they could not relate to the other person's story, their brain activations and physiological responses decreased. These results appear to reflect differences in people's ability to experience empathy, an emotional state. It's to the psychology of emotions that we now turn.

3

Understanding Our Ancestors, Understanding Our Emotions

Charles Darwin at the age of 31, portrait by George Richmond.

Charles Darwin proposed his theory of evolution based on three principles: "Superabundance" (production of more offspring than necessary for mere replacement), "Variation," and "Natural Selection." He also founded the psychology of emotions. Paul Ekman continued Darwin's investigation of emotional expressions and proposed that some emotions, which include happiness, sadness, anger, and fear, have distinct expressions and are human universals that derive from evolution. Although this proposal has become controversial, emotions are now central to psychology. They occur usually when an event in the world affects an inner concern. They involve the mind, physiological changes, and actions.

Charles Darwin

Charles Darwin was the founder of modern biology, and one of the founders of modern psychology. *On the Origin of Species*, in which Darwin presented his theory that human beings have evolved from other animals, has influenced psychology profoundly and has pervaded the way we think about ourselves.

At the age of sixteen, Charles was sent as a medical student to Edinburgh University but often, instead of going to classes, he would go out to study invertebrate creatures along the shores of the Firth of Forth.[1] In despair at the failure of his son's medical studies, Charles's father sent him to Cambridge where he obtained a BA in theology. He seemed destined for life as a country parson, with a hobby of collecting beetles. At Cambridge, however, he attracted the attention of scientists for his work in natural history. Perhaps most important, he became close to Adam Sedgwick, a clergyman who was professor of geology, and to John Henslow, also a clergyman, and professor of botany. It was Henslow who recommended Darwin be appointed naturalist on the British navy ship *HMS Beagle*, which set out on a voyage that would take nearly five years, to chart coastlines in South America. The *Beagle* returned to England in 1836, and a year later Darwin published his first book, *The Voyage of the Beagle*, presenting scientific observations he had made during the voyage, on geology, on living species of animals and plants, and on fossils. In 1839 he married his cousin, Emma Wedgwood, and at the opening of this chapter you can see a portrait of him that was painted shortly after this. The relationship was a long and companionable one. It resulted in a happy family with many children.

During his voyage aboard the *Beagle*, Darwin was looking to see whether the earth had changed during geological time, and whether—if it had—species were not fixed but had to change to fit the new environments that came into being. He found that new environments had indeed been formed. Coral reefs, for instance, were created by microorganisms after the Earth's creation, and new species had come into existence to fit these new niches.

Darwin's notebooks show that after his return from the voyage on the *Beagle*, he was working avidly through his observations.[2] One set of notes, which he called "Transmutation," would lead him to his theory of evolution by natural selection. Darwin's theory had three components. The first he called "Superabundance." Members of each species produce more offspring than are needed merely to replace themselves. The second he called "Variation." Members of each species produce offspring that differ from each other, with variations of anatomy and ways of behaving being passed on to the next generation by heredity. The third and most famous principle was "Selection." Offspring that had variations that fitted them most closely to their environment were selected. They survived and reproduced, to pass on some of their variations to their progeny. Those with different variations, which were less adapted to their environment, did not survive.

In *Darwin's Dangerous Idea*, Daniel Dennett wrote that this is the best single idea that anyone has ever had. In psychology Darwin's theory affects how we think. Much of our psychology derives from our animal inheritance. It isn't just that we share with our nearest animal relatives, the chimpanzees and bonobos, anatomical features such as eyes, ears, and fingers. Psychological features such as the way in which we protect our infant offspring from harm also derive from our animal heritage.

Darwin had conceived his theory of evolution by natural selection by 1838, but although he wrote private essays on it in 1842 and 1844, he didn't think himself sufficiently qualified as a biologist to publish it. Partly to improve himself in this regard, he spent eight years studying barnacles. He did not publish *On the Origin of Species* until 1859, more than twenty years after he conceived his theory.

A year later, when she heard of Darwin's theory of evolution, the wife of the bishop of Worcester is said to have remarked, "My dear, descended from the apes! Let us hope it is not true, but if it is, let us pray that it does not become generally known."[3] It did become known. We humans were not created specially and distinctly. We are descended from apelike ancestors.

Darwin and his wife Emma were devoted parents. They were devastated when their eldest daughter, Annie, died at the age of ten. Darwin's theory of evolution had not challenged his Christian faith, but this event did so.

Darwin was not just modest. He was anxious in public. His father had left him enough money to live on; even so, he worked almost every day . . . at home. Family life, in Downe Village, in Kent, was affectionate. The Darwins' son Francis remembers the tenderness his father showed his mother.[4] Although he didn't like going out, from time to time Darwin would stay at health spas to try and cure his many health problems that included anxiety and gastric symptoms, which he worried that he would pass by heredity to his children.

Darwin on Expression of Emotions

At the same time that Darwin was writing notes on "Transmutation" with equal fervor, he was writing a second set of notes that he called "Mind and Materialism." These would form the basis of

Figure 6. Photograph of a young woman smiling, from Charles Darwin's *Expression of the Emotions*. *Source*: Chapter VIII of Darwin, C. (1872). *The expression of the emotions in man and animals* (second edition, of 1889). London: Murray; image from book, photo taken by Keith Oatley.

his 1872 book, *The Expression of the Emotions in Man and Animals*, the first substantial scientific study of emotions. It was based on observations of both animals and people. When he lived in London, he made many visits to the newly established London Zoo, at that time open only to scientists for purposes of research.

Darwin's book on emotions was one of the earliest to use photography for scientific purposes. He had photographs taken of people expressing emotions naturally, such as you see in figure 6, and also of actors expressing emotions on request. Darwin was also one of the first to use the psychological method of questionnaires. He had a set of questions printed and sent to missionaries, government officials, scientists, and others in different parts of the world, in which he asked for observations of facial expressions in different societies, especially among people who had not associated much with Europeans. In the journal *Mind,* in 1877, he also made one of the first contributions to developmental psychology, with detailed observations of the emotional and cognitive development he had made of his son William, as an infant.

Darwin's book on expression was a kind of sequel to *On the Origin of Species.* He argued that if we are descended from animals that were not yet human, the study of emotional expressions could contribute to the evolutionary idea. He said that "some expressions, such as the bristling of the hair under the influence of extreme terror, or the uncovering of the teeth under that of furious rage, can hardly be understood, except under the belief that man once existed in a much lower and animal-like condition."[5]

Although we are descended from them, human beings are distinctively different from other animals. So, despite biologically almost inconsequential differences such as skin color or facial shape, we humans are very similar to each other psychologically. Some characteristics that are distinctively human are those we hold most dear. The ability to use language to communicate, the extended love of parents for their children and of people for their sexual partners, the capacity to cooperate with others in tasks that we cannot do alone, the ability to create and improve technologies and to make art, the ability to create societies and cultures. All these have been bequeathed to us by evolution. None of them is characteristic of species other than ours.

In modern times, among the best-known writers on evolution has been Richard Dawkins. In *The Selfish Gene*, he argues that every gene is selfish because its purpose is to make copies of itself. In this respect, all plants and animals, including ourselves, are merely the vehicles of genes. It makes sense for parents and offspring, and other close relations, to help each other (unselfishly) because they pass on copies of the same genes. In his book, Dawkins also introduces the idea of the meme, a cultural version of a gene, which transmits itself by being part of a belief system.

Emotions as Human Universals

Faculties shared by humans, but not other animals, are human universals.[6] The implication is that these have evolved since the time 6–10 million years ago when progenitors of both chimpanzees and humans lived in African forests. Some such universals would have been firmly established by the time modern humans emerged, some 300,000 years ago: distinctive human characteristics that are passed on, programmed by our genes into our brains.[7]

From his own observations, and from the results of the questionnaires he sent to observers in different parts of the world, Darwin concluded that "the same state of mind [a specific emotion] is expressed throughout the world with remarkable uniformity."[8] The idea is an important one. Could it perhaps be responsible for us being able to communicate as well as we do with others across boundaries of nationality?

The researcher best known for taking up Darwin's idea of universal emotions has been Paul Ekman. The study by which he became influential was conducted with Richard Sorenson and Wallace Friesen. From more than 3,000 photographs, they selected thirty white male and female faces, which expressed what they thought were six pure basic emotions: happiness, fear, disgust-contempt, anger, surprise, and sadness. They showed these photographs to people from the literate societies of the United States, Brazil, and Japan, and from two preliterate societies in New Guinea and Borneo. For each photo, participants were asked to choose one from a list of six names (for the six basic emotions). For the preliterate samples, the names of the emotions were spoken in the observers' native language, or another language with which they were familiar. For the literate participants, responses were between 97 percent and 63 percent as predicted across all six emotions, with people performing best with smiles, which they said indicated happiness. Among the preliterate participants, again smiles were the easiest: between 99 percent and 82 percent of these observers also labeled smiles as expressions of happiness. Preliterate participants were, however, less good than literate ones at labeling the other emotions as the researchers expected, although their scores were above chance levels.

From results of this kind, Ekman has argued for six basic emotions, each signaled by a facial expression that is universal.[9] Whereas some researchers have accepted this hypothesis, others have been skeptical. They have pointed out, for instance, that cross-cultural recognition of some expressions is not very good, and that alternative hypotheses about recognition of expressions across different cultures are plausible.

Ekman developed a theory proposed by his mentor, Sylvan Tomkins. It is that a human emotion is based on a program that is wired into the brain, and derived from evolution in a way that, among other things, produces distinct facial expressions. Ekman says emotions are "unbidden," meaning you cannot will them to occur; they are triggered automatically by events.[10] Each one, he asserts, includes a distinctive physiological change plus a distinctive pattern of muscular movements of the face in a recognizable display.

Physiology and expression were starting points for the famous theory of emotion proposed by William James. In 1884 he argued that the emotions that we feel are literally what we feel: our inner sense of physiological changes, along with inner perceptions of the bodily changes that Darwin called expressions. An emotion is the feeling of the tension, of tears, of running from a danger. If we subtract the sensation of such changes, said James, no emotion remains. The physiological changes that Ekman measured during emotions can be seen as contributing to James's theory.

Ekman developed the Facial Action Coding System (FACS) for recognizing emotions from live facial expressions, from still photographs, or from movies, based on the muscles involved in making the expressions.[11] Someone who has trained in this coding system is able to recognize what emotions a person is expressing. A smile, expressing happiness, for instance, involves contraction of muscles at the side of the mouth, and also muscles that crinkle the sides of the eyes. If a smile includes a curved mouth but lacks contractions of muscles around the sides of the eyes, which are not under voluntary control, the smile is likely to have been put on, not spontaneous. There are now computer systems that recognize expressions from photographs and video recordings, and do as well as people trained in expression coding.[12] This will benefit research and will enable people's faces to be monitored by tiny cameras as they engage in various activities.

Ekman used to practice emotion recognition by watching television shows in which politicians, pundits, and media personalities spoke on camera. He would turn the sound to mute, so as not to hear what they said and could concentrate on the facial expressions, which he thought were more truthful. If you do the same you will recognize happy expressions of friendliness. Anger is more difficult: look for eyebrows pulled down and together, staring eyes, lips either closed and tightened or showing a square mouth. Ekman used his knowledge to detect lying; he trained members of police forces and Homeland Security to observe its signs.[13] Ekman reached a pinnacle that few psychologists imagine: a television series, *Lie to Me*, was based on his work on emotion recognition and the detection of lies.[14]

What Emotions Really Are

Both Darwin and Ekman concentrated less on emotions as such and more on their expressions. But what are emotions, really, in our day-to-day life and in our inmost being? The best approach, which is widely accepted, is that of Nico Frijda.[15] He proposed that an emotion is a state of readiness to act in a certain way when some event is appraised as affecting a concern that we have. A particular kind of readiness may be to approach, or to acquire new information, or to avoid something. This readiness often involves physiological changes and expressions, but it's primarily mental and has to do with intentions. What an emotion does, proposes Frijda, is to give priority—an urge—to one kind of action rather than another, for instance to touch a friend on the arm with a feeling of affection, or to walk sullenly out of the room when we feel insulted.

Darwin wrote his book on emotions to offer contemporary evidence for his theory of evolution. He proposed that, as with hair bristling with terror, and tears of sadness, some expressions of emotions are residues of our evolution from animal states and from development in childhood. Had Darwin thought his theory was better established, he might have thought that emotions themselves had evolved generally to be functional in the kind of way that Frijda has explained.

Controversy has emerged recently with the proposal that emotions thought to be basic and discrete by Ekman and colleagues are not universal. Lisa Barrett, Batja Mesquita, and Maria Gendron say this paradigm should be replaced; also see Barrett's 2017 book, *How Emotions Are Made*. The alternative is that emotions are based on a simple system called core affect, founded on just two categories: positive-versus-negative feeling and the degree of energization or enervation It is proposed that a core affect can then prompt a range of culturally constructed and idiosyncratic ways in which we think about and talk about our emotions. Philip Kragel and Kevin LaBar have used pattern analyses of brain imaging results to see how far this idea of emotions as based on valence and arousal can explain brain activations of emotion. They conclude that the way in which emotions are represented in the brain does not fit well with the idea of two dimensions of valence and arousal, but is better understood in terms of brain regions that underlie discrete universal emotions.

One way to think of this is that the discrete states are evolutionarily derived bundles of types of action readiness.[16] In this way, happiness has evolved to prompt states of readiness to continue what one is doing, making modifications as necessary. Fear is the set of states of readiness that include stopping what one is doing, scanning the environment for signs of danger, and preparing to escape.

Sociality

A great deal of psychology focuses on the individual, but for emotions this is not ideal. Although we experience emotions personally, most of them are interpersonal.

Our sociality may be seen from emotion diaries, in which people are asked to keep a record of the emotions they experience in the course of their day-to-day lives, jotting down their name for each emotion, what it was about, who was there, and so on.[17] In a report of employed people who kept diaries of the next four emotions they experienced after being given a diary of this kind, it was found that 69 percent of the emotions were predictable from the kind of goal or concern that was affected. Most emotions were not individual, but interpersonal: 59 percent of episodes were caused by the action of another person, and for anger this proportion was 75 percent. In forty-nine episodes of the emotion of happiness, twenty of the incidents involved an urge to touch, hug, or caress. If you want to see this kind of emotion in action, visit the arrivals area at an airport. In those waiting and arriving—in people of all nationalities across a range of ages—you see emotions of happiness, warmth, and affection, expressed in waves and smiles and hugs.

Actors in the theater are given a script—the words of a play—and on the stage they enact emotion-based relationships with other characters. Everyday emotions are the other way around. An emotion occurs: love, or anger, or whatever it may be: a wordless script, and the person finds words appropriate for it.[18] With the emotion, the words that flow from the emotion-script enable the relationship to go forward.

Putting this another way, most emotions involve other people, and often emotions themselves are shared, in empathy and other ways.[19] So happiness is the emotion of cooperation; it can involve joint plans and shared concerns. It is not an accident that many advertisements include people smiling at you. Sadness is an emotion of disengagement but also a request to others to help. Anger is the emotion of something having gone wrong in a relationship so that it needs re-negotiation with the other person, who is likely also to feel angry. Expressing the anger can help you to sort out what's gone wrong. But anger is also the emotion of conflict, and can sometimes lead to disengagement from the other person. Fear, or anxiety, invites others to join with you in collective avoidance of danger. Contempt is the emotion toward another person, or group, that denies humanity in the relationship.

When we experience a strong emotion, we tend to talk to someone else about it. Bernard Rimé and colleagues asked people to think back to an experience of an emotion suggested by one of seventeen emotion-names, and asked if they confided it to anyone. As you can see from figure 7, for love and joy, about half the people talked to someone about it on the same day, and the other half later. For anger and fear, nearly all the confiding was done on the day the emotion happened. For sadness, people continued to confide beyond a week. In a theoretical and empirical review, Rimé reports on people who kept a diary of the event that had affected them most during the day. The majority of these incidents were confided on that same day, often to more than one person.

Confiding enables people to integrate their emotions into how they think and feel about themselves in relation to each other: What kind of person am I to have experienced this emotion in this way? What do you think of me for having experienced this emotion in this way?

Despite what Darwin said about some of our emotional expressions occurring, whether or not they are useful, emotions themselves are as useful as the psychological functions of perception or

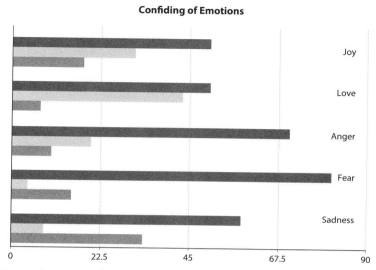

Figure 7. Percentages of occasions on which people spoke to someone else about emotions they had experienced, as found by Bernard Rimé and colleagues. The top bar for each emotion is confiding on the same day, the second bar is for later that week, and the lower bar is for later than a week. *Data source*: Rimé, B., Mesquita, B., Philippot, P., & Boca, S. (1991). Beyond the emotional event: Six studies on the social sharing of emotions. *Cognition and Emotion, 5,* 435–465. Figure drawn by Keith Oatley.

thinking. They are at the very center of mind and human meanings. Their function is to signal to us that an event is happening that affects one of our concerns: something potentially important. They displace other matters from our minds. They make the issue urgent. They make us ready for certain kinds of action.

The problem with emotions is that they don't in themselves let us know whether an event that prompted them is important or merely urgent. In the case of fear, for instance, is there really a danger or only the possibility of a danger? The emotion of fear is like a burglar alarm. Is someone really trying to break in? Or has the alarm gone off for some other reason?

We take our cues from emotions, each one usually prompted by an event that affects a concern or goal. Our mind can become filled with it. It can become an object of consciousness of what the event may mean, of what its implications are, of what our intentions might be in relation to it. It is we who must decide whether the event is not merely urgent but also important.

Erasmus was one of the most influential people of the European Renaissance. With the new availability of books, he promoted literacy and education. His own most-read book was *Praise of Folly*, in which Folly stands up and gives a speech in praise of herself, a very foolish thing to do. She points out that she is a woman, so already at a disadvantage, and says that although many people present themselves in public as very serious, if one looks beneath the surface one may see that some speak from pride in being superior and in the right while everyone else is wrong, while others speak from a desire to be the center of attention. Such people scarcely admit to emotions of these kinds; they prefer to think they are being rational. They do this, Folly suggests, because "It's confessed on all sides that the emotions are the province of folly. Indeed, this is the way we distinguish the wise man from the fool, that the one is governed by his reason, the other by his emotions."[20] Folly goes on to say that, really, "emotions not only serve as guides to those who press towards the gates of wisdom, they also act as spurs and incitements to the practice of every virtue."

It took several hundred more years for emotions to be regarded as important in psychology. Now it's becoming evident that in human lives and relationships they are central. The idea of empathy, with which we closed the previous chapter, is being able to experience an emotion within our self that is similar to an emotion being experienced by someone else. The emotion is shared, be it happiness, anger, sadness, or anxiety. It's one of the ways in which we can come to know others, and coordinate ourselves with them.

We are animals of a particular kind: among all the species, we humans are the most social. Among principles that emerge are ideas that emotions have been selected for during evolution, and that they are usually functional, especially in the ways that they enable us to relate to other people. In this way emotions mediate day-to-day interactions with people we know.[21] Over the longer term they include antipathy toward those with whom we are in conflict, and affection for those with whom we are close.

4

Individual Differences
and Development

Item from Alfred Binet and Théodore Simon's scale for measuring intelligence in children, who have to say, for each pair of faces, which one is the prettier.

Alfred Binet and Théodore Simon developed the first intelligence tests for children. Influenced by their work, Jean Piaget proposed that mentally we develop in stages. In the first stage, children come to know that objects in the world can be lost and found. In the next stage, children are influenced by surface appearances. Only in adolescence is a stage reached in which people start to think logically. Testing traveled to America, where multiple-choice tests were used to measure people's intelligence. What should we do for people who score less than average on such tests? The evolutionary process of variation gives us different intellectual abilities by mere luck. Might justice suggest that those who are fortunate contribute to those who are less fortunate?

The Testing of Intelligence

A turning point in psychology occurred with the testing of children's intelligence. At the beginning of the twentieth century, a law was passed in France that all children between the ages of six and fourteen should receive school education. The question arose as to whether it might be better for children who had difficulties with learning to be educated in special classrooms. But how might such children be identified? Partly in response to this, in 1908, Alfred Binet and Théodore Simon published a test with thirty items to measure children's intelligence.[1]

The test was administered by a trained person. The first item was easy: could children follow a beam of light with their eyes? A slightly harder task was to name body parts. More difficult tasks included naming differences between pairs of things, for instance, for the three pairs of cartoon faces shown at the chapter opening, the tester asked the children which of each pair was the prettier. Then the tester asked the children to construct sentences from three words, to repeat a list of seven random digits, and to make change from some money.

Binet and Simon asked teachers to select children who were average for their age. These children took the test and their results set standards for it. If a new child was then tested and could do all the tasks that average seven-year-olds could do, but not those that only older children could do, the child was given the mental age of seven.

The term "IQ" stands for "Intelligence Quotient."[2] It's the ratio of each child's measured mental age to actual age, multiplied so that the normal person has an IQ of 100. So, if Aimée can do the tasks that average nine-year-olds can do, she has a mental age of nine. If she is actually aged seven, her IQ will be 9 divided by 7 multiplied by 100 = 128. Nowadays IQ is assessed in relation to normal populations rather than in terms of mental ages. One hundred is the average; 95 percent of people have IQs between 70 and 130.

Alfred Binet was born in Nice, in 1857.[3] He took a law degree in 1878, then considered going into medicine, but he became interested in psychology, which was not much developed, so he taught it to himself. In 1894, he became director of the Laboratory of Experimental Psychology at the Sorbonne, in Paris. In 1903, he published *Experimental Studies of Intelligence*. Soon after this he was joined by a young physician, Théodore Simon, who was fascinated by his findings.

Work on testing opened up a range of issues in psychology: how people may see the world differently; how damage to our brains might be diagnosed by testing; how, amid the variation that Darwin observed, might we live in a world of people who are different?

Binet and Simon offered one kind of answer. It was that children who scored lower on their tests needed extra help in school so that they, like everyone else, could have a chance to reach their potential. To understand how education might be appropriate for children of different ages, and of different abilities, a theory was needed of how children develop.

Stages of Development

The most influential theory of cognitive development is that of Jean Piaget.[4] Born in 1896, Piaget grew up in Neufchatel, in Switzerland.[5] He went to school there, and he received his PhD in biology from the University of Neufchatel. After that he spent some time studying in Paris. There he taught at a school run by Alfred Binet, and studied with Binet's collaborator, Théodore Simon. In 1921 he returned to Geneva, Switzerland, where most of his career was centered. Earlier in life Piaget had been interested in psychoanalysis but, deciding that Freud's work was mainly about emotional development, he thought he would concentrate on cognitive development. In 1923, he married Valentine Chatenay. The couple had three children, Jacqueline, Lucienne, and Laurent, who became the main participants in his studies. The Piaget family is pictured in figure 8.

Jean Piaget proposed that children pass through stages, each based on a distinctive kind of understanding: an implicit theory of the world and how it works.

First, from birth to age two, is the sensory-motor stage in which children come to recognize the outside world. At this time, the children's implicit theory is that when they act on the world it changes, and that if an object disappears, it still exists somewhere, so they can search for it. Piaget called this object permanence. Next, from age two to age six, came what Piaget called the pre-operational stage. Children come to represent the world symbolically through language and mental images, but their understandings depend on surface appearances. In the third stage, from age six to age twelve, which Piaget called the stage of concrete operations, children are able to carry out mental operations—thoughts—that enable them to combine and transform objects and actions. In the fourth stage, from ages twelve to nineteen, which Piaget called the stage of formal operations, adolescents become able to think logically and to take an interest in abstractions.

Piaget and his colleagues worked to diagnose what stage children were in by giving them carefully arranged questions. The questions were influenced by those devised by Binet and Simon but, rather than having their purpose be to diagnose differences, they were intended to give insights into how children think. Thus, a four-year-old child might be shown a row of coins, and

Figure 8. Jean and Valentine Piaget in 1936, with their children who were the main subjects in Jean Piaget's research on cognitive development. *Source:* © Archives Jean Piaget, Geneva.

alongside it the same number of coins spread out so that the row is longer. When asked which row has more coins in it, four-year-olds tend to answer that it's the longer one. In their implicit theory longer means more. At this stage they don't know that a better theory would involve counting the coins.

One well-known test invented by Piaget, to distinguish the pre-operational stage from the stage of concrete operations, was to judge the amount of water in glasses of different shapes. Children before about the age of six think there is more water in a tall, thin glass than in a short, fat glass. And they think there is more in the tall glass even if the water is poured into it from the short, fat glass. They don't at that stage think: "Well none was spilled so it must be the same amount." Whereas some people in education ask what kind of teaching would enable children to move more quickly to the next stage, Piaget thought that enabling children to explore implications of their current theory-stage would be better for their development. Some of Piaget's tests, like the one with glasses of water, have become famous. Tasks of the kind Piaget developed have also influenced the measurement of intelligence.

Adult Testing and Eugenics

Mental testing was started not by Binet and Simon, but by Francis Galton, a half-cousin of Charles Darwin. In 1884, Galton established what he called an anthropometric laboratory at London's International Health Exhibition. People paid three pence to be tested and were given a copy of their measurements. Data were collected from more than 9,000 people, on each of whom seventeen measurements were made of keenness of sight, color sense, hearing, touch, breathing capacity, strength of pull and of squeeze, height when standing and sitting, body weight.

Galton took his research in a direction based on Darwin's idea of variation, but his new direction was one of which Darwin would probably have disapproved. Galton was keen to make the human race better, and his idea was to use selective breeding to increase the proportion of certain variations (superior people) and decrease the proportion of others (the inferior). For this, in 1904, Galton described a concept he had invented: eugenics.

When Binet and Simon's test reached America it was translated into English and became the Stanford-Binet test. Many of those who developed this test worked to use intelligence testing to promote eugenics. In the New World, rather than having testers work with individual children, new formats were devised.[6] One kind, the multiple-choice questionnaire, has become familiar. Questionnaires of this kind can easily be administered to large numbers of people, including adults. In this way, as Leo Kamin discusses in *The Science and Politics of IQ*, when the United States joined World War I, some two million recruits to the army were administered a multiple-choice questionnaire called the Army Alpha Test, and given grades from A to E. Grade A denoted an officer type. B denoted a non-commissioned officer, and C a private. D denoted fair soldiers who were often slow in learning. Those at a half grade lower, D-minus, were designated as barely fit for military service, and E were said to be unqualified for military service. Although the tests came too late to have any substantial effect on army policy at that time, subsequent analyses of the results shocked the testers.

Results of the Army Alpha Test of recruits who had been born in America and immigrants from Northern Europe (designated Nordic races) had the highest average scores, whereas the majority of those who had immigrated from Russia, Poland, and Italy had scored D or below. An implication seemed critical for eugenic policies. The recommendation was that immigration from Southern and Eastern Europe should be curtailed. These sentiments were different from those expressed by Emma Lazarus in the poem that in 1903 (just twenty years earlier) had been engraved on the pedestal of the Statue of Liberty.

> Give me your tired, your poor,
> Your huddled masses yearning to breathe free,
> The wretched refuse of your teeming shore.
> Send these, the homeless, tempest-tost to me,
> I lift my lamp beside the golden door!

Kamin describes how one theorist, Harry Laughlin, categorized D-minus people as follows: "Cost of supervision greater
than the value of labor,"[7] and of how, in 1923, Arthur Sweeney
wrote part of an appendix for the U.S. House of Congress Com-
mittee on Immigration which included the following:

> The D minus group can not go beyond the second grade . . .
> we shall degenerate to the level of the Slav and Latin races . . .
> pauperism, crime, sex offences and dependency . . . guided
> by a mind scarcely superior to the ox . . . we must protect
> ourselves against the degenerate horde.[8]

In 1924, the U.S. Congress passed a law to limit further immigration from countries of southern and eastern Europe. As
Kamin puts it: "The law, for which the science of mental testing
may claim substantial credit, resulted in the deaths of literally
hundreds of thousands of victims of Nazi biological theorists."[9]

Intelligence and Inheritance

The early American intelligence testers failed to consider how
long immigrant recruits who had taken the Army's Alpha Test
had lived in the United States. Had they done so they would
have seen that men's scores on this test were closely related to
how long they had lived in a country where the language was
English—the language in which the tests were written. It was
the language spoken by immigrants from Britain and Ireland,
but not by most of those from Poland and Italy. Had the testers
thought a bit harder, moreover, they might also have realized
that something other than inheritance was involved in answering questions of the Army Alpha Test, such as the one in which
it was asked whether the Overland car was manufactured in Toledo, Buffalo, Detroit, or Flint. (Toledo is correct.)

Many early testers were not trying to answer questions in a scientific way but were looking for confirmation of what they already knew. When standardizations began of the Stanford-Binet test, the issue of sex differences arose. Lewis Terman and Maud Merrill put it like this: "A few tests in the trial batteries which yielded the largest sex differences were eliminated early on as probably unfair. A considerable number of those retained show statistically significant differences in the percentages of success for boys and girls."[10]

The testers had found that when IQs of girls were measured, on average they were higher than those of boys. In the male-dominated society of that time, the testers thought this could not be true. The solution was that they altered some of the questions so that, on average, girls and boys scored the same. When, later, black children were tested, their average IQ scores were found to be lower than those of white children. This result was considered to be true. In the 1986 revision of the Stanford-Binet test, it is described how items have been reformulated to minimize differences of both gender and race.

In 1994, the psychologist Richard Herrnstein and the political scientist Charles Murray published *The Bell Curve*, in which they argued that IQ is associated with a range of personal factors such as income, job performance, and crime.[11] They don't claim that it is all a matter of genetics, but they do discuss the issue in terms of race, and this caused an outcry. In his review of the book in the *New Yorker*, Stephen Gould states, "The authors omit facts, misuse statistical methods, and seem unwilling to admit the consequence of their own words." The controversy continues.

In many modern studies of intelligence, scores are compared in pairs of identical (monozygotic) twins and in pairs of non-identical (dizygotic) twins. As Robert Plomin and Frank Spinath show, by adulthood, correlations between IQ scores of the monozygotic twins (who share 100 percent of their genes) are about 0.8, while correlations between scores of dizygotic twins (who share 50 percent of their genes) are about 0.4. This means there is a substantial inherited factor in IQ. Modern research makes it clear that single genes have only tiny effects on psychological functions such as ability to learn and succeed.[12] Such effects are due to large groups of genes, working together.

Twin studies show that IQ is an example of Darwin's idea that psychological characteristics, not just physical ones, can be inherited. It is an easily administered predictor of how well a person is likely to perform in school, at college or university, and in employment. It even helps predict, to some extent, how people are likely to manage against those slings and arrows of fortune that can threaten to precipitate emotional disorders. As a predictor, it is by no means exact. Individual lives, with their many opportunities taken and declined, are more telling than a simple number of the kind IQ provides.

We now recognize that it is unacceptable in society to have members of one group able to exercise power to curtail the life-chances of another group to which they do not belong. To be born with these parents rather than those, with one set of abilities rather than some other set, are matters of chance. They are arbitrary and potentially unfair.

In this book we discuss some answers that cognitive science has offered us. Perhaps even more important are questions. Here is one: how are different individual abilities and fairness to be related in society?

In 1972, John Rawls argued that what we mean by justice includes reducing sources of unfairness. He proposed the idea that he calls the "original position." In it we imagine that, before our birth, we take part in discussions in groups of others, about what kind of society we would like to be born into. These meetings take place before we know whether we will be female or male, whether we will be born into a family that is rich or poor, what ethnic group we will be in, whether we will be more or less intelligent. Rawls proposes that among the results of such discussions is a likely choice of a kind of society in which, if by chance we happen to have certain abilities, we should be able to develop them but, at the same time, from resources we would gather as a result of better life-chances and abilities, we would also contribute to the well-being of people whose life-chances have been less. Of course, not all societies aspire to fairness, but we can ask how societies that do aspire in this way can promote policies that embody this principle.

PART TWO

Learning, Language, Thinking

5

Stimulus and Response

One of Ivan Pavlov's dogs, showing container for collecting saliva.

In Russia, Ivan Pavlov discovered conditioning. In America, John Watson proposed that psychology should be the science of behavior; he went on to influence advertising, not to give information, but to offer stimuli designed to cause consumers to respond by making purchases. B. F. Skinner further developed behaviorism. In a Skinner box, a rat or pigeon that exhibited some piece of behavior that was followed by a reinforcement such as delivery of food, increased its probability of producing that behavior. Are we humans like dogs, rats, and pigeons, as behaviorists describe, or might we have minds, and make decisions?

Conditioned Reflexes

The first clues that it was possible to study learning in a way that was both simple and significant came from an unlikely source: experiments by a Russian physiologist on digestion in dogs. The researcher was Ivan Pavlov. He performed surgeries on dogs to move the duct of a salivary gland from the inside to the outside of the mouth and connect it to a tube, as shown in the chapter opening photo, so that salivation could be observed and measured.

Pavlov discovered that saliva started to flow not just when food entered a dog's mouth, but when the dog saw food. This is a useful mechanism because salivary juices, which are important to digestion, can start working immediately when food enters the mouth. Pavlov's most famous finding was that, when on several occasions he showed the dog food and at the same time sounded a buzzer, saliva would start to flow when the buzzer was later sounded alone, without food being offered. The original reflex, in which the sight of food caused salivation, had a learned reflex grafted onto it.

With this discovery, the terms "stimulus" and "response" first introduced by Descartes in his description of how the nervous system worked to produce reflexes, entered psychology. Many psychologists use the term "stimulus" today to mean a pattern of sensory events that can affect the nervous system, and they use the term "response" to mean a movement of muscles or glands in a particular circumstance.

Pavlov's dogs learned that the buzzer meant that food was about to arrive. This kind of learning is called "conditioning." The new stimulus is the conditioned stimulus. The dog has learned what event in the environment signals that something important is about to occur. The idea was that the nervous system becomes rewired, so that now the signal causes the response. Since Pavlov's time, there has been intense research to discover what kinds of rewiring in the nervous system happen during conditioning.

Ivan Pavlov was born in 1849 in the small town of Ryazan, 250 miles southeast of Moscow.[1] His father was a priest who inspired his sons with a love of learning. In his youth, Ivan was also strongly influenced by his godfather, abbot of a nearby monastery, who was known for his simple life and devotion to duty. Ivan Pavlov seems to have taken on these traits. He lived with an almost other-worldly concern for his work. Although at first he studied theology, Pavlov came to believe in science, and took up physiology. In 1861, he married Sara (Seraphima Karchevskaya). Their early years together were difficult because they had almost no money. Sara's first pregnancy ended in a miscarriage, and the couple's first child died while still very young, but they later had three children who survived to adulthood. From 1890, when he was invited to direct the Department of Physiology in the Institute of Experimental Medicine in St. Petersburg, Pavlov's career thrived, but he did not become interested in psychology until ten years later when, at the age of fifty, he discovered conditioning. In 1904, he was awarded the very first Nobel Prize in physiology.

Watson and Behaviorism

Ivan Pavlov had laid the foundation of behaviorism. For its next phase we travel from St. Petersburg in Russia to Baltimore, Maryland in the United States. Here a psychologist called John B. Watson became the protagonist.[2]

Influentially and independently of Pavlov's work (which he seemed not to have known about at that time), in 1913 Watson wrote an article for the prestigious journal, *Psychological Review*, entitled "Psychology as the behaviorist views it." In it, he made three points. First he argued that psychology had lost its way with the idea that its chief subject matter was consciousness and that its chief method was introspection. He said this had yielded nothing of importance in nearly fifty years. Watson's second point was that, as the proper alternative to introspection, psychology should use the observable data of behavior. In this way, the study of humans would become objective, and no different from the study of animals. Indeed, he said, humans should be regarded as animals from the point of view of psychology. Watson's third point was that, by observing and analyzing behavior, psychology would place itself among the sciences.

Following the establishment of psychological experimentation by Wilhelm Wundt, and following Wundt's principle that psychology should be a science, behaviorists tended to take physics as their model, with its theories such as gravitation, and with its laws such as Newton's laws of motion. Psychology, too, they said, should have its theories and laws.

All three of the points that Watson stressed in his article continue to be influential. Most psychologists now regard introspection as of minor interest. Many think that behavior, along with physiological observations, constitute the principal data of psychology. Most remain keen that psychology is a science.

It came to seem for the behaviorists that the best domain within which to search for psychological laws was learning. Learning by conditioning, in the way that Pavlov had demonstrated, came to be regarded as a fundamental mechanism. We humans, it came to be thought, are characterized not by instincts like the lower animals, but by our superior ability to learn. Unlike lower animals, we guide our lives by what we learn. The behaviorist idea included the promise that if we could find out how fundamental kinds of learning occur, we would discover how these processes are elaborated in humans. This would reveal the secret of our success, help us cure what goes wrong for human beings, and help us to become even more successful.

In 1919, a nineteen-year-old student, Rosalie Rayner, became John Watson's research assistant. It was with her that he performed a famous experiment on an eleven-month-old boy, who came to be known as Little Albert.

Albert was found to be curious about a friendly white rat, as you may see in figure 9. In the experiment, when the boy reached

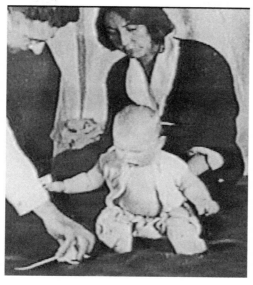

Figure 9. Rosalie Rayner holds Little Albert, who takes interest in a white rat that is being shown to him by John Watson. *Source*: "Rosalie Rayner holds Little Albert." http://www.nscpsychology.com/blog/who-was-little-albert. Archives of the History of American Psychology, The Drs. Nicholas and Dorothy Cummings Center for the History of Psychology, The University of Akron.

toward the rat, Watson banged an iron bar with a hammer so loudly that it startled the child. Albert withdrew his hand and whimpered. Over the next weeks, Watson and Rayner showed the rat to Albert several more times, and paired the boy's attempts at reaching toward it with the loud sound of striking the iron bar. Albert stopped reaching toward the rat. In those days there were no ethical considerations about what kinds of experimentation might be regarded as acceptable.

The experiment by Watson and Rayner, with Little Albert, published in 1920, began the American study of learning as conditioning. They called Albert's change of behavior toward the white rat a conditioned emotional response. From this time, they started to take an interest in the conditioning that occurs in the development of children, and how this can shape their behavior.

They also realized that conditioned emotional responses could be the basis of anxiety disorders. This idea that long-lasting anxieties can have been set up in this way is central today in behavior therapy and cognitive-behavior therapy.

As well as being the year of publication of a study that would make him famous, 1920 was the year in which John Watson's academic career ended. He had started an affair with Rosalie Rayner. Watson's wife, Mary, discovered letters between him and Rosalie, and the letters found their way to the president of Johns Hopkins University, who summoned Watson and required him to resign on the spot. Despite the influence he had won in psychology, Watson was never offered another university position. In describing the concept of "response" in his popular book *Behaviorism*, Watson would write: "Under sex excitement the male may go to any length to capture a willing female."[3] At the end of 1920, Mary and John Watson divorced, and at the beginning of 1921 Rosalie Rayner became the second Mrs. Watson. Along with a new wife, Watson needed a new career. He found one in advertising, at the J. Walter Thompson Company, where he worked until 1935.

Watson was responsible for bringing psychology into the advertising business. As David Cohen put it: "Watson . . . shifted the focus of American advertising. The potential buyer was a kind of machine. Provide the right stimulus and he will oblige with the right reaction, digging deep into his pocket."[4]

The ingenious Watson took to advertising as an opportunity for a new kind of learning experiment. One had to choose stimuli with a view to eliciting certain kinds of responses. One successful campaign was for Maxwell House coffee. Cohen describes how Watson "decided to appeal to the snob in the customer."[5] Under Watson's direction, Maxwell House advertisements pictured splendid historical scenes. At high society balls, what did the butler bring on a tray? Maxwell House. In elegant Southern mansions, beautiful women asked for Maxwell House. Cohen relates how in 1928 the *New Yorker* observed that Watson had "conditioned housewives and commuters into all sorts of prejudices about coffee." Cohen continues:

> It was not a drink that the advertisements were selling, it was a dream ... Drink Maxwell House and project yourself into a world of superb elegance and gorgeous glamour. Sip Maxwell House. Slip into the dream.[6]

Watson's third career was as a writer of popular books. In *Behaviorism*, Watson described his experiments on Little Albert and introduced, too, a series of other experiments on children to show, in perhaps the first examples of behavior therapy, how fears could be removed by methods he called "reconditioning" or "unconditioning."

Watson was successful as a popular writer because what he said was outspoken and often contrary to received belief. He became an authority on childcare. He argued that too much mother-love was bad for children. There was often something missing from the lives of parents, he said. What they did in kissing and coddling their children was largely for their own gratification. The effect of this was to make the children hopelessly dependent, and it destined them for neurosis in adulthood. He proposed that parents should regard their children as experimental subjects and work out what enabled them to learn whatever might be necessary for purposes the parents might have. All this, of course, both enraged and engaged the public.

Skinner and His Boxes

In the middle of the twentieth century, if you opened an American textbook on psychology, you were likely to read that "Psychology is the science of behavior." B. F. Skinner was a significant influence on this view. He promoted behaviorism so effectively that one might have thought that it was all there was to psychology.[7]

Among Skinner's contributions was the invention of the Skinner box: a cage in which a rat or a pigeon could be rewarded for some particular piece of behavior. A Skinner box designed for rats contains a food hopper into which pellets of food can be delivered. In the box, too, is a lever which, when it is pressed, causes a food pellet to be delivered. When a hungry rat is first put into the box, it tends to wander about, sniff here, climb up there, until by accident it stands on the lever. Then, with a click, a pellet of food arrives in the hopper. The rat finds it and eats it, then tends to hover around the food hopper, then wander about the box some more until, perhaps accidentally again, it stands on the lever. Another click, another food pellet. If you watch sequences of this kind, you see the rat spend more time near the lever, and then go to sniff around the food hopper, go back toward the lever, perhaps climb on it so that another click is heard, and another pellet arrives. As the rat starts to go back and forth between lever and food hopper, it becomes more efficient until it presses, goes to the food hopper, presses again and so on, to produce for itself a steady supply of food pellets. You might then say to yourself: "Now it's got the idea."

According to Skinner, you'd be wrong. In his behaviorism, anything like an idea was prohibited. The proper way would be to describe the observed behavior. You might say that the rat's behavior had been shaped to press the lever. You might describe the delivery of each food pellet into the food hopper. You wouldn't, however, call this a reward. You would call it a positive reinforcement. If you took a class with Professor Skinner and in a test you wrote "reward" instead of "positive reinforcement," you would not be reinforced. You would lose points.

Most important of all, according to Skinner's psychology, you would describe relationships between responses and reinforcements. So, you could say: "The rat is on a schedule of reinforcement such that when it presses the lever a food pellet is delivered." Whereas Pavlov's kind of learning came to be called "classical conditioning," Skinner called his kind of learning "operant conditioning," where "operant" meant an operation on the environment. Rather than responding to the pairing of a signal and an event that was significant for the animal (as in Pavlov's experiments), operant responses had to be emitted. Learning consisted of increasing the probability of emitting a particular response to which the experimenter had chosen to give positive reinforcement.

Skinner started to point out the parallel between operants selected by reinforcement and Darwin's idea of evolution by means of heritable variations being selected. This was a shrewd move. If natural selection enabled species to evolve across generations, learning by reinforcement enabled the individual to evolve within a generation. Skinner thus elevated his idea of positive reinforcement as the shaping of organisms to contingencies of the environment to a grand principle. He insisted that what he was doing was Science, with a capital "S," and he tended to belittle the work of other psychologists.

The principle of trying to shape children's behavior by positive reinforcement became important especially in schools and in therapy for children who were delayed or disordered in their development. Punishment, the delivery of some painful event after a response, does diminish the probability of that response, but it's not effective if it is delayed and, more importantly, Skinner found that it tends to disrupt behavior, so it is to be avoided if possible. If undesirable responses occur, instead of punishing children who emit them, these children are to be put on a time-out, comparable to when, for a rat in a Skinner box, the mechanism by which the lever causes food to be delivered is turned off. During a time-out period, children are not responded to at all. Instead, after the time-out interval, the teacher or therapist waits until the child does something thought to be appropriate and then delivers a positive reinforcement: a word of praise or something else the child is motivated to acquire.

Some principles based on Skinner's ideas have become useful. For instance, if parents want their baby to sleep at night on its own, the principle of not responding to crying when the baby goes to bed is critical. If a child is put to sleep at night, and the parent leaves the room, the child is likely to cry. Distressed by the crying, the parent tends to come back to pick up the infant, then hug and soothe it until it stops crying. Perhaps the parent takes the child into the parental bed. What the child learns is that crying is reinforced; when the child is put down to sleep, the crying increases. Many parents have despaired in this situation. The answer is to stop reinforcing the crying behavior. It is anguishing for parents to hear their infant howl for thirty minutes, which is likely to happen on the first night it has to sleep on its own. But if the child is left, it is likely to fall asleep after crying. Next night, it may cry for twenty minutes. The following night, it cries perhaps just for five minutes. The next night it may fall asleep without crying. If we weren't describing behavior in Skinner's terms, we might say that in this way the child finds its own resources for comforting itself and going to sleep.

Despite great professional success, Skinner aroused hostility. One target was his use, for his younger daughter, Deborah, of a temperature-controlled crib that was padded and comfortable. He called it the "baby tender." The idea was that a baby in the tender was in a completely safe environment, without aversive stimuli. If the baby cried, this response was not reinforced. Skinner saw his invention as a labor-saving device for mothers. In 1945, he published an article on this invention in the *Ladies' Home Journal*. He wrote that the device offered mothers better opportunities to schedule naps and feedings and that, in the tender, babies could be more active and mothers were freer to love their babies who, because they were happier, were indeed more lovable. There was no suggestion that children were to be kept in the tender all the time. The tender's function wasn't much different from that of a playpen, a device that had been in use since the beginning of the twentieth century. But an editor at the *Ladies' Home Journal*, perhaps intending to hint that Skinner was a bit of a crackpot, gave his article the title, "Baby in a box."[8] This was the second box

Skinner had invented and, because some people thought he was experimenting on his children in a Skinner box, criticism became intense. In 2004, Lauren Slater published a book entitled *Opening Skinner's Box*, in which she recounted rumors that Deborah was irreparably damaged from being experimented upon as a baby. When the book was published, Deborah, who was an artist at the time, married and living in London, happened to read a review of it, and wrote an article for *The Guardian* newspaper to say that no experimentation and no ill-effects had occurred. Skinner seems to have been a kind parent to both his daughters.

Skinner's biggest challenge to conventional thinking was to propose that mind and free will are both wrongheaded, both dangerous. He pointed out that we humans continue to go to war with each other, and that social inequality is pervasive. The conclusion that individuals are autonomous beings has not led to happy, well-regulated societies, and not led to much care for our environment. What we should do, Skinner argued, is to live in a simpler way, as he had outlined in his novel, *Walden Two*. He proposed that the environment should be carefully engineered to ensure a flow of positive reinforcements.

One might say that Skinner was not an innovator who made striking discoveries and challenging pronouncements about how to manage people and societies. One could say there was merely a history of environmental contingencies that reinforced certain responses in an organism called B. F. Skinner. But that would be unfair.

In 1971, Skinner appeared on the cover of *Time Magazine*. That year marked, perhaps, the peak of his influence. What are the lasting effects of Skinner's work? He seems not to have persuaded us that we can't make decisions about our lives. Among lasting effects of behaviorism are that principles of learning-by-reinforcement have become part of the language of psychology, in rats, in pigeons, and even in us humans. Nowadays, however, psychologists also talk about rewards, and even about whether one can experience pleasure in accomplishing our goals. This issue has become critical, for instance, in understanding addictions. Schoolteachers and children's therapists have rightly become wary of punishments, and think about how to offer positive reinforcements to children for their learning and for behavior that shows success in achievement, or demonstrates kindness and consideration for others.

What was discovered by Skinner? He showed, indeed, that learning often does occur by positive reinforcement, and that learned connections between stimuli and responses are determined by contingencies, and by whether responses are reinforced by certain events in the environment. He established too that if every response of a particular kind—a rat pressing a lever in a Skinner box, or a child correctly answering a teacher's questions at school—is positively reinforced, then the schedule of reinforcement can be called continuous, and the probability of that response is increased. If positive reinforcements are discontinued then, after a while, responses are no longer emitted: the probability of response is diminished. Don't even think that the rat or the child may have given up. One needs to say the response was extinguished. If positive reinforcements are re-established, re-learning is quicker than for the original learning. If a response is positively reinforced only intermittently, the schedule is called partial reinforcement. Here, responding becomes more rapid than for continuous reinforcement, and when reinforcement is discontinued, extinction takes longer. Negative reinforcement is the removal of aversive stimuli. Application of aversive stimuli, usually called punishment, is unreliable for learning and is to be avoided, since it disrupts behavior and generalizes too widely. There are a few more wrinkles, but this paragraph might be regarded as about 70 percent of the principles and findings of Skinner's behaviorism.

It was thought by Skinnerian behaviorists that the operations of 86 billion neurons, in processes of human perception, learning, emotion, development, and imagination, could be summed up in a paragraph like the previous one. Some processes of reinforcement remain important, for instance in special education and behavior therapy, but behaviorism as a movement drained psychology of meaning. It seemed almost like a disease. As discussed in the next chapter, the remedy would come from an unlikely source—from linguistics. But further into the future, as we see in chapter 8, learning processes not unlike those outlined by Skinner would make a comeback in artificial intelligence.

6

Language

Noam Chomsky in 1977.

Noam Chomsky was influential in the cognitive revolution with his proposal that language is not based on learning by reinforcement. He developed the idea of deep structures, of inner rules of grammar that underlie all languages. They enable people to learn the language of their social group, and to generate and transform deep structures into talking and writing. Katherine Nelson found that when infants start to speak they do so in a way that is based on grammatical structures that have a relation to Chomsky's idea, but differ from it in important respects.

Deep Structures in the Mind

A turning point in the influence of behaviorism occurred in a book review.[1] The book was B. F. Skinner's *Verbal Behavior*. The year was 1959. The book's reviewer was Noam Chomsky, whose photograph you can see at the head of this chapter.

Before this book review, Chomsky had written mainly technical works such as *Syntactic Structures*, based on his PhD thesis, which he had completed two years previously. In *Syntactic Structures*, Chomsky argued that grammar and how it works could be understood independently of how words relate to concepts. Part of his argument was that a sentence could be grammatical without meaning anything. Consider these sentences.

Colorless green ideas sleep furiously.
Furiously sleep ideas green colorless.

Both are nonsense, but the first is grammatical nonsense. Using arguments of this kind, Chomsky went on to show how minds contain inner structures to which we have no conscious access, but which are fundamental for the human use of language.

In *Verbal Behavior*, Skinner argued that language is learned by principles of stimulus, response, and reinforcement. In his review of the book, Noam Chomsky writes that it is difficult to see how this view affords any insight. He argues that the concept of control by stimuli means that one might listen to a piece of music and say "Mozart" or look at a painting and say "Dutch." Skinner would say that such verbal responses were due to subtle properties of the musical or visual stimuli. But, says Chomsky, what if one were to say of the painting: "it clashes with the wallpaper"? Skinner could only say that this response, too, derives from properties of the stimulus: "wallpaper-clashfulness." "The device," says Chomsky, "is as simple as it is empty." The idea of control by a "stimulus" is without objectivity.

The difficulty for behaviorists in defending themselves against Chomsky's arguments was that, with their system of thinking, all they could say about the mind being based on inner structures is that it is of no interest. For them the mind is unnecessary. But inner operations and the working of the mind were, and are, of interest to many. Chomsky's proposals were influential and they helped unite cognitive psychologists, linguists, and computational theorists in their exploration of mind. Kept out of psychology for two decades, the mind was back, and it is now—once again as it used to be—the principal focus of psychology.

Language, argued Chomsky, depends on a system that has been bequeathed to us by evolution. He called it a "universal grammar." The word "universal" is important in the way that we reviewed in chapter 3, in discussion of emotional expressions. Of all the human universals in psychology, language has been the most widely accepted. Chomsky emphasized how the ability to speak grammatically and the ability to learn any of Earth's many languages depend on particular genes that characterize our species. Although the languages of the world are different, they all have a grammar, based on universal principles.

Imagine asking an English-speaking person questions about grammar. You might say: "Please decline the past-perfect tense of the verb 'to think.'" Or you might ask: "What is a gerund?" The person might not know, but have no difficulty in producing or understanding such a sentence as: "I had thought you didn't like eating after seven o'clock in the evening." In this sentence, "I had thought" is the first-person past-perfect tense of the verb "to think." This tense is used to refer to a completed act that took place in the past. The word "eating" is a gerund derived from the verb "to eat." The gerund is a form in which a verb works grammatically as a noun. But we don't need to know about such technical issues consciously to use such forms correctly. Our implicit knowledge enables us to form and understand sentences in which they occur. Chomsky pointed out that for us to talk and understand each other, our mind-brains must contain and use

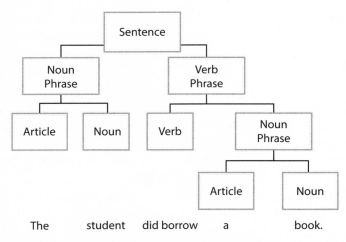

The   student   did borrow   a   book.

Figure 10. Deep structure and surface structure of a sentence. Diagram by Keith Oatley.

such pieces of grammatical knowledge without knowing consciously how we do it. This was the same kind of argument that Helmholtz had used about how we see.

Chomsky argued that two kinds of rules constitute people's implicit knowledge of language. One set is generative. Language is innately and continuously creative: generative rules enable us to produce an infinite number of new sentences that are grammatical. The second set of rules is transformational. It's a set that allows people to do different things with one underlying idea, one underlying structure.

Chomsky called underlying arrangements of sentences "deep structures." They are different from the surface forms of word orders in sentences. Figure 10 shows a deep structure and surface structure of a sentence. The simplest deep structure of a sentence is a noun phrase plus a verb phrase. A noun phrase can be an article ("the" or "a") plus a noun. A verb phrase is a verb and a noun phrase.

The surface structure of the sentence in figure 10 is "The student did borrow a book." With the deep structure, one can make transformations. So, to say that an action was in the past and was completed (the past-perfect), the verb "did borrow" is transformed into "had borrowed" and everything else stays the same. To form a negative, the deep structure is transformed by inserting the word "not" into the verb phrase, to produce the surface structure: "The student did not borrow a book." To ask a question, the transformation involves keeping the noun phrases and their positions intact, while splitting the verb in two and moving the first part to the front: "Did the student borrow a book?" Other transformations involve elaborating noun phrases by adjectives, "a slim book," verbs by adverbs, "did previously borrow," and the addition of other phrases that augment the noun phrase in which the word "book" is contained: "about the psychology of language." In similar ways, other changes of tense can be made, and forms such as requests, warnings, and so on can be constructed.

This is grammar at work. There are no languages in the world, says Chomsky, that change tenses or make negatives, or ask questions, by operating on surface structures of words. For instance, there are no languages in which a question is generated by any operation such as interchanging the order of the first and last words of the surface structure to produce such forms as: "Book student did borrow a the?" The mind, therefore, contains deep structures, of the kind illustrated in figure 10, and works to perform transformations that are involved in making sentences, and generating meaning.

Larissa MacFarquhar begins the biography of Noam Chomsky that she published in the *New Yorker* in 2003 by saying that on Thursday evenings Chomsky, "one of the greatest minds of the twentieth century," would teach a class on politics to two hundred students at the Massachusetts Institute of Technology (MIT). Though she says he is not an activist by nature, he is outraged by injustice. He is also a very determined arguer, so he has spent a good deal of the second part of his life on political issues, and has become a public intellectual by denouncing immoral actions of governments, including the government of the United States. He argues that although people are free and self-determining, states behave in their own selfish interests. In doing so, they often disregard others and hence act very badly indeed.

Chomsky's university office, wrote MacFarquhar in 2003, was a narrow room with two windows that looked out onto an alley. It had many bookshelves and two desks, both piled high with books. He would sit at one of the desks with his feet in an open drawer. It was typical of him, she said, to have created a space with nowhere comfortable to work. MacFarquhar wrote that Chomsky and his wife Carol had a companionable marriage with three children: Aviva, who taught at Salem State College; Diane, who had moved to Nicaragua and fallen in love with a Sandinista activist; and Harry, an aspiring violinist.

MacFarquhar wrote about how Chomsky's students felt they were in the vanguard of a revolution. For half a century the mind had been seen as murky and amorphous. Now, with his universal grammar, the operations of which he would spell out, Chomsky declared that the mind was a beautiful system, and that it is possible to understand some of its workings. Rather than the mind being a non-place as the behaviorists supposed, it is a place that contains complex structures, a place where transformations and other procedures take place that can in principle be understood.

Part of Chomsky's argument against Skinner's supposition that children learned languages by reinforcement was that, although some parents may instruct their children on how to talk, many children learn languages without anyone systematically reinforcing them. Children of immigrants, for instance, whose parents can't speak the language of their adopted country, learn to speak the language by being exposed to it in a rather haphazard way. Of course, growing into a language requires learning. We learn the language of the community in which we grow up, and not some other language. But, argued Chomsky, the very fact of being able to learn a language at all means that we must be innately provided with grammatical structures into which words can be assimilated, so that an inborn proclivity to operate on them by means of grammatical rules can get to work. We need to postulate, said Chomsky, that being able to learn language is based on an inherited language acquisition device.[2]

Case Grammars, Verb Islands, Cooperation

Charles Fillmore took up Chomsky's idea of grammar that is generative and transformational, to suggest Case Grammar. He proposed that the most basic deep structure of sentences across a range of languages is a Verb (an Action) with a set of slots around it, which include Agent (who does the action), Object (on which the action is done), Location (where it happened), Recipient (to whom it is done), Means (how it is done). This deep structure based on verbs can then generate a set of surface structures, in which specific Agents, Objects, Recipients, and so on could then fit in the slots. Here is an example: "Chomsky (Agent) gave (Verb) the world (Recipient) transformational grammar (Object)."

How do children learn a language? Some recent research indicates that they learn it in terms of something close to case grammars. Michael Tomasello and his collaborators have shown that as children progress beyond one-word utterances, they take an early interest in actions and the verbs that represent them, like "eat" and "go." Tomasello calls the structures "verb islands."[3] Like case grammars, these islands are verbs with slots for Agent, Object, Means, Location, and so on.

Children concentrate at first on a fairly small set of verbs. Katherine Nelson asked the parents of a child named Emily to put a tape recorder by her bed before she went to sleep, to record what she said to herself before she fell asleep. At age twenty-one months, Emily said: "The broke. Car broke, the . . . Emmy can't go in the car. Go in green car."

Emily here illustrates Tomasello's proposal that children first learn to speak by learning and using a small number of verbs, which stand for actions in the world, and that these verbs are islands with slots around them to depict particular actions, in particular ways. The verb "broke" has its slot for the agent, which was the car. The verb "go" has slots for Agent, "Emmy," and Means, "in the car."

Language is not just abstract, it's cooperative, and we come to the principle of cooperation in chapter 14.

7

Mental Models

Succession of faces, starting at the top left and progressing to the bottom right, from an experiment by Frederic Bartlett in which a succession of people each looked at one of the images, remembered it, drew what they remembered, and passed it on for another person to look at, remember, and draw.

Frederic Bartlett found that remembering isn't like retrieving a stored photographic image. It is based usually on a few salient details and involves schemas, outline theories of how the world works, from which we construct what must have happened.

Following this, Kenneth Craik proposed that we think by making models of the world, and operating with them to reach new conclusions. The theory of mental models has become a fundamental principle of cognitive psychology.

Remembering

When we are asked to explain something that is familiar to us, or when we arrange a plan, we usually know what we're talking about. But with much of our knowledge, we don't know what we know. Our knowledge comes from processes that are unconscious in the sense that Helmholtz proposed—we couldn't possibly know about all the operations accomplished by the brain's 86 billion neurons—we know only some of the conclusions that these neurons offer us, shaped as they are into forms that we can understand. We have unconscious knowledge of how to use language to talk with other people. We can recall memories, although we have no conscious idea of how or where in the brain the information is stored. Some other parts of our knowledge may be unconscious in the sense that Freud proposed. There may be aspects of our desires that we could know but don't—at least, perhaps, not until we undertake some psychological therapy.

The foundational experiments to show how the mind organizes knowledge were done by Frederic Bartlett and published in his 1932 book *Remembering*. The image at the start of this chapter is from Bartlett's paperback book cover. It's from results of a method that Bartlett called serial reproduction in which a person looked at an image, then after a short interval reproduced what she or he remembered by drawing it on paper. The resulting image would then be shown to another person, who would remember it and draw it, and so on. In the above picture, the sketch at the top left corner is what someone remembered and drew from an image entitled *Portrait d'homme* from a different culture than the British participant's own. Then, moving rightward and downward you see the third, fifth, and eighth reproduction in a series. Over this series, the pictures move from an unfamiliar kind of image toward an image of a kind familiar in Western culture. This experiment showed that, within our minds, we are influenced by conventions from societies in which we have grown up, and that these conventions affect what we see, and what we remember.

In Bartlett's most famous experiment, which reaches this same conclusion, he describes how he asked participants to read a Native American folk story called "The war of the ghosts," which had been recorded by the anthropologist Franz Boas. Bartlett chose a story from a culture that was different from the one to which his participants belonged. British participants were asked to read the story twice at their normal reading speed, and then write down what they could remember of it, as exactly as possible. Bartlett then asked them to return to his laboratory at intervals over the next few years, and make further reproductions. The story starts like this.

> One night two young men from Egulac went down to the river to hunt seals, and while they were there it became foggy and calm. Then they heard war-cries, and they thought: "Maybe this is a war party." They escaped to the shore, and hid behind a log. Now canoes came up, and they heard the noise of paddles, and saw one canoe coming up to them. There were five men in the canoe, and they said:
> "What do you think? We wish to take you along. We are going up the river to make war on the people."
> One of the young men said: "I have no arrows."
> "Arrows are in the canoe," they said.
> "I will not go along. I might be killed. My relatives do not know where I have gone. But you," he said, turning to the other, "may go with them."
> So one of the young men went.[1]

Then there are eleven lines about how the young man went with the men who had come up to them in the canoe, and took part in a fight. He was shot but he did not feel sick and he thought, "Oh, they are ghosts." The young man then returns home. Here are the story's last lines.

> He told it all, and then he became quiet. When the sun rose he fell down. Something black came out of his mouth. His face became contorted. The people jumped up and cried.
> He was dead.

What happened when participants were asked to remember the story? One person had reproduced the story several times in the first months after reading it, but had then not thought of it for two and a half years. Here's what he then wrote.

> Some warriors went to wage war against the ghosts. They fought all day and one of their number was wounded.
> They returned home in the evening, bearing their sick comrade. As the day drew to a close, he became rapidly worse and the villagers came round him. At sunset he sighed: something black came out of his mouth. He was dead.[2]

A great deal had been forgotten. But the emotionally charged detail "something black came out of his mouth" was remembered by this person, and indeed by most of Bartlett's participants.

An even more significant finding was how a story was transformed according to the culture and idiosyncrasies of the person who remembered it. When we remember something, we assimilate it to a structure of meaning, which Bartlett called a "schema."[3] Although he doesn't mention it, this idea of "schema" comes from Immanuel Kant who, in *The Critique of Pure Reason*, argued that when we see something, such as a sphere or a triangle, what we perceive does not come entirely from the image, because images can never include the concept of roundness, or of triangularity, and can only ever be limited to a single part, or a single view. In this way, by proposing that we see the world not just as input from senses, but by means of our representations of the world, Kant can be thought of as laying a foundation for cognitive science.

It's in schemas that our knowledge about the world is represented. In the memory of Bartlett's participant whose reproduction of "The war of the ghosts" is cited above, we see how, in the schemas of Western industrialized countries, not only are wars carried out by groups of people who become "comrades," but it's more appropriate to die in the evening than in the morning.

When an incident occurs, in our lives or in a story, we remember only a few significant details and a general attitude of how we have been emotionally affected. When asked to recall, we can recollect some details along with our attitude. We then use our schemas—our implicit theories of the world and how it works— to generate what must have happened.

"Schema," wrote Bartlett, "refers to an active organization of past reactions, or past experiences, which must always be supposed to be operating in any well adapted organic response."[4]

Although performed many years ago, Bartlett's experiment on "The war of the ghosts" is still among the most important in cognitive psychology: significant for our understanding of how we remember and what we remember. Bartlett put it like this:

> Remembering . . . is an imaginative reconstruction, built out of the relation of our attitude towards a whole active mass of organized past reactions or experience, and to a little outstanding detail . . . It is thus hardly ever really exact . . . and it is not at all important that it should be.[5]

Both in popular thought and in psychology, there is an idea that memories are stored in the kind of way that a pattern of light is stored in a photograph, or a pattern of sound is stored by an audio recorder.[6] The researches of Bartlett and, following him, of Elizabeth Loftus have shown that although information is stored somewhere in the brain, the idea of memories being stored as immutable traces is not very helpful for understanding how our minds work.

Loftus has shown that memory is malleable; we are easily influenced by others in what we remember. She has shown, too, that although the testimony of eyewitnesses is often used in courts, it is seldom accurate.[7] Not only when we witness something and remember it are we influenced by biases, stereotypes, and expectations, but memory remains active and changeable. Under interrogation it can be affected by how questions are put.

If you are worrying that your memory of something you did last week is fragmentary and vague, and that you can't recall exactly what happened, you can stop worrying. As Bartlett said, in most circumstances, exactitude is "not at all important." Instead, from our memories we derive our own personal sense of meaning. What we remember is used to organize our relationships with others, to make our plans, to shape our aspirations.

Bartlett didn't publish *Remembering* until 1932, but he ran the experiment on "The war of the ghosts" in Cambridge toward the end of World War I. At that time, he wrote, anxieties about separations from relatives were salient. In one group of twenty participants whom Bartlett tested, only ten remembered that in the story one of the young men's excuses was that he had no arrows, but eighteen of the twenty remembered the excuse that the young man's relatives would not know where he had gone. Our remembering, our knowledge, our understanding, are organized in our minds following the principle Bartlett called "the effort after meaning."[8] They depend on our culture, our interests, our relationships.

Mental Models

The most brilliant of Bartlett's PhD students was Kenneth Craik. Bartlett had been told by James Drever, professor of Psychology

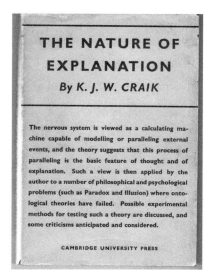

Figure 11. The cover of Kenneth Craik's 1943 book. *Source*: Book cover of Craik, K.J.W. (1943). *The nature of explanation*. Cambridge: Cambridge University Press, reprint of 1952. © Cambridge University Press 1943.

at Edinburgh University, "Next term I am going to send you a genius." This person was Craik. Bartlett wrote of Craik's

> tall, rather powerful, spare frame; a face pale but full of life . . . a shock of black hair. From the beginning he was wholly "at home" . . . with any amount of genuine modesty, but not a scrap of false humility.[9]

The work by which Craik is chiefly known is a small book, published in 1943, called *The Nature of Explanation*. A photo of its cover is provided here as figure 11. In the book Craik extended Bartlett's idea of schemas. He proposed that really these schemas are models of the world: mental models, and these models aren't just used in remembering, they are the means by which we think, the very basis of mind.

Craik proposed that to think is first to translate a problem into a mental model, then to set the model to work to produce a new result, then to translate the result from the model back into terms of the world again, into words or actions.

When people start to become interested in psychology they come across facts, and more facts, and theories, and more theories. Without some way of putting them together, all this material can seem haphazard. Craik's idea of the mind as a model and as a maker of models can help organize the material wonderfully.

The mind is the means by which we make models of the physical world and of the minds of other people. We make models of our own minds, too, so that we can think, and know about ourselves: the kinds of things to which we aspire, the kinds of things we are likely to do, whether we are outgoing, whether we are generally reliable, and so on.

Why do we need models? Why shouldn't we just respond to the world?[10] The reason is that only in terms of some inner understanding can we make inferences. With a mental model, we can access the model, put it to work so that its state is transformed, and thereby see what could happen next when it hasn't yet happened in the outer world. With an inner model, we can imagine what someone is thinking when they don't tell us. The idea that the mind makes models that enable us to think and understand, to make hypotheses about the world, is the principle at the very center of modern cognitive understandings of mind as shown, for instance, by Philip Johnson-Laird.[11]

Kenneth Craik didn't just think about inward models of the mind; he made outward models. People who knew him admired his ability to make things. Among the things he made were little model steam engines. He would often produce one from his pocket. In place of steam, Craik would blow through a little tube he'd attached to the model so that a wheel on the model would go whirring round.

When World War II broke out, Craik wasn't eligible to join the forces because of a congenital hip dislocation. At the beginning of the War, he designed and built the Cambridge Cockpit, an early flight simulator, a model based on the cockpit of a Spitfire fighter plane. It enabled Air Force pilots to learn more, and to learn more quickly than usual, by having safe experiences of different airborne situations. It also allowed psychologists to experiment on ways to improve pilot training, and to avoid error-producing fatigue. If, now, you learn to fly a plane, you would do well to spend time in a flight simulator, because in a few hours you can experience more situations and contingencies than you would be likely to encounter in a lifetime of flying. In an emergency, if you have experienced what to do in a simulator, you might save your own life, and those of your passengers.

Those who knew Craik remember his quick-thinking, his practicality, and his penchant for getting to the heart of a matter. With a mixture of mechanical, electrical, and psychological skills, as well as working on the Cambridge Cockpit, he worked during the War on many other practical problems. These included pilot aptitude, gun aiming, visual location of submarines, attention, and signal detection. His work involved working with other scientists, as well as people who ranged from generals, admirals, and air marshals to privates, ordinary seamen, and airmen.

People who knew Craik thought of him as a person of outstanding intellect, far ahead of his time, as well as being endlessly helpful and friendly. But within, he was terribly lonely. He seems to have had no really close friends of either sex. Oliver Zangwill, who wrote an obituary, cites Craik as writing: "Emotionally I have always felt life to be a struggle to break down a wall that enclosed me on every side ... It is a wall composed of one's ignorance of other people's thoughts and feelings."[12] So, like Helmholtz, Craik was modest. Perhaps for both of them this contributed to their curiosity about how the mind works.

Although Craik was manually dexterous, perhaps because of his hip dislocation, he often seemed clumsy in his larger movements. One colleague said of him that as a cyclist he was a menace on the roads. On May 7, 1945, a day before the end of the

War in Europe, when he was thirty-one, Craik was cycling along Cambridge's main street, King's Parade, and the door of a parked car opened. He collided with the door, and was thrown into the path of an oncoming lorry. He was taken to the hospital. Without recovering consciousness, he died a few hours later.

Theory-of-Mind

Jean Piaget and his colleague, Barbel Inhelder, made a model of three mountains arranged on a large board. Each mountain was a different size and shape and had something distinctive on its top. On one was a snow cap, on another a church, on the third a small hut. Piaget and Inhelder had children who were in the pre-operational stage of cognitive development walk round the model, so that they saw it from all sides. Then the children were asked to sit at one side of the model, and were shown pictures of what the mountains might look like to a doll who had been placed at one of the other sides. At the pre-operational stage, the children couldn't do it. They tended to pick the picture of the model that showed it from their own point of view. Only when they were older could they make a mental model, to imagine the perspective of someone else.

An important extension was made in 1983, by Heinz Wimmer and Josef Perner. They told children a story about a boy called Maxi, who had some chocolate, which he put in a blue cupboard while he went out to play. When he was out, his mother used some of the chocolate to make a cake and, instead of putting the rest of the chocolate back where it had been, she put it in a green cupboard. Then Maxi came back indoors. The experimenters asked the children to whom they were telling the story: "Where will Maxi look for his chocolate?" Figure 12 is a picture of Maxi, wondering which cupboard to look in.

Children under the age of about four tended to say that Maxi will look for his chocolate in the green cupboard. They knew that's

Figure 12. In which cupboard will Maxi look to find his chocolate in the study by Heinz Wimmer and Josef Perner? *Source*: © Susan Beattie, with permission.

where it was. Only children of four or older thought that Maxi would look in the blue cupboard, where he had left it. Both the younger and older children had a model of the world. But the older children were also able to make a mental model of Maxi's mind with its belief of something different from what they knew about the world. Research on this issue—of how we come to understand and consider the minds of others—is now called theory-of-mind.

Perhaps, although he was brilliant at the idea of inward and outward models and their uses, Kenneth Craik found for himself that to make models of other people—theory-of-mind (also called "perspective-taking" or "mind-reading")—was an enigma.

A fundamental issue for theory-of-mind is how it affects interactions with others. Jennifer Jenkins and Janet Astington tested twenty children on three occasions, three and a half months apart, when the children were between three and four years of age. The children's theory-of-mind was assessed by three tasks.

One was a change-in-location task similar to that in which children had to say where Maxi would look for his chocolate. Another involved containers that had unexpected contents: for instance a Smarties box (which looked as if it contained candies called "Smarties") was shown to contain crayons instead. Children had to say both what they thought the box had first contained, and what they thought a friend would think. A third task was similar to this, but was about appearance-and-reality, for instance with an object that looked like a rock, but was actually made of foam. The children were video-recorded in play that included toys and dressing-up clothes with a friend. Scores were obtained for joint planning. An example was when a child said, "Pretend you're squirting me again," and for role assignments, as when one child said to the other, "Hello teacher." Their abilities at theory-of-mind predicted how well they did in joint planning and role assignments. That is to say, when children were better able to construct mental models of the other's mind, during their play they were better able to make cooperative plans and take part in roles that involved interdependence.

Jenkins and Astington found that, in general, earlier language abilities predicted earlier abilities in theory-of-mind, but better abilities in joint planning during play did not predict children's subsequent scores in theory-of-mind tasks. It seems that theory-of-mind emerges somewhat as language does, in an individualistic way during the course of development.

There has now been a great deal of research on how and when theory-of-mind develops in children. The deep issue is that in order to be human, that is to say in order to interact with others in relationships, we need to make mental models of each other. We do this by interacting with them, by seeing whether their emotions are affectionate or stand-offish, by knowing whether they are reliable in arrangements they make, by what friends and relations say about them in conversation.

We humans not only have mental models of our acquaintances, but we know—and we need to know—what mental models these others have: what they think about others including what those others think. In *The Human Story*, Robin Dunbar puts it like this. Shakespeare's *Othello* involves several levels of theory-of-mind. Here they are with mental states italicized and numbered in square brackets.

> Shakespeare *intended* [1] that we in the audience would *realize* [2] that Othello *believed* [3] that his servant Iago was being honest when he claimed to *know* [4] that his wife Desdemona *loved* [5] his lieutenant, Cassio.[13]

To be in the audience and understand this play, we must have at least four levels. As author, Shakespeare needed the five levels depicted above.

As humans we make mental models of the people we know. Some of us, too, find it easy to make models of others' models, three or four deep. Our social worlds are intense, but without understanding the kinds of people that others are, and the kind of person each one of us is in our own self, these worlds could scarcely work. Perhaps it was at the next level or two deeper, of understanding what others understood about him and what they thought and felt about how he thought and felt about them, that Kenneth Craik felt unsure, and hence isolated.

8

The Digital World

Prototype of the Automatic Computing Engine (ACE) based on a design by Alan Turing.

Alan Turing invented digital computing, and proposed the idea of artificial intelligence, which also provides bases for theories of how we perceive, think, and use language. Geoffrey Hinton has shown that learning can occur by changes of connections in networks of artificial neurons, which make generalizations and construct inner models from being offered many examples. The means by which Google now offers translations from one language to another is based not on rules of the kind Chomsky proposed, but in this way.

The Turing Machine

The first article by which Alan Turing became famous was published in 1936. In it he demonstrated that any problem that is computable by a human can be computed by a machine, for which he gave specifications. It has become known as the Turing Machine, and it is the basis of all computers. A pilot version of one of the earliest computers, the Automatic Computing Engine designed by Turing, is shown in the chapter opening photo.

Turing's innovation is fundamental to modern life. If you have a smart phone, it's a small computer, based on Turing's idea. Computation became fundamental to cognitive science as well. The new cognitive science was a real revolution. Before Turing's work, psychological theories involved metaphors or analogies. Memory, for instance, was said to include a trace like that which occurs in a photograph or a tape recorder, stored somewhere in the brain. Turing's new idea, which has become fundamental to cognitive science, was to program computers actually to remember, to make decisions, and to think.[1] Theories began to be produced that were not just about mental processes. They were based on processes that do what the human mind does. The principle was, and is, that both the mind and a computer make models of the world and, from such models, draw inferences and generate actions.

Although Alan Turing and Kenneth Craik were both at Cambridge at the same time, they seem not to have met. Their ideas were in many ways similar. Craik, too, had thought of the mental models he proposed as being like calculating machines. But these two young people were at colleges on opposite sides of the university.

Turing would cross to the other side of the university to attend courses given by Ludwig Wittgenstein, who had written in *Tractatus* (4.01): "The proposition is a model of the reality as we think it is."[2] In 1936 Turing went to Princeton University, in the

United States, to complete his PhD. When World War II started in 1939, he returned to England and began work at the secret British Government Code and Cypher School at Bletchley Park, a forty-minute train journey from London's Euston Station.

Computation at Bletchley Park

During World War II, Turing's idea of mind-like models that could be programmed in computers was developed at Bletchley Park to crack the codes used by Nazi commanders to send messages to their military forces. The initial focus of Turing and his team was on a coding machine called Enigma, which was used by the Germans.[3] It had typewriter keys, and above them letters in typewriter layout with lights behind each one that lit up to show what each coded output letter was when a typewriter key was pressed. The machine allowed an operator to type in a message in which each letter of the message, called the "plain text," was transformed into the coded output, seen as a letter with the light behind it.

One part of the Enigma mechanism worked by means of a plugboard that the operator would set up in a different configuration each day, using a coding book that all the operators possessed. It enabled the machine to be set up in some 150,000,000,000,000 ways. The second mechanism was based on three rotors, chosen by the operator out of a set of five. The rotors worked so that with each letter typed in, they first routed the electrical signal to produce a coded output letter and then, for the next letter, they rotated to a new setting, and hence a new code for the next letter. To choose three rotors from a set of five gives 60 possibilities. The number of settings derived from the three rotors, each with 26 positions, is 26 x 26 x 26 = 17,576. So, given these processes, the overall number of configurations was 150,000,000,000,000 x 60 x 17,576: a very large number. If a human being were to work through all the possibilities for a coded message of 20 letters at the rate of one per second, it would take several billion years to do so. The Nazis thought that Enigma codes were unbreakable.

Before the War, Polish code-breakers knew of the Enigma machine and had started work on decoding its messages. They knew that each coding operation was symmetrical: if an A were input and the coded output was R, then if an R was input its coded output was A. Because of this pairing, to receive a coded message, the operator would type in a coded message to a properly set up Enigma machine, and the original German plain-text message appeared in the sequence of the machine's letters lighting up one at a time. The Polish code-breakers also knew that the instructions for how to set the rotors, which were different for each day, were sent over the airwaves as three-letter signals, transmitted twice.

With Gordon Welshman, a Cambridge mathematician, Alan Turing was able to build on the work of the Polish code-breakers, to make inferences from the pairings of plain text and coded letters of the initial rotor-setting messages and other regularities in the system. Based on a Polish prototype, called the Bomba, Turing and Welshman constructed an improved version, the Bombe, which was a model of the Enigma machine. It was designed to work backwards from coded letter sequences picked up as Morse code messages over the radio to the settings of the plug-board and rotors, and hence to messages that had been sent.

The Bombe was a specialized computer, constructed to search its model of the Enigma machine. The task for Turing, Welshman, and their colleagues was to exploit regularities of the Enigma machine to reduce the amount of searching that had to be done, and to use the Bombe to work through possible settings much faster than a human could do. The goal was to eliminate settings that produced contradictions, for instance settings that would not work because of German spelling rules, until the model could offer a small number of hypotheses about what the settings were, from which humans could infer the plain-text words in German. Search was then, and continues to be, central to computational models of mind.

It's said that Turing's work in decoding messages from Hitler and his commanders shortened the War by as much as two years, and hence saved millions of lives. By the end of the War, ten sizable electronic computers, called Colossus, were in use at Bletchley Park. But during the Cold War years, everything that had taken place there was kept secret. Beyond just a tiny number of people, no one understood the whole operation. One consequence was that the history of computation had huge holes, which have only gradually been filled.

The Imitation Game

The 1936 paper on the idea of the Turing Machine, which could calculate anything that a human being could calculate, was fundamental for the development of cognitive science. In 1950 Turing published another paper, which took the idea further. It began the study of artificial intelligence. The paper was entitled "Computing machinery and intelligence." In it Turing outlined what he calls "the imitation game." As described in the paper, two humans, let's call them Amy and Beatrice, and a computer, let's call it Chloe, interact with each other by means of teletypes; nowadays they would send text messages. Beatrice answers questions that Amy puts to her. Chloe is an imitation of a human mind that can think in the sense that Craik outlined by operating on models and it, too, answers Amy's questions. Amy knows that one of the two, Beatrice or Chloe, is a human and the other is a computer. From their answers she must work out which is which. Turing proposed that in the future a person in the role of Amy, in this game, would not be able to tell the difference between a human being and a computer-based model of a human.

Here is part of a conversation that Turing imagined.[4]

QUESTION: Please write me a sonnet on the subject of the Forth Bridge.

ANSWER: Count me out on this one. I never could write
    poetry.

QUESTION: Add 34957 to 70764.

ANSWER: (Pause about 30 seconds and then give as answer)
    105621.

QUESTION: Do you play chess?

ANSWER: Yes.

QUESTION: I have K at my K1, and no other pieces. You
    have only K at K6 and R at R1. It is your move. What
    do you play?

ANSWER: (After a pause of 15 seconds) R-R8 mate.

What do you think? Are these answers being given by Beatrice
the human or Chloe the computer? The answer to the first question is cute, but ambiguous. As to the second, we know that computers can add numbers. They are better at it than people, and they
can do it quickly. If Chloe computer were answering, she would
have inserted the 30-second pause to imitate a human. What about
the third question, about the chess problem? If Beatrice were answering she would make a mental model of the chessboard with
the positions of the three pieces on it. Chess players can do this;
the better they are at chess, the easier they find this kind of mental-
modeling. Chess was among the earliest problems on which artificial intelligence programmers worked. In 1997, a computer program called Deep Blue beat the reigning chess champion Garry
Kasparov in a six-game match.[5] Deep Blue was a chess-playing program with mental models of a chessboard, of chess pieces, and of
chess rules, that ran on an IBM computer.

    A 2014 film directed by Morten Tyldum, called *The Imitation
Game*, is mainly about Alan Turing's code-breaking at Bletchley
Park. A clever idea in this film is that we human beings often
speak to each other in codes. Turing was dedicated to truth, and
wondered why we don't just tell each other what we mean. In
the film, he realizes that he has spoken in code to the mathematician Joan Clarke, who came to work at Bletchley Park. Turing

and Clarke went together to the cinema a few times, and Turing proposed marriage. Clarke accepted. Turing felt affection for her and was pleased for the two of them to visit both her parents and his, but his model of himself was that he was homosexual. When he told her this, she was unfazed. How would you have decoded these messages? Turing later thought he should not marry, so the relationship had to be adjusted. He and Clarke remained close friends.

There are now many computer models that can give answers to a range of questions in a human-like way, and can even hold conversations. Turing's idea, which he put forward with "the imitation game," has become known as the Turing Test. So far no computer program has passed it over a range of questions, but many experts think that this will happen in time, perhaps a fairly short time.

There are deeper issues to consider. Computers and artificial intelligence brought a new principle into psychology. If you understand some mental process, really understand it, then you should be able to write a computer-based version of this process. Now, for instance, following some of the principles that Helmholtz laid out, as discussed in chapter 1, robots have been programmed to perceive an environment and its objects as they move around in it.

To do good research in cognitive science, the ability to write computer programs has become central. It works like this. To understand a psychological process—to perceive, to hold a conversation, to reason—one can put together parts that have been discovered by experimentation and other methods into computational models. Programming such working models can then give one lovely insights into what it takes for the mind to work as it does. Writing programs enables one to create understandings and new hypotheses about mental processes in a way that nothing else can. We can think of this principle as synthesis, and put it alongside the principle of analysis that derives from hypothesis and experimentation.

Artificial Intelligence

Among the most common computational models, or simulations, today are the kinds used in video games. If you play such a game, or watch a trailer for one, you will see a landscape through which you or your avatar can move. You may see castles and ravines. You may decide to go along this path, or through that gate. Birds of prey may hover above. Sword-wielding warriors may approach you. All this is made possible by understandings developed over the last fifty years of the relation between three-dimensional models and projections of these models onto two-dimensional surfaces such as the screens of your computer or television set. Understanding how to use these models has derived from developments in the cognitive understanding of perception.

The people who write the programs for video games start with three-dimensional models for which they can specify the coordinates of principal parts. Think of a map. A map reference is a coordinate in an east-west direction and a coordinate in a north-south direction. In three-dimensional space another coordinate is needed, too, in the up-down direction. The three coordinates define exactly where some part of an object is, for instance the tip of a sword. Then, with coordinates for other parts of the model object, one can know where the whole object is in three-dimensional space and how it is oriented. Then, by algebra, one can work how images of the object would look when projected on a two-dimensional screen, from any viewpoint. And it can be calculated how the object will look when it moves or changes.

Video games and virtual reality involve solving puzzles and, often, interacting with adversaries. The games derive from Craik's idea of models, and Turing's ideas of how to program computational implementations of them. The computational processors that video-gamers use to play their games conduct billions of algebraic calculations to generate from their models the two-dimensional views of the simulated world that the gamers see as they move through it.

In 1951, having done more than almost anyone else to help win the war against the Nazis, and having designed computers at the National Physical Laboratory in Teddington, near London, a prototype of which is seen in a photo at the beginning of this chapter, and in Manchester, Turing was charged with homosexual practices. He was subjected to chemical castration by injection of female hormones. In 1953, at the age of forty-one, he died, perhaps by suicide. He was pardoned posthumously for an activity that few people now think should ever have been made illegal.

Turing's principles of search over many possibilities in a model, and of narrowing the search space, became basic to artificial intelligence. It was by these methods that Deep Blue was able to think ahead through variations for each move and their possible replies to beat Garry Kasparov at chess. More recently the process of search, done in clever ways to narrow the search space, is what provides the oomph inside Google's success on the Internet.

The New Cognitive Science

In 1985, Howard Gardner published *The Mind's New Science*, a brilliant introduction to the cognitive approach to mind. In it he discusses research by Bartlett and Piaget. He mentions Craik, and reviews Johnson-Laird's experiments on reasoning, based on Craik's ideas. He writes, however, that "the logical-mathematical work that ultimately had the greatest import for cognitive science was carried out by . . . Alan Turing."[6]

A proponent of the new cognitive approach was George Miller. Gardner tells us of Miller's proposal that September 11, 1956 was the date of the real turning point,[7] the day on which cognitive science really got started, when a meeting was held at the Massachusetts Institute of Technology (MIT) on information theory. Noam Chomsky presented a paper at this meeting, called "Three models of language," in which he sketched his ideas on transformational grammars. Allan Newell and Herbert Simon presented the first proof of a theorem by a computer: the "Logic theory machine." George Miller presented his idea that short-term memory has approximately seven slots in it, with each slot able to carry something as simple as a number or as complex as a concept. The idea would issue in a paper called "The magical number seven, plus or minus two." Miller came away from the meeting with a "strong conviction ... that human experimental psychology, theoretical linguistics, and computer simulation of cognitive processes were all pieces of a larger whole."[8]

With Eugene Galanter and Karl Pribram, Miller published *Plans and the Structure of Behavior*. They weren't quite bold enough to call it *Plans and the Structure of Mind*, but it was a step toward showing how the human mind is indeed based on structures, and on plans and other processes that can produce outcomes. A plan is made by starting from a goal in a mental model of the world as one would like it to be, then working backward through a se-ries of states of the world to the current state. These states are stored, and for each one an action is conceived to accomplish it. To enact the plan, each step is taken in reverse order, from the current state to the goal. At last the mind was beginning to be seen as made up of operations that are able to construct outcomes that are not so much behavior, but that much more important entity, action.

To start with, the only method in artificial intelligence was to write programs by hand, as sequences of instructions based mainly on "if-then": if this is the case, then do that, or if the result of a computation is this, then the state of the model-world is that. It was a development of Piaget's idea that in adulthood a person thinks by means of logical operations. Programs were written to analyze visual scenes, starting with visual images and making inferences about the structure of the three-dimensional world. A

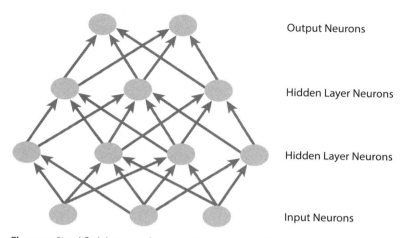

Output Neurons

Hidden Layer Neurons

Hidden Layer Neurons

Input Neurons

Figure 13. Simplified diagram of a system that learns by adjusting the strengths of connections among artificial neurons in layers. *Source*: Diagram by Keith Oatley.

good deal of what we know about vision can now be performed computationally and this has been helpful in understanding how the human visual system works.[9] Another informative application has been for language in which programs have been written to implement grammatical rules, including those of the kind Chomsky proposed.[10]

A different approach has been pioneered by David Rumelhart, Geoffrey Hinton, and colleagues. According to this approach, operations are not based on logic and rules but on artificial neurons, which have activations. The simulated neurons are simpler than the brain's neurons, but they embody an idea, which physiologists have established, that information is stored in the strengths of the connections among them. In this kind of system, illustrated in figure 13, there is a set of input neurons (equivalent to receptors), layers of intermediate, or hidden, neurons, and output neurons (equivalent to motor neurons) that implement actions.

Imagine that in a network of the kind pictured in figure 13, the pieces of information given to the input neurons (at the bottom of the diagram) are digits (ten of them rather than just the three represented in the figure), and that the network's task is to classify each as odd or even. Imagine digits being offered to the system, one by one, as activations of one of the ten input neurons. Imagine then that activation of the output neuron at the top right of the diagram is taken to mean that the input digit is "even," while activation of the output neuron at the top left means it's "odd." When each example digit is presented—say 2, 4, 6—the programmers have arranged that a signal is sent backward (a process called back-propagation) from the right-hand output neuron to change the strengths of the connections in the network in the hidden layers. Connection strengths that tend to activate the "even" output neuron are increased, and connection strengths of those that tend to activate the "odd" output neuron are decreased. Many iterations of back-propagation are applied for each input digit, with each one reducing errors in the system's connections by small amounts. The result is that, when any digit is offered to it, the system will indicate whether it is even or odd. This is called supervised learning, because someone has had to specify whether each output is correct. The approach is like learning by reinforcement, of the kind the behaviorists proposed.

Deep Learning

Far more important, now, is unsupervised learning, in which there are no signals to say whether an output has been right or wrong, no reinforcements. Instead, huge networks can be offered millions of digitized pictures as inputs, and from these inputs the systems learn regularities in the visual world, which become embodied in the strengths of the systems' connections. The systems work not by logical operations, but by forming distributed mental models of these regularities. This unsupervised learning occurs by a process related to the making of associations, as proposed by David Hartley in the eighteenth century.

Generalizations are based on associations between things that are close in time and place. Two hundred years after Hartley, the idea was augmented by a proposal from Donald Hebb, that connections among neurons are strengthened when neurons fire together.

Geoffrey Hinton calls the new unsupervised mode—the making of associations by changing connections in a neural net—"deep learning."[11] For one system of this kind, designed by Hinton and his colleagues, input is given to the input-receptor layer from a digital video camera directed at a real scene. If the system moves the camera, then in the same way as occurs when the human eyes move, the system knows how much change to expect in the input image. From such movements, changes of pattern on the input-receptor layer allow the system to calculate the changes of the three-dimensional coordinates of the parts of the objects that gave rise to the input pattern: perhaps corners of objects, perhaps pieces of bright reflection. In this way the system can build three-dimensional models of objects in the world.

Hinton went to work for Google and, using one of his deep learning systems of visual perception, Google will show you pictures, from the Internet, of something you request verbally. You can try it yourself. Go to Google and type "Houses." Now select "Images." You will see a range of images of houses. If you type, "Jewelry," you will see pictures of jewelry. Houses are not too difficult. Features that are regularly associated with them include straight-line edges, rectangular windows, and so on. But jewelry? Such images might have features that are bright; but light-bulbs are bright. The jewelry might be on people's necks, or ears, or laid out in rows. The system is able to generalize from millions of examples to show you a wide range of images of jewelry, in different ways in which they might appear.

To see is to pick up information from the two-dimensional patches of activation of receptors of the retinae, in patterns that act as cues and prompt us to construct three-dimensional models of the world. In this kind of way, Hinton's system is the modern version of unconscious inference as explained by Helmholtz, on which we reflected in chapter 1.

An important accomplishment of deep learning has been in translation of text from one language to another, say English to French. This kind of translation used to be done computationally by making lists of phrases and, by hand-coding, matching each English phrase to its equivalent in French. In the kind of unsupervised learning networks invented by Hinton and his colleagues, sentences have been input from Wikipedia, with a total of half a billion words. The system finds what other words each input word is associated with in sentences, and makes generalizations, that is to say mental models, which are meaningful deep structures. So, when Google Translate is now given a sentence in English, it creates something like a thought, distributed among the network's connections: something like a meaning of what the writer might have intended.[12] To do the translation, the model is run in reverse, and offers an output in French based on this inner meaning.

In figure 14, you can see a map of meaning derived from the kind of system that is used by Google Translate: the closeness of associations of 2,500 English words from the input from Wikipedia, derived from vector models, and represented as spatial closeness on the map. In the figure, the cluster near the top and just to the right of center is of place names. At the top of it is Virginia, close to Missouri, and to Washington. At the bottom of this cluster, with the two words very close in meaning-space to each other, are Vietnam and Iraq.

On Google, now, you can find examples of something in which you are interested by typing in words and phrases. Using a meaning-based system, in the future you will be able to ask Google to find passages based on meaning: as Hinton suggests, you might want to find passages that seem to support efforts to slow down climate change but which really try to undermine the evidence that climate change is occurring.

Figure 14. Joseph Turian's map of meaning derived from input of half a billion words from Wikipedia, and their associations with each other in the sentences that were input. *Source*: Joseph Turian from Collobert, R. & Weston, J. (2008, July 5–8). *A unified architecture for natural language processing: Deep neural networks with multitask learning.* Paper presented at the ICML '08 Proceedings of the 25th international conference on machine learning, Helsinki. © Joseph Turian, with permission.

In another application, Ethan Fast and colleagues have analyzed more than a billion words from novels, to see what human beings do with objects. Their system, Auger, trains models that predict human activities from their contexts, for instance, eating food with a friend, attending a meeting, taking a selfie. Human evaluations of Augur's predictions were rated as 94 percent sensible.

Among controversies prompted by artificial intelligence is the question of whether the operations of computers to perceive, to translate languages, and to play games are helpful in understanding how humans do such things. Current conceptions support the idea that perception occurs in the way that Helmholtz proposed, and that the properties of neurons, as discovered in neurophysiological experiments, are important. Other views are that the ways in which computers do things need have no relation to how the human mind does them.

In the world beyond cognitive science, big controversies arise about whether artificial intelligence will take away people's jobs and cause unemployment. In an interview with the BBC, the physicist Stephen Hawking said:

> Humans, who are limited by slow biological evolution, couldn't compete, and would be superseded . . . The development of full artificial intelligence could spell the end of the human race.[13]

When computers pass the Turing Test and become difficult to distinguish from humans in their mental abilities, will they, as Hawking suggests, go further and surpass us as human beings? Hinton's answer is that this will not be a matter of science and technology. It will depend on political arrangements.

We might decide how to use computationally based abilities of a human-like kind for purposes that Francis Bacon proposed, for the betterment of the human state.[14] On the other hand, we might decide that the new artificial beings are too threatening to us and do away with them. To make decisions of this kind we must do research not just on how to make machines that work in mind-like ways, but also on social cognition to understand how beneficial arrangements can be created in society, and be chosen by people as worthwhile. The issue has begun to be aired in the short-story collection by Isaac Asimov, entitled *I Robot*, and in films like Alec Garland's *Ex Machina*. Might new beings, based on silicon rather than carbon, have feelings and rights?

During human development, technology has helped. Gutenberg's introduction of the technology of printing to Europe led to widespread education, which in turn enabled people to read. Among the books people read were novels, with a surge that started in the nineteenth century. In the twentieth century, Virginia Woolf wrote, "In or about December 1910, human character changed." In part she was referring to the inwardness of novels, in their exploration of character. In an article in the *New York Review of Books*, Edward Mendelson wrote that Woolf was "a hundred years premature." He says that "human character changed on or about December 2010 when everyone, it seemed, started carrying a smartphone."[15] He went on to say that human life is no longer mainly private, relational, inward, and that more of it has become public, broadcast, outward. In civil life, new methods include surveillance and monitoring. In international life, drones are employed along with other devices that have long-distance effects on others.

Might there be new ways to think about how to take part in our new digital world? Might we, for instance, use some of the new digital connectedness among us to join in with more engagement and consequence, to help make political decisions about how we should live?[16]

Deep Principles for Psychology

The preceding implications of digital technologies are timely and important, but there are also other fundamental principles for psychology to reflect upon.

Psychological theories employed in artificial intelligence are not just analogies—memory is like a tape-recorder—the models that are produced can actually work in human-like ways. The success of deep learning, based on neurons and their connections, has demonstrated that learning can take place in the kind of way that it does for babies, by encountering many examples, with generalizations being made by associating things that are close in time and place. Ideas such as those of Jean Piaget and Noam Chomsky were that thinking occurs by an inner machinery of logic or of rules. It seems now, however, that rather than inner logical processes and grammars, being the bases of thinking and conversation, logic and rules are not themselves the bases of inner mechanisms. They are summaries of outcomes.

The best current hypothesis is that mental models are first constructed as inscrutable intuitions based on associations in distributed neural networks, and that these intuitions can then be offered into consciousness or externalized to others (and ourselves) as verbal and non-verbal languages of our conversations and interactions.

PART THREE

Mind and Brain

9

You Need Your Head Examined

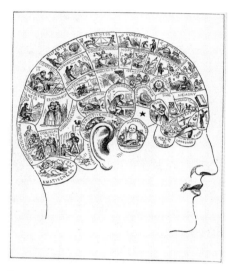

Phrenological diagram of propensities localized in the human brain.

The proposal of phrenology was that traits of personality are localized in specific parts of the brain. Modern psychology includes traits of personality, but not with this kind of localization. Carol Magai and Jeannette Haviland-Jones developed the idea of personality as psychological biography, based on early relationships, and expressed in emotion-based interactions with others. David Kenny showed that our personalities have different aspects. In one aspect we show the same traits to most of the people we are with. In another we can elicit certain kinds of

moods from others. A further aspect occurs in the emotions of relationships with specific others.

Phrenology

It's 1840 and you go to have your head examined. A specialist takes a tape measure to your skull, runs fingers across your
head, and notes protuberances and indentations. You receive a
diagnosis. Perhaps you are told that your Philoprogenitiveness,
love of your children, is well developed. Perhaps you are told
you are low on Cautiousness. The specialist is telling you about
two powers of the mind, each localized in a particular part of the
brain. When a part is well developed it has pushed out a bit on
your skull to make a bump. If less developed there is a dent.

The person who examined your head would have been a specialist in phrenology, a system of thinking about the mind and
brain that became popular in the first half of the nineteenth century.[1] You can see a diagram of phrenological regions of the brain
at the opening of this chapter. The inventor of phrenology was
Franz Gall. Some of his early studies were conducted on inmates
of lunatic asylums and jails. He found a region, at the side of the
head, an inch-and-a-half or so above the ear, that was especially
well developed in pickpockets. This region contained the organ
of Acquisitiveness.

When Franz Gall was a schoolboy, he thought the shapes
of the heads of some of his schoolmates showed something
about their mental characteristics. As a medical student, he
continued to make such observations. Those who had promi-
nent eyes seemed to have good memories. In 1800, after he had
qualified in medicine, he was joined by Johann Spurzheim, and
the two of them began to lecture all through Europe. Spurzheim was the popularizer; it was he who introduced the term
"phrenology."

Gall's main work began to be published in 1810. It has one of the most overdeveloped titles of any book in the library. In English, it is, *On the Functions of the Brain and of Each of Its Parts: With Observations on the Possibility of Determining the Instincts, Propensities, and Talents, or the Moral and Intellectual Dispositions of Men and Animals, by the Configuration of the Brain and Head*. The first volume deals with the whole nervous system, the sensory nerves, the spinal cord, the cerebellum, and so on. It isn't until volumes 2, 3, and 4 of this work, the last of which was published in 1819, that Gall enters into phrenology proper.

Gall's head was—of course—examined. A phrenological biographer wrote:

> The organs of Amativeness, Philoprogenitiveness, Adhesiveness, Combativeness, and Destructiveness, were all very well developed in Gall. His Secretiveness was also rather large, but he never made bad use of it. He was too conscious of his intellectual powers to obtain his ends by cunning or fraud.[2]

Gall proposed that there are thirty-seven mental dispositions, each of which is generated by a specific organ in the brain. By 1840, commentators had started to say this was pseudoscience, and its popularity waned, although phrenological societies and journals continued into the twentieth century.

Here's a phrenology of the automobile. We open the hood and see a big lump. That must be its Goingness. What about its Stoppingness? Perhaps that's somewhere down near the wheels. What about other parts—the organ of Speediness, the organ of Economicalness, the organ of Noisiness? Might there perhaps be an organ of Stuckness-in-Traffic? We know that's not quite right. To understand how cars work, we need to know about the functions of such parts as ignition systems and pistons and camshafts.

Despite this, historians such as John van Wyhe have argued that Gall's influence was important. In his multi-volume book, Gall proposed that the brain is the organ of the mind, that it is not homogeneous but an aggregate of functions, each localized in a specific part of the brain. We now accept that the brain is the organ of mind, and also that specific parts have specific functions. Two hundred years ago many thought that those who were mentally ill were possessed by evil spirits. Phrenology was one of the influences that helped people realize that some of the inmates of insane asylums might be suffering from diseases of the brain.

Now if someone says, "You need to have your head examined," that person isn't just referring back to an outmoded system, but is being rude. The person is telling you that some propensity is overdeveloped and that you should recognize it so that you can suppress it. The idea of diagnosis and self-therapy helped make phrenology popular. Although some phrenological propensities had peculiar names, the idea of psychological functions was appealing, and the proposal that they are produced by the brain made them seem objective. At the same time, the message of hope in phrenology was inviting. You could improve yourself by developing or diminishing a propensity. This kind of thought would, one hundred years after Gall's lectures on phrenology, become central to the practice we recognize as psychotherapy.

Personality

Modern psychology tells us we each have enduring dispositions: traits of personality. In the manner suggested by those who developed the test questions asked by Binet and Simon, these traits are detected from the pattern of answers to questionnaires. You are given such statements as: "You are emotionally stable, not easily upset," or "You are talkative," and then asked to rate these statements on scales that range between "Strongly disagree" and "Strongly agree." People who strongly agree with the first of these statements will get a high score on Emotional Stability. People who strongly agree with statements such as the second will get a high score on Extraversion.

Emotional Stability and Extroversion are traits in a system that has become standard: the Big Five test of personality developed in the 1980s by Paul Costa and Robert McCrea.[3] The other three traits are Agreeableness, meaning sociability and friendliness; Openness to new experience, including fantasies, emotions, and aesthetics; and Conscientiousness, which includes being dutiful and striving for achievement. This last trait, Conscientiousness, made it into the Big Five from Gall's list of thirty-seven powers of the mind.

It follows from Darwin's idea of variation, and from his idea that mental abilities are inherited along with physical characteristics, that personality may have genetic foundations. Based on studies of identical (monozygotic) twins who share 100 percent of their genes, and non-identical (dizygotic) twins who share 50 percent of their genes, Melissa Moore and colleagues have found that the genetic component of each of the Big Five traits of personality is around 50 percent, with a component of almost the same size that is unique to the individual's own experience of the world.

Personality traits have an emotional quality. One can even think of them as long-term moods. Low Emotional Stability is a tendency toward anxiety and sadness; Extraversion involves cheerfulness; Agreeableness is warmth and friendliness; Openness involves eagerness: Conscientiousness includes a tendency to earnestness and disapproval.

There have, of course, been studies to see how the Big Five traits are represented in the brain.[4] Here, research has not shown very clear results. Low Emotional Stability, in which people tend to take a negative view of events, with tendencies toward anxiety disorders and depression, has been considered to involve areas of the brain such as the amygdala. Extraversion is associated with brain systems that mediate reward.

In comparison with the forty-seven propensities suggested by Gall, the idea of having only five traits may seem stingy. But Colin

DeYoung and his colleagues have proposed that each trait has two facets. Low Emotional Stability is Volatility and Withdrawal, Extraversion is Enthusiasm and Assertiveness, Agreeableness is Compassion and Politeness, Openness is Intellect and Openness, Conscientiousness is Industriousness and Orderliness.

If you wonder whether a self-report questionnaire method is valid, in 1988, Costa and McCrea published a study in which they report on 167 people who answered the Big Five questionnaire and also had their spouses rate them on the scales of Emotional Stability, Extraversion, and Openness.[5] The spouses agreed fairly closely with those to whom they were married. In this same paper the researchers reported on how constant 983 people's Big Five personality traits were over six years. For both men and women the stability of their ratings on all five scales was high, after the age of thirty. Before the age of thirty, although there is stability there is also change, as has been shown by Brent Roberts and Daniel Mroczek. They found that between the ages of about twenty to thirty, people on average became more self-confident and warmer toward others. They also tended to increase their Emotional Stability and their Conscientiousness.

Costa and McCrea start an article with this question. "How will you feel two months and three days after your 78th birthday?"[6] You might say you would feel old, or that it would depend on circumstances. Costa and McCrea say that you are likely to be wrong: more likely you will feel much as you do today. Emotionality and mood have continuity with childhood temperament. They will have pervaded your life so far, and are likely to pervade it in the future.

Personality, Character, Biography

A different way of understanding people is in terms of character, as depicted in novels. In "The art of fiction," Henry James wrote, "What is character but the determination of incident? What is incident but the illustration of character?"[7] This also applies to biography, and it is closer to the mental models we make of people we know, and of ourselves, than are traits of personality.

Rather than being about general tendencies such as "You are talkative," character in biography and fiction is about how a person handles particular circumstances. Famous among biographies is *Eminent Victorians*, by Lytton Strachey, in which he gives accounts of the lives of famous people from the century previous to his own, which emphasize features that were rather different than the myths that had circulated about them. In it he recounts, for instance, how in the first part of her life Florence Nightingale was active as a nurse, working with soldiers in the Crimean War, where she became known as "The lady with the lamp." Much less widely known was that after the war she became formidable and effective in her promotion of public health measures in the army and in civil society in Britain. At the age of forty-five she moved into a house in South Street, near Park Lane, in London, where she stayed for another forty-five years, going out very little, and spending much of her time in bed. There she engaged in the development of statistics and epidemiology, and was visited by dignitaries from the government and abroad.[8]

A fascinating advance of modern times, which combines personality, character, and biography, is the work of Carol Magai and Jeannette Haviland-Jones in their study of three psychotherapists, Carl Rogers, Albert Ellis, and Fritz Perls. The authors analyzed the three men's emotional expressions as they each interviewed a psychotherapy client, Gloria, in the first film made of psychotherapy.[9] They also analyzed themes as they had appeared in the three men's academic work, together with autobiographical and biographical writings. Their theoretical approach is developed from Freud's idea that it is from our relationships with parents that we develop a certain set of emotional modes of being, which become habitual, and form the bases of our character and our interactions with others.

Here is a sketch of Magai and Haviland-Jones's portrait of Carl Rogers. He was one of six siblings in a well-off Christian family.

He was unwell as a child, sufficiently so that his parents gave him a lot of attention. The family atmosphere was affectionate, but anger was forbidden. Rogers attended university and soon afterward started a long and, for the most part, happy marriage. He also started an extraordinarily successful career, in formulating a mode of psychotherapy that has become known as counseling. Those he knew found him gentle and lacking in anger, though he got into disputes with colleagues in psychiatry. It was probably to escape these conflicts that, during his career, he moved his place of employment several times.

Magai and Haviland-Jones write that he had a good relationship with his parents, perhaps especially his mother:

> Yet, his interactions with other social partners could be fractious . . . Rogers could also be painfully shy, and yet he was drawn to people and even did group encounter therapies. He often made others the center of his existence. He was also often in conflict with others, but he was not a particularly "angry" or hostile man.[10]

It was as if Rogers longed to recreate, for himself and his clients in therapy, the warm and close relationship that he had as a child with his parents. But his makeup also included a great deal of shame that seems to have been fostered by a mother who was keen to point out shortcomings. Throughout his life he maintained his longing for closeness with others, but he remained shy. When he spoke there were many "ums" and "ers" and his non-verbal signals were also of shame. The therapy he pioneered could be thought of as escape from shame, with the goal of attaining closeness and self-acceptance.

In the film with Gloria, Rogers showed a great deal of interest, but with eyebrows slightly slanted to express sadness. After the session Gloria said that with Rogers she was her more lovable self, and to her surprise she found it possible to talk openly with him about sex. The character who was Rogers, then, included an invitation to Gloria to express a certain aspect of herself, her more loveable aspect. After the session, Rogers spoke to the camera and said he felt the session had gone well. Magai and Haviland-Jones draw attention to a moment when he said, "When I'm able to enter into a relationship, and I feel it was true in this instance." Magai and Haviland-Jones write that, as he said this, his voice rose and that:

> He was being spontaneous here and the excitement and proud pleasure mounted. At the height of this juncture, the configuration of his face changed into a more open and unguarded one, and at this point we see the only "pure" prototypic interest expression (brows raised and arched) of the whole film. Furthermore, what happened next is even more revealing. The raised brow lasted only a flicker of a second before the muscles controlling the outer brow were drawn into play to pull the outer corners down, thus creating the sad brow.[11]

Magai and Haviland-Jones speak of how Rogers seemed to experience an instant of excitement here, but the emotional structure of his character would not enable him to dwell on it, because it is shameful to express self-satisfaction or pride.

Magai and Haviland-Jones had spotted an incident which, although small, reveals something central to Carl Rogers's character. In his novel *À la Recherche du Temps Perdu*, Marcel Proust had put this idea as follows:

> The features of our face are scarcely more than expressions that have been made so often that they have become fixed by habit. Nature, like the catastrophe of Pompeii, like the metamorphosis of a nymph, has immobilized us in a habitual movement.[12]

Personality derives from the temperament with which each of us is born, which has a large genetic component. It's an individual matter. Yet much of our life is social. So, is there an association between individuality and sociality? In a study in which people were given personality-questionnaire-type descriptors from individuals, and asked how each one would behave in particular circumstances, participants were able to make mental models of the people they imagined.[13] All the same, generalizations of personality are a long way from the specifics of mental models we make about our loved ones, friends, and acquaintances. How might traits of personality and habits of emotional engagement with others, of the kind depicted in biographical incidents, be brought closer together?

Social Relations

Traditional ideas of personality are generic and free of social context. She is talkative, he keeps to himself. David Kenny and his colleagues proposed a social relations model in which people affect each other and are affected by each other. One kind of influence is the actor effect. It's the style in which a person expresses herself or himself generally with other people. One person is typically warm and friendly to others, another is generally assertive. Another aspect is the partner effect, which is what a person elicits from others. One person might tend to cheer people up. Another may make them irritable. In the film with Gloria, Carl Rogers elicited from Gloria aspects of her more loveable self. Another kind of effect occurs only in specific relationships, in a way that is different from what occurs in other relationships. This is called the dyad effect. In one dyad we may spend a lot of time laughing, in another we may be more earnest. To estimate dyad effects, actor effects and partner effects that occur across all relationships are subtracted out, and the remaining effects include those that are distinctive to particular relationships.

Jon Rasbash, Jennifer Jenkins, and colleagues studied 687 non-divorced families and step-families that each included two parents and two adolescents, to observe actor effects, partner effects, and dyad effects, as well as to see whether a certain kind of relating was distinctive to particular families. The design included analyses of genetics, so in the non-divorced families there were monozygotic and dizygotic twins as well as non-twins, and in the step-families there were full-siblings, half-siblings, and genetically unrelated siblings. Each pair (for example mother-father, mother-older-child, mother-younger-child) was video-recorded for ten minutes as they conversed to resolve two issues that they had agreed were problematic between them. Problematic issues included actions toward themselves and toward other family members, chores, sharing, homework, money, in-laws.

The researchers focused on emotional Negativity and Positivity, which were coded from video recordings: from what was said, tone of voice, facial expressions, and gestures. Negativity included irritation, disapproval, criticisms, and hostility. It was exhibited in harsh parenting, sibling rivalry, and marital conflict. People who have high scores on this measure have been found to have lower well-being both as they remain in a family and when they leave it. These effects can last a lifetime. Positivity included warmth, affection, and closeness. High scores on this measure are associated with fewer disorders in children as they grow up.

In this study, a statistical analysis called multi-level modeling was used to distinguish actor effects, partner effects, dyad effects, and family effects. Actor effects derive from scores of emotional Negativity and Positivity expressed by a person across all relationships in the family. Partner effects derive from scores when the person, with each particular other, elicits a particular kind of emotion from all these others. Dyad effects (when actor and partner effects are subtracted out) are distinctive to particular relationships: for a sibling, for instance, when just with the other sibling, or just with the mother, or just with the father. Family effects are those common to all family members.

As you can see from figure 15, as actors, the fathers and adolescent children in the study by Rasbash and his colleagues

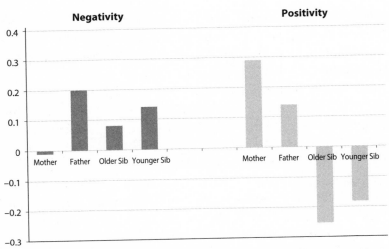

Figure 15. Mean amounts of Negativity and Positivity of actor effects in family members, as found by Jon Rasbash, Jennifer Jenkins, and colleagues. *Data source*: Table 1 of Rasbash, J. Jenkins J. M., et al. (2011). A social relations model of observed family negativity and positivity using a genetically informative sample. *Journal of Personality and Social Psychology, 100*, 474–491. Drawn by Keith Oatley.

expressed more Negativity (irritation, grumbling, criticism, and the like) and less Positivity (warmth and affection) than did the mothers. Overall, actor effects—which in this model are closest to traditional personality measures—were stronger for Positivity and explained 28 percent of variance (technical term for differences among people in the study) than for Negativity, which explained 20 percent of the variance. Actor effects were larger than partner effects, but a substantial partner effect was found for Negativity, and explained 9 percent of the variance.

An important finding was that around 50 percent of the variance in Negativity and Positivity was due to dyad effects: specific combinations of each pair of participants (a certain father and his fifteen-year-old daughter, a particular pair of step-siblings, and so on).

In addition to these, in this study and others, Jenkins and her colleagues have found substantial family effects in which the emotional atmosphere of each family influences all its members in the same way.[14] Leo Tolstoy opened *Anna Karenina* by writing that "All happy families are alike; each unhappy family is unhappy in its own way." Putting this in statistical terms, there is more variability among unhappy families, and this has been confirmed.

As to genetics and environment: for Negativity expressed by the adolescent children in the study by Rasbash, Jenkins, and colleagues, some 35 percent was due to genetic factors and 19 percent due to the shared family environment.

So, unlike what one might believe from standard theories, such as the Big Five, personality is not all in one lump. We each have an emotional style (actor effect) but we also tend to elicit certain kinds of emotions from others (partner effects). We each tend to be affected by the family in which we live (family effects), and we are different in our relationships with the different people we know (dyad effects).

What about the most celebrated dyad effect in industrial societies: falling in love and starting to live with someone? Lisa Neff and Benjamin Karney found from questionnaires and observed interactions in two samples of newly married people that both members of each couple were taken up in a strong positivity with their partner. Although they did not use methods based on actor and partner effects, we can say that Neff and Karney's finding was that newly married people were in a distinctive kind of dyad effect. They call it "global adoration." To some of the people in this study, it would come as a surprise to find that the person with whom they had started to live had what one might call a personality with an idiosyncratic way of being and acting (an actor effect), as well as characteristics (in a partner effect) that elicited from them particular kinds of emotion that were not necessarily of adoration. After the positive global sense of the other, only some of the newlyweds attained accurate perceptions of specific attributes of their new loved ones. On average, the wives, but not the husbands, were able to construct accurate perceptions of such specific attributes to improve their supportiveness toward their spouses and make it more likely that the marriages would last.

10

Mental Illness, Psychosomatic Illness

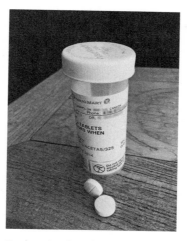

Psychoactive drugs have become widespread for treatment of mental disorders.

Mental hospitals have been replaced by psychoactive drugs. Some mental illnesses derive from malfunctions in the brain, but George Brown and Tirril Harris found that the most common kind of mental illness, depression, usually starts with something going wrong not in a person's brain, but in a person's life. Higher rates of mental illness in different countries, and in different regions within the same country, relate to the amount of inequality between people's incomes in that country or region. Different kinds of psychological therapy have been found helpful. Psychosomatic illnesses can be brought on by certain kinds of stress and these, too, have been shown to be influenced by psychological therapy.

Can We Be Right in the Head?

The nervous system employs many chemicals, and in the brain they are distributed unevenly. Most drugs that affect the mind do so by influencing the metabolism of transmitter substances, hormones, or other chemicals in certain systems of the brain. One drug might make people alert, another can diminish pain, another changes mood. Such drugs, of the kind shown in the photo at the opening of this chapter, have become familiar. Although some psychoactive drugs, such as alcohol, have been known for thousands of years, the supply of prescription drugs intended to affect psychological functions didn't really get going until the 1950s; now it's widespread.

In the 1950s and 1960s in Europe and North America, psychiatry was transformed. You can read about this in Andrew Scull's *Madness in Civilization*. Although one reason for the change was the coming of the new drugs, another was the anti-psychiatry movement in which doubts were expressed about the ways in which people with mental illnesses were kept, sometimes involuntarily, for long periods in mental hospitals, not all of which were well staffed or well maintained. At that time, people who suffered hallucinations or delusions, or who were manic or depressed, were kept "under observation" in hospital. In the 1950s, says Scull, "in England and Wales 150,000 patients were to be found locked up in mental hospitals on any given day . . . in the United States the figure was nearly four times that many."[1] In this way, "In New York State in 1951," writes Scull, "one third of the amount spent on state operations went to underwrite the costs of its mental hospitals, compared with a national average of 8 percent."[2] Despite this, at that time, there was no standard system of psychiatric diagnosis, and agreement on specific diagnoses and recommendations for specific treatments was about 65 percent.[3]

Leaders in the anti-psychiatry movement were Thomas Szasz in the United States and R. D. Laing in Britain. Both had trained in psychoanalysis, which at that time was the principal approach to psychological therapy. Also at that time there was a biological approach to psychiatric treatment: Electro-Convulsive Therapy (ECT). Popular sentiment became involved as concern grew with how people were treated in mental hospitals. This may be seen in Milos Forman's film *One Flew over the Cuckoo's Nest*, in which Randle McMurphy is involuntarily hospitalized and tormented by the authoritarian Nurse Ratched. When he disobeys the rules he is given ECT as punishment. In the end Ratched succeeds in having him undergo surgery with a frontal lobotomy.

The target of the anti-psychiatry movement was psychiatric practice. Long-term hospitalization came to be seen as inappropriate and, at the same time, local authorities became alarmed at the expense of mental hospitals. These changes combined seamlessly with the coming of drugs such as the anti-psychotic Thorazine.[4] The result was that mentally ill people were to be cared for, as the phrase stated, "in the community." Huge mental hospitals that were built in the nineteenth century still stand on the borders of cities, some decrepit, some repurposed to other uses. And, in turn, people who previously would have been in-patients at these facilities are now among those who sit on upturned milk crates outside grocery stores, asking for change. If a person is admitted to the hospital with a mental illness in the current environment, there is pressure to put the patient on a drug regime, and discharge her or him within a few days.

One way in which psychoactive drugs work is by keeping a transmitter substance in synapses for longer or shorter periods. Lengthening this time can occur by preventing re-absorption. Drugs called selective serotonin reuptake inhibitors (SSRIs) are thought to reduce reabsorption of the transmitter substance se-rotonin, so it remains in synapses and continues to activate the next neurons in the chains of connection. The best-known selec-tive serotonin reuptake inhibitor drug is Prozac, which began to be marketed as an antidepressant in 1987.

A book in which the regulation of society is assisted by psy-choactive drugs is Aldous Huxley's *Brave New World*, in which the genetics of intelligence are regulated by having people born in special breeding units to be *alpha, beta, gamma, delta, or epsilon*, with alpha being the more intelligent, and epsilon the grade of those to whom menial jobs will be assigned. Conditioning helps fit people without complaint to their societal roles, and the drug *soma* is universally used to promote happiness.

Prozac is not *soma*, but this is from a blurb of Peter Kram-er's 1993 best-selling book, *Listening to Prozac*. According to the blurb, the book

> announces a revolution in the science of the self. Tess takes Prozac because she's always been depressed; Julia takes it because she doesn't know who she is; when Sam takes the drug it makes him feel "better than well." Four and a half million Americans have taken this anti-depressant since it has been introduced, and many have become more confi-dent, popular, mentally nimble, and emotionally resilient.

In a 2008 article Marcia Angell argues that drug companies now control most research on psychoactive drugs and, she says: "there is mounting evidence that they often skew the research they sponsor to make their drugs look better and safer."[5] Three years later, in the *New York Review of Books*, she reviewed books that questioned the efficacy of Prozac and other such drugs. In her re-view, Angell reproduces an advertisement for Prozac from a 1995 issue of the *American Journal of Psychiatry*. It includes a color pho-tograph of a lively looking woman, smiling happily. The heading of the advertisement says: "For your patients with depression: The Prozac Promise." Below that, the advertisement lays out the promise: "It delivers the therapeutic triad: Confidence, Convenience, Compliance." What this means is that if you are a psychiatrist, you can have Confidence that your patient will like your prescription, that despite all the problems of depression this solution will be best for your Convenience, and that you can expect the patient to show Compliance with your treatment regime. Depression is the most prevalent mental illness in the Western world.

The marketing of Prozac and other selective serotonin reuptake inhibitors is based on the drug companies' idea that depression is an imbalance of serotonin in the brain's synapses. By correcting such imbalances, these companies say, drugs of this kind will solve the problem. Angell reports that that in 2011, 10 percent of people over the age of six in America were taking antidepressants, and many said the drugs were helpful. One problem with the drug companies' theory of depression is that it is not to be found in the scientific literature. In *The Emperor's New Drugs: Exploding the Myth of Anti-depressants*, Irving Kirsh writes: "It now seems beyond question that the . . . account of depression as a chemical imbalance in the brain is simply wrong."[6] This account is equivalent to the aspirin theory of pain: the theory that pain is a deficiency of aspirin in the blood.

In his book, Kirsch explains that obtaining approval of a drug by the Food and Drug Administration requires a far lower standard than showing that the drug actually works better than alternatives. Kirsch has found that in analyses of properly conducted trials in which people have been randomly allocated either to take a placebo or drug, then in comparison with placebos, specific selective serotonin reuptake inhibitors had either no effect, or a tiny effect. Placebos are inert substances, given as pills, that patients believe in. Kirsch says placebos have been found in such trials to be more effective than no treatment and 82 percent as effective as antidepressants.

Approaching the issue by way of brain chemicals assumes that depression is simply something wrong in the brain. Although brain processes are no doubt involved, the evidence is that people start to become depressed when something goes seriously wrong not in their brains but in their lives.

Life Events and Vulnerability

Our understandings of physical illness have been established in two stages. In the first, known as epidemiology, surveys have been conducted to find who has a particular illness, and what their life circumstances are. Then, in a second stage, hypotheses derived from this first stage have been explored to find particular mechanisms and to work on remedies. The first definitive epidemiological discovery was by John Snow in 1854. Among other findings, he traced an outbreak of cholera in the Soho area of London and showed that people had acquired the infection by getting water from a particular pump. He inferred that the disease was spread by germs. A hundred years later, Richard Doll and Bradford Hill found in a survey of doctors that smoking was associated with lung cancer. It wasn't until ten years after that that the epidemiology of mental illnesses began with a study of children who lived on the Isle of Wight, in the south of England. The most important psychiatric epidemiological study in adults was made ten years after the study of children. It was on the topic of depression. It was made by George Brown and Tirril Harris, on women who lived in the south of London. Women were chosen as participants because whereas addiction is more common in men, depression is more common in women.

Brown and Harris used a standardized method of diagnosis, by means of a semi-structured interview. They found that those who had a diagnosis of depression were likely to have had a serious life event or difficulty that had adverse consequences for them. Among 458 women interviewed, 37 had an onset of depression during the year before the interview. Of these 37 women, 33 had experienced a severe life event or a severe difficulty before the onset of their depression, a far higher rate of adversity than that for women who were not depressed. A severe event was something such as a loved one dying, or being fired from a job with no prospect of reemployment. A difficulty was a longer term problem, something such as serious illness, or a child being in trouble with the police. When such an adversity occurred to women who also had what was called a vulnerability factor—such as having no one in their lives to whom they were close and with whom they could share their emotional lives—then they were likely to become depressed. The support one gets from interaction of friends and intimates, called "social support," is now recognized as a major factor in preventing depression when adversity strikes. A common case of someone likely to become depressed is a woman who has two small children, no job, few friends, and a very small income, who suffers the adversity of her marriage breaking down.

Since Brown and Harris's work, it has been found that having one episode of depression makes further episodes more likely, even without further adversity. At this point changes do seem to occur in the brain to increase the probability of becoming depressed.

An important piece of early work on these issues was carried out in 1930 by Marie Jahoda, Paul Lazarsfeld, and colleagues on effects of unemployment in the village of Marienthal, near Vienna, where the main source of work was a textile mill, which closed down.[7] The research was interdisciplinary and innovative. Methods included observations, interviews, and asking inhabitants to keep diaries. The research team also introduced the idea of unobtrusive measures, which included numbers of books borrowed from the local library; these numbers declined, although people had more time on their hands. Poverty became severe. More severe were demoralization, apathy, and depersonalization: depression. Although income is, of course, important, Jahoda and colleagues concluded that the most important benefits of work are social and personal.

In the twenty-first century, an important study of depression is that by Avshalom Caspi, Terrie Moffitt, and their collaborators. They showed that serotonin does seem to be involved in depression, although not as a chemical imbalance of the kind implied by how drug companies say selective serotonin reuptake inhibitors like Prozac are supposed to work.

In 2003, Caspi and his colleagues published a study of 1,032 people (52% male, 48% female) in Dunedin, New Zealand, whom they had followed up from age three to age twenty-six. Participants were tested for the 5-HTT transporter gene, the function of which is to promote the transmitter substance serotonin. The gene comes in two forms, long and short. The long form is more efficient at promoting serotonin. Since everyone has paired chromosomes, one set from their father and one set from their mother, everyone has two of these 5-HTT transporter genes. So these pairs can be long-long, long-short, short-long, or short-short. In the cohort, 31 percent of people had two longs, 51 percent had a long and a short, and 17 percent had two shorts. The participants also had an assessment of how many severe life events they had experienced between their twenty-first and twenty-sixth birthdays.

The results were that people who suffered a severe life event and who had at least one short form of the gene were more likely to become depressed than those with two long forms of the gene. The greatest risk was for those who suffered a severe life event and had two short forms of the gene. Those with one or two short forms of the gene but no adverse life event did not become depressed. The long form of the gene protected people from depression even when severe life events occurred. Many follow-ups have been done. In one meta-analysis, Katja Karg and colleagues found both a role of adversity in the causation of depression, and the moderation of this effect by the 5-HTT transporter gene. In another meta-analysis, Neil Risch and colleagues found evidence for adversities in the causation of depression, but not for the role of the 5-HTT transporter gene in this relationship.[8] In the most modern studies, for example by Saskia Selzam and colleagues, it is now recognized that it's not single genes, but large groups of genes, which have substantial psychological effects.

Mental Illness, Societal Conditions, Therapy

Depression is the most common single diagnosis in psychiatry. It occurs as a pervasive sadness, or low mood, often together with loss of interest in activities that had been enjoyable, along with five other symptoms such as inability to concentrate, disturbances of sleeping, loss of weight, being slowed in one's movements, feelings of worthlessness, thoughts of suicide.

Longer-term adversities that increase the risk of depression include having been neglected in childhood, being socially isolated, being unemployed, being in an abusive marriage. Although modern industrial society has many benefits, disparities of income increase adversity and so are a major risk to the many people who live in poverty, surrounded by advertisements, television coverage, and physical evidence of what they do not have. To become depressed is to become despairing about life, and about what could ever be done to make it better.

The degree of income inequality in a nation contributes to risk of psychological disorders such as depression in that nation. Figure 16 shows the percentages of people in the populations of four countries who suffer from some form of mental illness. Beneath the column for each country is a number that represents income inequality: the ratio of income of the top 20 percent of incomes in that country to the bottom 20 percent. In Japan, that ratio is 3.4. In the United States, which is among the most unequal societies in the industrialized world, the top 20 percent of the

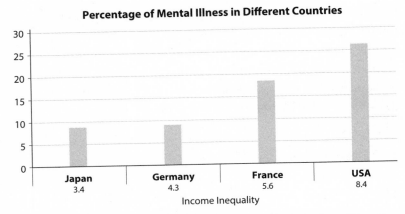

Figure 16. Percentages of people with mental illness in countries that have different levels of income inequality, as found by Kate Pickett, Oliver James, and Richard Wilkinson. *Data source*: Pickett, K. E., James, O. W., & Wilkinson, R. G. (2006). Income inequality and the prevalence of mental illness: A preliminary international analysis. *Journal of Epidemiology and Community Health, 60*, 646–647. Drawn by Keith Oatley.

population have incomes 8.4 times those of the bottom 20 percent. You will see, too, that the higher the income inequality, the more people suffer from a mental illness. In the United States, the percentage of the population with a diagnosis of mental illness is 26 percent. Most frequent is depression but mental illness in this study included anxiety disorders and addictions. Richard Wilkinson and Kate Pickett show that negative effects of income inequality apply similarly to physical illness, longevity, obesity, and many other outcomes. They show, too, that the patterns seen across countries are replicated across the different states of America. Although culture and customs across the United States are broadly similar, states with greater inequality of income have higher rates of mental and physical illnesses.

Neglect and abuse of children have been shown to be exacerbated by poverty, and they have been shown to set up vulnerabilities and risks, in adulthood, for states that include depression. These vulnerabilities have been shown to be ameliorated when parental incomes are improved, because the parents become less worried about how to live and can provide better care for their children.

Depression is hopelessness, giving up. It can occur for people whose problems in life have become overwhelming. In this state, people become less able to solve their problems, and so although we don't yet have a good theory of the brain processes of depression, drugs that enable people to feel less depressed can be helpful to people in coping with their lives. But there is some distance to go before drugs enable people to feel less hopeless, or less anxious about the slings and arrows of fortune. Drugs don't solve problems such as those induced by inequalities in society, by adverse life events and difficulties, and by childhood neglect and abuse. And, importantly, they should not distract us from the seriousness and pervasiveness of these problems. At the same time, they can sometimes enable people to cope better with their problems and with dispositions that arise from genetics and early childhood experience.

Disorders of depression and anxiety are helped by psychological therapies—talk therapies—for which Freud was an early proponent. Psychoanalytic therapy has been evaluated by Rolf Sandell and colleagues, who found substantial improvements after three years in 156 patients who had severe symptoms.[9] After their analyses, these patients continued to improve so that their mental health became indistinguishable from that of the ordinary population.

Psychoanalytic therapy takes a long time and it's expensive. Another problem is that it's very difficult to do well. Even Freud said he wasn't very good at it, or Dora would not have left before her therapy was finished. In her book, Janet Malcolm called psychoanalysis *The Impossible Profession*. There are now hundreds of psychological therapies, many of which aim to make therapy quicker and easier to conduct. Almost all follow Freud in being based on a therapist listening carefully and striving to understand psychologically what the patient (or client) says.

A form of psychological therapy that has been shown consistently to be worthwhile is cognitive-behavior therapy. For treatment of depression it has been found more effective than drugs, and it has a lower rate of relapse.[10] A new principle is that mindfulness meditation is now often combined with cognitive-behavioral therapy or psychoanalytic therapy.[11] Mindfulness derives from Buddhist meditation, in which each day one takes a period of time to be secluded and quiet, and concentrate on something of one's own choosing such as one's breathing. In this practice, when anxious and depressive thoughts come into the mind during this quiet time, as one returns to what one is concentrating on, those negative thoughts leave it again.

In *Ordinarily Well: The Case for Antidepressants*, Peter Kramer draws back from the claim in his previous book that antidepressants can make one "better than well." He offers an extensive review of evidence, statistical and clinical, and concludes that drugs can be helpful to some people some of the time. He also writes that in his practice as a psychiatrist, he relies heavily on psychotherapy, and postpones prescribing drugs.

Psychologists need to work on improving therapies. Perhaps even more important is prevention. Studies by Vincent Felitti and colleagues, including follow-ups such as that by Van Niel, Felitti, and others, have shown that adverse events in childhood—physical or sexual abuse, violence against the mother, having family members who were substance abusers or mentally ill, or had been in prison—are strongly predictive of poorer physical health, as well as psychological disorders including depression and addiction, in later life. They found that the larger the number of childhood adversities, the greater is the risk.[12] As well as improving therapies, therefore, psychologists need to work on reducing such risks, all of which are exacerbated by the long-term difficulty of poverty. We all need to work on reducing such factors as income inequality, which negatively affects mental health, starting in childhood, and is also a risk for conditions as disparate as obesity and the number of homicides in society.

Stress

The word "psychosomatic" refers to the connection between mind and body. The central issue here is stress. It's the same kind of idea as adversity, in the epidemiology of depression, but its use tends to be broader and to include mild as well as severe problems. One can read about stress in the newspapers, and ponder the solutions: exercise, yoga, meditation, lead a less hectic life, make more time for yourself.

When we experience a stress, the body responds in two phases. The first is rapid and involves the nervous system and hormones. Adrenaline increases blood flow and cortisol increases levels of blood glucose. The body switches from a state of equilibrium to a state of emergency, ready, as the phrase has it, for fight or flight. In terms of Darwin and emotions (chapter 3) we could say that the stress response is an expression of fear.

In a second phase of stress that is severe and long-lasting, changes can occur in the body's immune system, presumably from having been in a state of emergency for a long time. First of all, wounds take longer to heal. Second, the immune system can become less efficient in recognizing and destroying infectious germs. Third, the system can fail to recognize the body's own tissues, so that autoimmune problems such as rheumatoid arthritis (in which the immune system attacks the body's joints) can get worse. Fourth, the immune system can fail to detect and destroy cancers. Fifth, cardiovascular disease (heart attacks and stroke) can also become more likely, again perhaps mediated by changes in the immune system.

Among innovative researchers is Janice Kiecolt-Glaser, who proposes that stress is fundamental to the integration of psychology and the health sciences. In a study on wound healing, she and her colleagues made a small, standardized 3.5 mm wound on one side of the mouths of eleven dental students during their summer vacation.[13] Some weeks later, three days before the students' first major examination of the following term, the researchers made the same size wound on the other side of each student's mouth. The wounds made just before the examination took an average of three days longer (40% longer) to heal than those made during the vacation. This study has been replicated.

In a series of studies of long-term stress, Kiecolt-Glaser and her colleagues compared people who were long-term caregivers for spouses who suffered from dementia with similar people who did not have caring responsibilities.[14] They found that in the chronically stressed people a substance called interleukin-6 (which is involved in signaling in the immune system) was raised four times above its levels in the non-stressed group. This substance plays a role in promoting heart disease.

A third kind of study was published by Jamie Pennebaker and Sandra Beall, who randomly assigned forty-six psychology students to write for fifteen minutes on four consecutive evenings, either about a trauma in their lives or about incidental issues. Some students who wrote about the trauma were asked to write just about the facts, some about the emotions involved, and some about both the facts and their emotions. Those who wrote about both the facts and emotions of the trauma had higher blood pressure and more negative moods immediately following the writing, but during the next six months they had fewer medical consultations at the university health center than those of the other groups.

Joining with Janice Kiecolt-Glaser and Ronald Glaser, Pennebaker ran a replication of the study described in the previous paragraph with fifty participants who came into the laboratory. They were assigned either to a trauma condition or to a control (no-trauma) condition. Those in the trauma condition were instructed: "During each of the four writing days, I want you to write about the most traumatic and upsetting experiences of your entire life." Those in the no-trauma condition were given a neutral topic to write on at each session, and asked to write about it without discussing their own thoughts or feelings. On the day before the first session of writing, and again an hour after the final writing session, and then again six weeks later, all participants underwent measures of heart rate, blood pressure and skin conductance, blood tests, and psychological tests. The people assigned to write about traumatic events found the actual writing more subjectively distressing than did the control participants, but they later had more resilient responses to an immunological challenge than did the control subjects. As with the study by Pennebaker and Beall, the participants who wrote about trauma as compared with those who wrote about neutral topics also made fewer visits to their university health center.

Replications of these effects have been made many times by Pennebaker and his group, as well as by several groups of independent researchers. There seems no doubt that therapeutic effects follow from reflecting on traumatic experiences, either in writing or by talking to others. Pennebaker proposes that we are often unable to suppress effects of traumatic experience. It produces a stressfulness that is reduced by confiding to others about the event and its emotions, as well as by reflecting on them by writing.[15]

Overall, says Kiecolt-Glaser, effects of chronic stress are more severe in women, and in people of both sexes as they get older. One problem in this field, however, is that although some studies, such as the one on stress and wound healing, seem straightforward and conclusive, results on the relation of stress to major categories of illness such as cancer and heart disease are more complex.

In the industrialized world, heart disease kills millions of people each year. The evidence is that it can be precipitated by stress. One major investigative group, led by Kristina Orth-Gomer, has started to make sense of the area in the Stockholm Female Coronary Risk Study. In 2000, Orth-Gomer and her colleagues found that among married women who had suffered a heart attack and were followed up for 4.8 years, those with marital stress were almost three times more likely to have a further heart attack than those without marital stress. In contrast, those who suffered work stress were not more likely to have a further heart attack than those who did not. In another result, in 2009, Orth-Gomer and her colleagues studied 237 consecutive patients hospitalized for acute heart disease (patients with myocardial infarction, coronary bypass, or other kinds of coronary event). They were randomly assigned either to the usual post-hospital care or to a psychosocial intervention program in which groups of four to eight patients met for therapy with a female group leader for twenty sessions of two to two-and-a-half hours over the course of a year. Each group session began with relaxation training, then focused on education about risk factors, cognitive restructuring, coping with stress from family and work, counteracting depression and anxiety, and improving social relations and social support. Leaders made sure that every patient talked at each session. During seven years from the time of randomization, twenty-five women (20%) in the usual care group died, but only eight in the intervention group (7%) died. The intervention, then, provided an almost threefold protective effect.

The first substantial advances in modern medicine came with the epidemiological discoveries of John Snow that cholera was spread by contaminated water and that germs were involved. Then came prevention in the form of provision of uncontaminated water to households, and the removal of sewage and waste. Only after that did antibiotics arrive.

Another advance is in progress, in understanding how psychological illnesses and psychosomatic conditions can be provoked by adversities, such as severe life events, chronic life difficulties, and other major stressors. We have only just started with prevention, on improvements for those whose lives for themselves and their children are difficult, for instance because of poverty, and with psychological therapies that help to enable people to cope, within themselves and in relation to others.

11

fMRI and Brain Bases of Experience

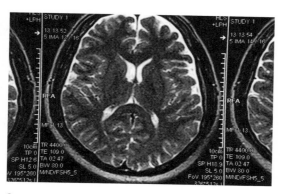

Computer-generated functional Magnetic Resonance Image of a slice through the human head and brain.

Brain imaging enables us to see what parts of the brain are active when people are engaged in different experiences. Gabrielle Starr used fMRI to study what happens when people engage with poetry, visual art, and music. She suggests that when art moves us, it reaches within to networks that are active when we reflect on others and ourselves. Other researchers such as Samir Zeki have found that influential pieces of art can be ambiguous, with the same image resonating for us in different ways, which can set off different associations within us.

Where It Happens

Since the early 1990s, functional Magnetic Resonance Imaging (fMRI) has become important in psychology. To take an fMRI image, a person lies in a space within a large magnet that can detect localized changes in blood flow in the brain. The process is expensive, so the numbers of people in fMRI studies tend to be small, but it is free of ill-effects on participants. It works because brain regions increase their blood flow when they become active. This can be detected magnetically because oxygenated blood being taken up into neurons has different magnetic properties from blood that has given up its oxygen and is leaving them. A computer then constructs images of the kind you can see at the start of this chapter to show which brain areas have been active.

Among those who have been energetic in this field is Gabrielle Starr who, although she is a professor of English, uses fMRI to study people's inner experience. Her research is on what she calls the three sister arts of poetry, painting, and music.

Among the most influential statements of what poetry and other arts do was that from the Roman poet Horace in *Ars Poetica*. He said poetry gives pleasure and instructs. Pleasure? Well, yes, I suppose so. But this does not take us very far. And instruction? Parents may instruct their children, politicians instruct us about how we should vote, advertisers instruct us to dig into our pockets. But does art instruct?

Starr has a better proposal. She writes:

> I argue that the arts mediate our knowledge of the world around us by directing attention, shaping perceptions, and creating dissonance or harmony where none had been before, and that what aesthetics thus gives us is a restructuring of value.[1]

Starr says "value" involves the quality of the emotional response. The significance of experiencing an emotion is central to human meaning because it indicates that something is important. Works of art can prompt transformations in how we see, feel, and think.

The proposal Starr makes is that "aesthetic experience calls on the brain to integrate external perceptions with the inner senses."[2] Art engages our emotions and reorders our perceptions. She argues that motor imagery is a good way of thinking about what goes on with the arts because it can give us the sense of "what would it be like *if we actually were to do what we are thinking.*"[3] In this kind of way Adam Smith said, in his *Theory of Moral Sentiments*, that sympathy starts at first within us, and then moves outward to others, as we imagine ourselves to be in their situation.

But art doesn't make us do things. A toaster makes a piece of bread turn into toast. That's not what happens with art. Art doesn't make things happen; it enables, it invites. In the imaginative activity of a person who engages with a poem, a novel, or a picture, the art can enable the person to experience an emotion as she or he changes a perception. It's the person who imagines.

In her book, Starr reflects on John Keats's poem, "Ode on a Grecian urn" which is about the relation of art, which endures, to ordinary life, which is ephemeral.

Here are the last four lines of the ode's second stanza, addressed to a fair youth depicted on the urn as he approaches a maiden:

Bold Lover, never, never canst thou kiss,
Though winning near the goal—yet do not grieve;
She cannot fade, though thou hast not thy bliss,
For ever wilt thou love, and she be fair!

As I read this, I find tears coming to my eyes, an instance of Starr's proposal. I have read these lines before, five times, maybe ten. So the reordering of perception, the directing of attention, the mental associations that are made, in harmony or dissonance, invited by what Keats has written here don't just happen once. For some topics that art addresses—and the relation of the eternal to the ephemeral is one—there are more and more things to think about, to reflect upon.

Part of Starr's discussion is of how art can affect the mind, and of how imagery works in ways that bring the imagined close to the perceived. The most famous lines in the poem are the last two:

Beauty is truth, truth beauty,—that is all
Ye know on earth, and all ye need to know.

These lines continue the theme of the eternal in relation to the ephemeral, but as I read them, after contemplating Starr's discussion, I wonder whether Keats, perhaps, was closer to presenting not just "this" is "that"—an identity—but a hypothesis of the kind that Starr is proposing: beauty is beautiful because it can suggest a step that we might take for ourselves, to come closer to truth.

Neuroscience of Experience

Are different experiences associated with activations of different regions of the brain? How about the experience of love? In a study published in 2000, Andreas Bartels and Semir Zeki asked seventeen participants who said they were deeply in love to be scanned in an fMRI machine while they looked at photographs of their loved ones. Two brain regions of the cortex, the medial insula and the anterior cingulate region, as well as two subcortical regions, were found to have higher activation when the participants looked at pictures of their love partners than when they looked at photographs of other people of similar age. Some other regions underwent deactivation when participants looked at photos of their beloved partners. In a similar study of ten women and seven men who had been married, and in love with their partners for an average of twenty-one years, Bianca Acevedo and colleagues found similar patterns of brain activation, which were distinct from those that occurred when looking at photos of long-term friends, or of acquaintances.

Phrenology was mistaken in its proposal that particular brain regions could be identified with whole propensities, for instance a region called Amativeness, responsible for sexual desire and attraction. We have to be careful that brain imaging does not become the new phrenology, and ask what imaging studies really tell us. At the same time, in a survey of 100,000 Americans, Jonathan Freedman found that it wasn't money, or worldly success, or health, that most people thought made life meaningful. It was love in marriage. Living happily with a love-partner can be thought of, therefore, as a state of well-being: an opposite of mental illness. The fMRI results may invite us to think that this kind of love is indeed distinctive.

In a study of 2004, Bartels and Zeki had twenty mothers view pictures of their own children and of other children they knew. With their own children the insular and cingulate cortex areas of the mothers were activated in the same way that these areas had been activated in people who viewed pictures of those with whom they were romantically in love. Changes in subcortical activity also showed a similar overlap. A further implication is that romantic love has a relationship with attachment love for infants.

Perhaps, however, we shouldn't yet jump to this conclusion, because the activations may occur in a more general way, by means of a system that mediates reward in the brain. Consistent with this idea was that at the same time as there was activation in some areas when mothers viewed their children, there was suppression of activity in areas known to be associated with critical assessment of other people. At the end of their paper on romantic and maternal love, Bartels and Zeki say modestly:

These results have thus brought us a little, but not much, closer to understanding the neural basis of one of the most formidable instruments of evolution, which makes the pro-creation of the species and its maintenance a deeply reward-ing and pleasurable experience.[4]

A neuroscience of engagement with art is beginning to de-velop.[5] Hideaki Kawabata in collaboration with Zeki studied the brain's response to beauty. They had ten participants look at 192 paintings—abstracts, still life pictures, portraits, and landscapes—and rate them on a scale of 1 (ugly) to 10 (beautiful). A few days later in an fMRI machine, participants were shown pictures that had been rated as ugly (1 and 2), neutral (5 and 6), and beautiful (9 and 10). As compared with pictures that had been rated as ugly, those that had been rated as beautiful strongly activated areas of the visual cortex and areas of the orbitofrontal cortex that are associated with reward and with emotional engagement. Ugly paintings tended to activate the motor cortex, and this perhaps was associated with actions of avoidance and rejection. Once again, therefore, the brain seems to be holding on to its secrets. We are reminded once more that some things are rewarding, and we want to approach them, while others are aversive, but we still do not know why. In a study of the experience of literary works, Adam Zeman and colleagues found that passages of poetry and prose that people found moving not only activated areas associ-ated with reading, but also those associated with music.

Studies of brain imaging in relation to consciousness and ex-perience are on the increase. Most are correlational. Georg Nor-thoff and colleagues review imaging studies and conclude that experience of the self is mediated by medial regions of cortex and mid-brain that are densely connected to other brain regions. Such studies do not tell us in what ways brain regions that are ac-tive may be responsible for certain psychological states. A newer kind of study is, however, under way. Julie Yoo and colleagues have investigated a causal relationship. They have found that when some parts of the brain, but not others, are active, people can learn better. In this way, researchers are coming closer to understanding which brain areas have some responsibility for some kinds of psychological functions.

Ambiguity

Art is not just beauty. In a paper published in 2004, Semir Zeki hypothesized that great art tends to be ambiguous. To look into the idea further, he studied what happens when people in an fMRI machine view ambiguous figures, such as shown in figure 17, which looks like a duck but then seems to look like a rabbit. As the interpretation of such images changes, so does fMRI activation in different parts of the brain.

Figure 17. Duck-rabbit, ambiguous figure, after Joseph Jastrow. *Source*: Drawn by Keith Oatley after Jastrow, J. (1900). *Fact and fable in psychology*. New York: Houghton, Mifflin & Co.

Zeki goes on to discuss not visual ambiguity of this kind, but cognitive ambiguity: how one's interpretation can change as one thinks deeply on some subject, or on a work of art. He offers an example of Johannes Vermeer's "Girl with the pearl earring." The picture itself, he says, is not itself ambiguous. It is a single, stable image. All the same the girl's face can be seen in several ways:

> She is at once inviting, yet distant, erotically charged but chaste, resentful and yet pleased. These interpretations must all involve memory and experience, of what a face that is expressing these sentiments would look like. The genius of Vermeer

is that he does not provide an answer but, by a brilliant subtlety, manages to convey all the expressions, although the viewer is only conscious of one interpretation at any given moment. Because there is no correct solution, the work of art itself becomes a problem that engages the mind.[6]

Zeki points out that Michelangelo left two-thirds of his works unfinished. Cezanne, too, left paintings unfinished, and said that he was not interested in finishing them because a painting only becomes finished in the mind of the beholder. To be art, a painting must both engage the mind and suggest something that is not in the painting itself, but invites the mind to do something: to offer meaning to the work.

Art Reaches Within

Ed Vessel, with Gabrielle Starr and Nava Rubin, asked how the workings of the brain could inform us of how art affects experience. They used fMRIs to study people as they looked at 109 paintings in randomized order. The works were from the fifteenth to the twentieth centuries, Western and Eastern, in different genres, representational and abstract. The works were chosen because they were not commonly reproduced in art books so they would be unfamiliar to the participants. The participants were told: "The paintings may cover the entire range from 'beautiful' to 'strange' or even 'ugly.' Respond on the basis of how much this image *moves* you." Participants were asked to rate each painting on a scale of how moving they found each one, from being the least moving to the most moving. The rating of most moving was given to 16.7 percent of the paintings.

There was, however, very little agreement among observers as to which paintings were the most moving. This indicates that being moved by an unfamiliar painting is personal and idiosyncratic. To start with, as the participants followed the instruction to look at each picture, a network called the default mode network was deactivated. This kind of deactivation happens when people perform a specific task in the outside world, for instance one that they have been asked to do. But with pictures people found most moving, activation began to occur in this network. This network has been found to come alive when a person is not concentrating on anything in the outside world, but when she or he is thinking about her- or himself, alone or with close others, or musing, or reflecting.

The implication is that with art that is moving to us in a personal way, we think for ourselves, in reflection. The paintings that participants had rated as most moving for them had reached within, and touched the self. Vessel and his colleagues say:

> [C]ertain artworks can "resonate" with an individual's sense of self in a manner that has well-defined physiological correlates and consequences: the neural representations of those external stimuli obtain access to the neural substrates and processes concerned with the self.[7]

12

Feeling within the Self, Feeling for Others

Drawing of Wilder Penfield's sensory homunculus, showing areas that are elaborately supplied with sensation, such as the hand, lips, and tongue, enlarged to correspond to the large amount of sensory cortex devoted to them.

Giacomo Rizzolatti and his team discovered mirror neurons, which are activated in monkeys when they see another individual doing an action and also when they do the same action themselves. Although controversies have arisen about the interpretation of functions of these neurons, the phenomenon of mirroring is established. It's a component of human empathy. Tania Singer and colleagues have shown that some brain areas that are activated when a person is feeling pain are also activated when that person knows a loved one is in pain. Empathy has bases in the brain and in experience. We are not just selves, but selves-with-others.

Neurons and Their Activities

Among early findings of how brain makes mind were the terrible effects of damage reported by John Harlow from the accident suffered by Phineas Gage. Neuroscientists call damaged brain parts "lesions." Sometimes in animals for purposes of research, and sometimes in humans for therapeutic purposes, for instance when there is a tumor, lesions are made deliberately, and groups of neurons are destroyed. This was the case with the modern Phineas Gages, studied by Antonio Damasio. Also, for the relief of intractable epilepsy that would spread from one side of the brain to the other, sometimes the neuronal tracts that join two hemispheres of the brain have been surgically cut. When this has occurred, the effects have enabled researchers to see something of the functions of each hemisphere. In most right-handed people, language depends on the left hemisphere, while spatial reasoning and non-verbal activities are more dependent on the right hemisphere.

In the eighteenth century, Luigi Galvani found that the leg of a dead frog could be made to kick when electricity was applied.[1] It was a discussion of these effects that prompted the eighteen-year-old Mary Shelley on holiday in the Alps with her new husband, Percy Shelley, and some other friends, to form the idea of writing *Frankenstein*. In this novel, the researcher Victor Frankenstein uses electricity to bring to life a creature he has constructed from human body parts collected from charnel houses.

Following Galvani's demonstrations it came to be recognized that the brain works, at least in part, by electricity. Consequently, a new method became available: stimulation with electrical currents. Studies conducted by Wilder Penfield and colleagues, of stimulation of groups of neurons of the human brain, for instance during surgical operations while the patient was under local anaesthetic but still conscious and able to report on effects, resulted in the discovery that the parts of the brain concerned with sensation are laid out in a kind of map of the human body, with the areas that are most important, the fingers and regions around the mouth, having more cortex assigned to them than areas such as the back. The amount of cortex associated with each body part has been drawn as a cartoon. It's called the "sensory homunculus," seen in the picture at the start of this chapter, with the size of each body part shown as larger or smaller according to how much sensory cortex is assigned to it. There is a comparable cartoon for the motor cortex.

In the twentieth century, with the new understandings of electronics that made radio broadcasting possible, another method became available. In addition to lesions and stimulation, it became possible to record the brain's activities. At first electrical activity of large areas of the brain was recorded, averaging across billions of neurons. These recordings were ElectroEncephalo-Grams (EEGs), and findings from them led to advances in our understanding of epilepsy.

Then, recordings of single neurons began. When the neuron's activities are turned into sounds, researchers can hear the neurons firing: "click . . . click, click, click . . . . click click"; the faster the rate of firing, the more active the neuron. Among the most famous findings of this kind were that neurons of the visual region of the cortex of cats fired when little straight lines (line segments) were shown to the cat's eyes, and that each neuron fired for lines in just one orientation: vertical, or horizontal, or various axes of oblique.[2] These findings gave a clue as to why outline drawings are so effective for us in seeing objects.

In 1996, the report of recordings from single neurons that caused a big stir came from Parma, Italy, by Giacomo Rizzolatti and his team. When they recorded in an area involved in the control of action, in the brains of monkeys, they found some neurons that fired when the monkey saw a hand picking up a raisin, and also fired when the monkey itself did the action. They called these "mirror neurons."

In a theoretical article, Vitorio Gallesi, with Rizzolatti and Christian Keysers, explain how mirror neurons enable us to take a step forward in our understanding of social cognition, the way we know other people. Think of it like this. If you see something happening in the physical world, perhaps a cloud moving across the sky, or a leaf dropping from a tree, you use your perceptual system to know what is happening. Cues on the retina pick up signs of movement, to which the visual system is attuned, and they connect with your knowledge of clouds or of leaves. You then project your understanding onto the input to the retina and see what is happening. When we see a fellow human rising from a chair or picking up a paper from a table, the same kind of process occurs in the visual system, but in addition something else happens. The part of your own brain that works the legs for you to rise from a chair, or the hand when you pick something up, is also brought into action, so that you get an intuition within yourself of standing up or picking up a paper.

Rizzolatti and his colleagues argue that empathy, in which one feels something that another person is feeling, is also based on a mirroring process. If we see someone make a facial expression of disgust, it has been found that we too feel disgusted. Areas of brain, which includes a region called the insula, are activated both in the person we observe and in ourselves. We don't just analyze the facial expression, we know the emotion within ourselves by mirroring it.

In human participants, one cannot record directly from mirror neurons, so Giovanni Buccino and colleagues used a method called "transcranial magnetic stimulation," which could be applied gently from outside the skull to parts of the motor cortex.

Figure 18. Hands playing a piano. *Source*: Photo courtesy of Keith Oatley.

When this stimulation was applied to an area of the motor cortex concerned with making hand movements, a movement occurred in the muscles of the hand. When applied to an area concerned with foot movement, muscles of the foot moved. Next the researchers gave their participants three-word sentences: "Suonava il piano" ("He played the piano," as you may see in figure 18) or "Calciava la palla" ("He kicked the ball"). When a sentence about a hand movement was offered, the activity of the hand muscles in response to transcranial stimulation was reduced. A comparable result was found for sentences about the foot and movements of foot muscles. These reductions did not occur when participants listened to sentences that were not about hand or foot movements. The researchers argue that the reductions in response to the magnetic stimulation occurred because when the participants had listened to sentences about hand movements or foot movements, the areas of the brain concerned with these movements were already occupied.

This result may seem a bit indirect, but we can get closer to the brain's secrets with a study by Nicole Speer and colleagues who trained twenty-eight people to read a story with words flashed one-by-one on a screen. This method was used to avoid eye movements that interfered with fMRI recording. After they had practiced, and were in the fMRI scanner, participants read four short stories, each of which took about ten minutes to read. The stories were about events in the day of a seven-year-old boy named Raymond.

When the story said, "Raymond laid down his pencil," fMRI recordings showed that regions of the motor cortex concerned with picking up and putting down objects were activated. When a character changed location, regions in the frontal cortex were activated. Another finding was that when a character's goal or intention changed, regions in readers' superior temporal cortex (at the side of the brain) and in the prefrontal cortex were activated. It's as if, to understand what someone says to us, or to understand what we read, we ourselves perform parts of these actions mentally, or we undergo for ourselves inner versions of changes that are referred to. It's quite different from seeing a leaf drop from a tree.

Here I think we may be getting close to something that we could not have glimpsed without the methods of brain science. With the idea of mirror neurons, and with studies of transcranial stimulation, and of fMRI changes while reading, we glimpse how we create within us imagined actions and perceptions that can derive from words we are told, or words we read. To understand and imagine, we use parts of the brain that we would use if we ourselves were to act in a way that is verbally suggested, or if we were actually to see the kind of thing that is spoken about.

The Coming of Empathy

A study by Tania Singer and colleagues has become perhaps as famous as John Harlow's paper on Phineas Gage. It was a study of empathy: a feeling that is similar to an emotion one sees, or imagines, another person to be feeling, while knowing the other person to be the source of the emotion. In their laboratory, the researchers recorded from the brains of sixteen women while a loved partner was sitting next to the scanner. Mirrors were arranged so that each woman in the scanner could see her partner. The researchers studied brain activity of each participant when she received an electric shock to the back of her right hand, and when pain of the same kind was applied to the back of the hand of her partner. In some parts of participants' brains, activation occurred when they themselves received a shock. These sites mediated the physical basis of pain. But then, in other areas of the brain, activation occurred both when the participant received pain and when the participant received a signal that her loved one was receiving pain. These areas mediated an emotional aspect of pain.

In addition to her work in neuroscience, Tania Singer has been influential in economics. She has argued that "Research in the fields of psychology and neuroscience shows beyond doubt that the assumptions about human nature that underpin mainstream economic models are simply wrong."[3]

The assumptions to which Singer refers are those that are central to economic theory: that humans act only in their own self-interest.[4] Of course we humans are selfish—sometimes we can be very selfish—but, says Singer, to say that human economic activity is guided only by this selfishness is to mistake a part for the whole. We are also motivated to care about others, and to think about what they might want. Psychology and neuroscience have shown that other people are important to us and with more compassion, societies and their economies would become more cooperative and responsible. "If we are to address some of our most pressing global problems, such as climate change and inequality," she says, "we need to devise new economic models that accommodate the real complexity of human nature."[5]

One might go further. One might say that when economists argue that individual self-interest and exchange are what make the commercial world work, they have it backwards. We humans cooperate with each other. Exchange and industry, which provide the wherewithal for all of us, are a happy result of our cooperativeness.

In an extension of the study of Singer and her colleagues, Lane Beckes, James Coan, and Karen Hasselmo monitored the brains of people in an fMRI machine when they were threatened with an electrical shock, when a friend was threatened with the shock, or when a stranger was threatened. Certain areas of the brain were activated when the participants were threatened themselves. Almost identical areas were activated when the friend was threatened, but not when the stranger was threatened. The researchers say that these results mean that those whom we love become part of us, not just metaphorically, but in a physical sense. The researchers conclude that "from the perspective of the brain, our friends and loved ones are indeed part of who we are."[6]

Researchers have tended to think of results of studies of the brain as being about the individual. But the findings of Singer, and of Beckes and colleagues, show this is not so. "Who we are" is seldom who we are on our own. "Who we are" is ourselves with others.

Ryszard Praskier has argued that mirror neurons enable people to synchronize their thoughts by means of empathetic relationships, and cites also a study in which children have been taught empathy, with positive results.[7]

The discovery of mirror neurons made an impact on how we think about the brain. It also evoked controversy. Among the claims are that mirror neurons offer a way to explain how we understand people and because some words can affect brain areas concerned with enacting their meanings, they may help to explain how language is based on processes of mirroring. Among arguments against such claims are that mirror neurons have been recorded only in monkeys, who don't understand other minds and who don't have language, and that there are people who have had strokes that have damaged motor areas of the brain (where mirror neurons are thought to be) who can still understand language.[8]

Although some proposals about the functions of mirror neurons are controversial, the phenomenon of mirroring is not. It happens when a parent smiles at a three-month-old baby, and the baby smiles back. In an experiment in which adult participants saw videos of people expressing happiness or anger while their own facial expressions were unobtrusively video-recorded, it was found that the people mirrored these expressions themselves, in a process that indicates both a component of inner recognition and a component of communication.[9] This kind of mimicry seems to have been an essential step in the evolution of the human mind in its sociality.[10]

The existence of mirror neurons is an established finding, and their significance is still being understood. Together with the study of empathy of the kind begun by Singer, perhaps the most fundamental issue is that neuroscience and psychology have started to deal with something that has been ignored or overlooked. It is that we humans are not just individuals. For the most part, we are not very individual at all. We are us-with-our-loved-ones, us-who-hang-out-with-friends, us-who-work-with-colleagues. We take part in cultures. Even when we are alone, we often think of ourselves in relation to others.

Sociality

How do we understand others? One idea is that we use ourselves to simulate others' minds. When we converse with someone, or consider an action another person has done, we often look into ourselves and imagine what we might think and feel in the other person's situation. We project an understanding of our selves onto that person, and we correct for what we know of her or him (from our mental model of the person). The mind is a somewhat private place, without windows through which we can gaze when we look into someone's eyes, so inference is necessary. The difficulty is that inference about other minds is indirect; it's a kind of projection. It does not have the immediacy of the way in which we perceive a leaf falling. Ray Nickerson has put it like this: we tend to project too much and correct too little.

The film *The Third Man* is set in Vienna in the years after World War II, when the city was occupied by the Allies.[11] Harry Lime, played by Orson Welles, has been stealing penicillin from a hospital and diluting it to increase its quantity, then selling it at a very high price. Diluted, it no longer works properly, so that young children to whom it is administered for treatment of meningitis are permanently brain-damaged. In one scene Lime, with his friend Holly Martins, is high up on Vienna's big Ferris wheel. "Look down there," says Lime. He points to people moving about on the ground, far enough below to seem like mere dots. "Would you really feel any pity if one of those dots stopped moving forever?" he says. "If I offered you twenty thousand pounds for every dot that stopped moving, would you tell me to keep my money?"

Holly Martins has liked Harry Lime, but as we watch the film we realize that Lime is a heinous man. He is without empathy. To reinforce his suggestion to Martins that he should turn Lime in, the British army officer, Major Calloway, who has been working on prosecuting Lime for his penicillin racket, takes Martins to a hospital to see some of the children who have been affected.

Empathy is just a part. The whole is that, among all the animals, we members of humankind are social. We are not just selves. We are selves-with-others.

PART FOUR

Community

13

In Affection and Conflict

Photograph of a chimpanzee, a member of a species in which faces are as individual as they are in humans.

Jane Goodall found that chimpanzees in the wild live affectionately together, but that they fight for status in male and female hierarchies. They have also been observed to hunt down and kill others of their own species, who live in smaller groups. Among humans more men than women commit murder; rates of murder depend not just on biology but on the kinds of societies in which we live. Muzafer and Carolyn Sherif found that boys in summer camps formed hierarchies, and when two groups were set to compete in games such as tug-of-war, a self-glorifying attitude started to occur within each in-group and derision began toward the out-group. This oppositional attitude could only be set into decline by having everyone in both groups cooperate on joint tasks.

The Chimpanzees of Gombe

We humans tend to think ourselves superior to other animals. Among our words for animal-like are "bestial" and "brutal." Charles Darwin linked this idea to his theory of evolution. In one of his notebooks he wrote: "The devil in the form of baboon is our grandfather."[1]

Our line branched off from that of the chimpanzees' between four and seven million years ago, and we share some 98 percent of our DNA with them. Chimpanzees live more or less together in communities with up to about fifty others: adult males and females and their offspring who know their mothers but, because chimpanzees are promiscuous, don't know their fathers.

The person who introduced us to the life of chimpanzees was Jane Goodall. In *The Chimpanzees of Gombe*, she describes how she and her colleagues spent many years making careful observations. Gombe, in Tanzania, is about the same size as Manhattan. It is densely forested, and has deep valleys in which streams run down to its shoreline on Lake Tanganyika.

To make her observations Goodall had two ideas without which she could not have done her research.

First, Goodall realized that she needed to spend time sitting quietly in the presence of groups of chimpanzees to accustom them to her presence. They seemed frightened at first, of this strange creature, this human, but gradually they got used to her, which enabled her to sit closely enough to them to see what they did, and to follow them where they went. She encouraged this closeness by making fruit available to the chimpanzees near her camp. After a particular group had become used to her or to one of her research colleagues, she or the colleague would be able to sit just a few meters away, observe actions and interactions, take photographs, and make notes.

The second thing Goodall did was to learn to recognize each individual and to give her or him a name. This may seem a quirk, like giving a pet a name, but it has a deeper significance. The chimpanzees are like us in that they relate to each other as individuals. You can see the face of an individual chimpanzee in the photograph at the beginning of the chapter. So, by giving the chimpanzees names and learning to recognize them individually, Goodall and her colleagues were able see who was fond of whom, who was competitive with whom, who was where in hierarchies of status, who had what kind of personality—pushy and aggressive perhaps, or retiring and reclusive.

Jane Goodall was born in London in 1934 to novelist Vanne Morris-Goodall and businessman Mortimer Morris-Goodall. Jane was always fascinated by animals. She saved up enough money so that she could live among Africa's wildlife, and, when she was twenty-two, she had enough to travel to Kenya to stay with a friend whose family had a farm outside Nairobi. When she was there, she phoned Louis Leakey, a leading palaeontologist, and was offered a job. Leakey sent her to London to study primatology, and in 1960 Goodall returned to Africa to work on a project that Leakey suggested, to study chimpanzees in the wild. Two years later, at Cambridge, she was one of only a very small number of people allowed to enroll in a PhD program without having an undergraduate degree. In 1964, she married the photographer Hugo van Lawick, and he took photographs of the chimpanzees at Gombe. Goodall and van Lawick later divorced, and Goodall married Derek Bryceson, head of Tanzania's national park system. He was able to protect Goodall's research in Gombe and prevent it from becoming a destination for tourists. In her later life, Goodall has devoted herself to advocacy for chimpanzees.

Chimpanzees are often affectionate and companionable. Here's an example:

Melissa and her daughter Gremlin have made their nests [in the trees] some 10 meters apart. Melissa's son Gimble still feeds on *msongati* pods . . . Gremlin's infant, Getty, dangles above his mother, twirling, kicking his legs, and grabbing at his toes. From time to time Gremlin reaches up, idly, tickling his groin . . . Suddenly from the far side of the valley come the melodious pant-hoots of a single male: Evered, probably in his nest too. It is Gimble who starts the answering chorus, sitting up beside Melissa, his hand on her arm, gazing toward the adult male—one of his "heroes."[2]

Goodall found that chimpanzee groups were organized into hierarchies, arrangements that are accepted by everyone in the group, which allow resources to be distributed relatively peacefully. The alpha male is at the head. He wins his position by defeating a previous holder through threats, intimidation, or fighting, and he holds the position usually for several years. Other males are organized roughly in a hierarchy beneath him. Females have a parallel hierarchy.

For the most part chimpanzees eat fruit, but they also hunt small animals, such as monkeys or piglets that they happen to come across. Males are usually more involved than females in hunting. When they have been successful in a hunt, they may squabble over the food, but sometimes they share it, sometimes so that favors are returned.[3] High-ranking animals obtain part of a catch, even when they have taken no part in the hunt, and usually they let only relatives and allies take shares.[4] Neither the gathering of a group to eat from trees, nor this kind of sharing, is equivalent to human sharing of food.

Chimpanzees are also quite competitive. They fight a good deal, often with others who are close to them in the hierarchy, in attempts to improve or maintain status. Goodall categorized fighting into three levels. At level one is a push or a hit, or a kick. Level two is an attack. It includes dragging, pounding with a fist, and the like, and it lasts less than 30 seconds. Level three is a severe attack, like that of level two, but lasting more than 30 seconds. Goodall found that attacks (levels two and three) made up 15 percent of fights, and in a quarter of these blood flowed, or an injury was inflicted.

Goodall found that, in 4,900 hours of observing thirteen individuals over two separate years, and excluding hours of darkness or when an animal being observed was just on its own or only with dependent offspring, attacks (at levels two and three) occurred every 62 hours in males, and every 106 hours in females. One particularly aggressive alpha male managed an attack every nine hours. The least aggressive animal, a female, did not attack in 230 hours. When a fight has occurred, the animals often later get together for reconciliation, for instance with a hug. When a dominant animal is approached by an inferior after a fight, the dominant one "responds to the submissive gestures of the subordinate with a touch, a pat, or even an embrace."[5] Mutual agreement has been reached about status. The dispute is resolved.

It had been thought that we humans are the only mammals that kill members of our own species. In her 1986 book, Goodall says she was appalled to observe a group of chimpanzees going around in a gang to hunt down and kill other chimpanzees they found alone or in small numbers. What had happened was that the original community whom Goodall and her colleagues were studying had divided. At first, after the separation, the two groups met occasionally, for instance when they came to get fruit at the camp. Although some meetings between individuals were friendly, in general members of both communities were tense at these encounters.

After the split, one of the communities was substantially smaller than the other. It had just six adult males and it tended to range south of Goodall's camp. The southern males started to avoid visiting the camp, and members of the two new communities started to avoid each other. Then Goodall and her colleagues noticed that northern males were starting to patrol, in a gang, along their borders, and then to make incursions into the southern area. On one such incursion, a group of six adult males, with one female and one adolescent male, encountered a southern male on his own. He tried to run away, but was caught by members of the northern patrol. While one male held him, other males beat him with fists for about ten minutes, and one bit him several times. Goodall says he was severely injured. He was never seen again, and Goodall inferred he had died from his injuries. Goodall and her colleagues observed that one by one all the other adults in the southern community were killed in a similar fashion, and they had no doubt that this was the intention. Adolescent females from the southern community joined the northerners.

It wasn't that the members of the southern community were strangers. Some of them had been friends with those who had become northerners. The attacks that were observed between northerners and southerners lasted longer than any that had been seen previously within a community, and they involved tearing and biting flesh in the way that occurred when eating animals of another species. The killing groups were largely male, and their attacks were made either on individuals or on numerically weaker groups of southerners they came across during their incursions. No members of the southern community were observed making incursions into the northern area, so the conflict could scarcely be regarded as territorial. For the northerners, the southerners had become an out-group, with hostility directed to others who had become "them," no longer "us."

There was considerable controversy when Goodall reported lethal attacks by chimpanzees, with some people saying such attacks did not occur naturally, but were an artifact of Goodall having provided fruit for the animals at her camp. This idea has been refuted by reports from other sites where no such provisioning had been made; intercommunity killings are rare, but they do occur.[6]

Us versus Them

Henri Tajfel and his colleagues have shown that the phenomenon of Us-versus-Them is very basic. In order to perform their experiments, they would assign people randomly to groups. Participants were told they were in one group or another. For instance, a coin would be tossed and, depending on the outcome, a participant would be in the heads group or the tails group. Then participants were asked to assign rewards to members of the group of "heads" and "tails," even when they did not know who was in the group they were in (their in-group) or who was in the other group (an out-group). They gave preference to people who were members of their in-group, even when this preference had no effect on their own rewards. Daniel Yudkin and colleagues found a similar bias in punishment. Participants played an economic game in which they thought other players were or were not supporters of their favorite sports team, and in which they thought others were or were not members of their nationality. In the game, they witnessed another player stealing. They inflicted more severe punishments when they thought the perpetrator was not in their in-group.

Another set of studies was conducted by Muzafer and Carolyn Sherif, who observed groups of boys at summer camps in 1949, 1953, and 1954. The researchers wanted to understand informal groupings that would arise without external pressures. For their participants they chose boys of slightly above average intelligence aged eleven to twelve. They interviewed potential participants' parents and teachers, and chose boys who were in good health, from well-adjusted, stable, middle-class homes. The camps to which the boys were invited were of a kind that are common for American children. The boys didn't know each other before they arrived at the camp, and they didn't know the purpose of the study. Members of the Sherifs' research group took on roles as camp staff directors, counselors, and so on. The first study, in 1949, consisted of twenty-four boys at a camp in northern Connecticut. The camp was arranged in three stages.

In stage I, which lasted three days, the boys were all housed in one large bunkhouse, and they quickly formed friendships.

In stage II, the boys were assigned to two equal groups, making sure that those who had become best friends were separated. The pain of separation was lessened by taking the two groups of boys on separate bike trips and campouts, which they found exciting. Each group developed a hierarchy, with a leader, in much the same way that Goodall had recorded for chimpanzee communities. Each group gave itself a name: Bull Dogs and Red Devils. Each established a territory, developed its own customs and culture. The leader of the Bull Dogs "rose to the leadership position by his greater contribution in the planning and execution of common activities and by regulating and integrating the tasks and roles of the group members."[7] He devised and regulated tasks to improve the bunkhouse, to build a latrine, and to create a secret swimming place. He supported the other boys in the group, praised them for their work, and made sure the boys lowest in the hierarchy were included. In contrast, the leader of the Red Devils was "recognized primarily for his daring, his athletic skill and his 'toughness.'"[8]

Both groups devised methods of punishment for those who did not properly carry out tasks assigned to them. For the Bull Dogs, punishments included moving large stones from the secret swimming place. Only once was the leader of the Bull Dogs seen to threaten another boy, and he did this verbally. The other boys in the group thought that generally he was "fair." By contrast, methods used by the leader of the Red Devils included threats and "roughing up."

The two groups were different in their organization. The Bull Dogs were compact, without much emotional distance between boys of higher and lower status. The Red Devils had a much steeper hierarchy. Their leader had a great deal of prestige but was cliquish, with three close lieutenants to whom he gave favors, and with whom he preferred to spend his time. Boys at the bottom of the hierarchy were emotionally distant, and sometimes were bullied.

After five days in which the boys had been separated into the two groups, approximately 90 percent of friendships of the boys had come to be within their own group. In each group, there was a great amount of affection, loyalty, and solidarity. A few boys who wanted to maintain friendships formed in stage I, with boys who were now in the other group, were called traitors. When the groups met, relationships were generally friendly, with any unfriendly trends that occurred being referred to as "play."

Stage III involved competitions between the groups. These included baseball, tug-of-war, and football, with points being awarded for each, and cumulative points contributing to coveted prizes of a hunting knife for each member of the winning group. As the competitions began, a proud, self-glorifying attitude arose within each group. The boys believed their own group to be strong and fearless. Accusations of the other group began. Within the group there was closeness and inter-reliance, toward the other group there was anger and contempt, with fights starting to break out.

When, in stage III, relations between the two groups had deteriorated, the researchers became alarmed and tried to find ways of improving them. One year, they had the idea of arranging for the two groups to share a meal together. But one of the groups arrived before the other and ate most of the food. When the other group arrived they were angry, and a fight broke out. The meal was abandoned. The method the Sherifs finally hit upon to reduce conflict between groups was cooperation in joint projects. In one, the researchers arranged for the water supply into the camp to be cut off. The boys had to cooperate to search the long pipeline that brought water into the camp, and to repair it. In another, when the boys were hungry, it was arranged that the truck that was used to go into town to get food failed to start. The boys

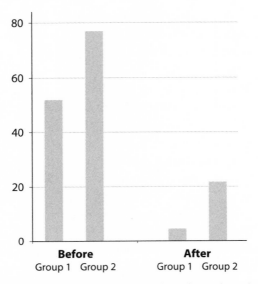

Figure 19. Hostility and reconciliation in the studies of Muzafer and Carolyn Sherif: percentages of boys in each group who thought all those in the other group (rather than some or none) were cheaters, sneaks, and the like, at the end of stage III, before and after cooperative activities. *Data source*: Sherif, M. (1956). Experiments in group conflict. *Scientific American, 195* (November), 54–58. Drawn by Keith Oatley.

decided that they needed to work together and use a rope (which had been used for tug-of-war) to pull the truck so that it could be put into gear in order to start it. Although hostilities did not cease immediately, they were much reduced by the joint projects. The results of cooperative activities for one year are shown in figure 19.

Human Killers

Among humans there exists not only a problem of Us-versus-Them, but also of Male-as-compared-with-Female. Martin Daly and Margo Wilson have found that many more men than women kill unrelated people of the same sex; for instance, in such cases, male-

male killing was found, in England and Wales, to be twenty-three times as likely as female-female killing, and in Canada, forty times. The populations of perpetrators and victims are similar, and the peak age for being a killer is the mid-twenties.

For humans, the body type of females is more basic than that of males. A geneticist who remains nameless has said that the male body type is "customized." He was drawing a comparison with the way some people buy an automobile, then customize it to make it faster and stronger.

Daly and Wilson point out that, on the subject of killing others, a purely biological explanation won't do. Societal factors play a part, as we can see from murder rates that vary by country, with same-sex murders being fifty-eight times more frequent in Detroit, United States, than in England and Wales. More likely, say Daly and Wilson, the male proclivity to homicide is a hybrid of biological and social factors, with males being in competition with each other, including competition for sexual partners. Unmarried males are three or more times more likely than married males to kill other males.

A large societal component has also been found by Steven Pinker. He found that rates of homicide in proportion to the size of populations, worldwide, both in groups (as in wars) and among individuals (as in murder), have been in decline. Among reasons for a ten- to fifty-fold decrease of violence in Europe since medieval times to the present has been the set of civilizing processes described by Norbert Elias. He showed that from the thirteenth century onward, starting among groups of aristocrats as they ate together, especially in the presence of women, lack of self-control and displays of violence became unacceptable. To behave without consideration for others became shameful. At the same time, acts of feuding and vengeance, which were personal, began to be replaced by processes of justice administered by the state. People's preference for reading and watching stories of detection and court trials suggests that we are still very interested in these issues.[9]

Since the time of the split between the line that led to chimpanzees and the line that led to humans, there have been twenty or more other hominid species who were not our direct ancestors.[10] The species that became extinct most recently is that of the Neanderthals, who lived in Europe until our ancestors colonized the area, some 30,000 years ago. Paul Mellars has inferred that groups of the two populations met and there was conflict. Humans had better technology and better skills of cooperation than the Neanderthals, and these gave our ancestors the advantage in carrying out aggressive intentions. With Jennifer French, Mellars has also found that with the colonization of Europe, our human ancestors came to outnumber Neanderthals by ten to one, and this too contributed to the Neanderthal extinction. There is evidence for some interbreeding, and it is estimated that about 1 percent of human genes derive from the Neanderthals, but as a species, they became extinct.[11]

Knowing this, and knowing what we do with our proclivity for Us-versus-Them, it seems likely that our human ancestors were responsible, at least in part, for eliminating other hominid groups. We continue to see the anti-social goal of such elimination in war, in genocide, in colonization, in class struggle. But then, as Steven Pinker has found, there are better angels in our nature. Despite two terrible world wars of the twentieth century, over time our proclivities to kill each other have diminished.

14

Cooperation

The hand of a mother pointing out something to her 18-month-old daughter: pointing is universal in humans but occurs in no other species.

Michael Tomasello and his colleagues have found that we humans know that other humans are like us, and that we and others can act in the world. The fundamental basis of human life is cooperation. This has evolved in two stages. In the first, which is of joint intentions, we do things together, which includes taking on roles, and sharing in what occurs. In the second, there are group intentions, which involve commitments to groups, and of group moralities, such as loyalty and fairness. Conversation is a kind of cooperation in which we turn things over, verbally, with another person. It's a human means of establishing friendly relationships, and maintaining them, in a way that involves making mental models of other people.

Doing Things Together

In the opening photo for this chapter you see a mother's hand as she points out something to her eighteen-month-old daughter. Starting in the second half of a child's first year, children, too, point to things of interest. On the day I wrote this I saw a baby, who didn't look more than six or eight months old, point at a dog to draw the mother's attention to it.

Pointing is a human universal. It's an early sign of cooperation: "Let's look at this together." Among all the animals, only we do it.[1] From Charles Darwin we learned of the survival of the fittest. From Richard Dawkins we learned of the selfish gene. We have learned, too, that our close animal relatives, the chimpanzees, are quite competitive. In the course of evolution, however, a whole new world opened up for us humans: a world of cooperation.

Daniel Povinelli and Daniela O'Neill worked with a group of seven chimpanzees who knew each other and got on well together. Using methods of reinforcement, they trained the chimpanzees separately to pull on a rope to draw toward them a box with fruit on it. Next, the box was made heavier so that one chimpanzee could not move it. Then two of the seven chimpanzees were selected and trained, by individual reinforcement, to pull on ropes together to bring the heavier fruit-bearing box toward them. These two practiced the cooperative skill and became good at it.

What would happen if a chimpanzee who had learned with the partner to pull in the heavier box were given a new partner who had only been trained to pull on the rope alone? Would the experienced chimpanzee show the inexperienced one what to do?

When an experienced and an inexperienced chimpanzee were given the joint rope-pulling task with the heavy box, the experienced one would pick up a rope, perhaps pull a bit, but then give up. Sometimes it would wait for while, even look over toward the new partner. Often, then, it would go into a bit of a sulk.

Among the five chimpanzees who had no experience in the joint task only one of them, Megan, did pick up the rope and start to pull in such a way that, with the experienced chimpanzee, the two were able to pull the box in. Megan did this with both of the chimpanzees who were experienced at the joint task. But neither of the experienced chimpanzees were able to carry out the joint task with any of the four other inexperienced chimpanzees. Also, not once, with Megan or with any of the other inexperienced chimpanzees, did either of the experienced chimpanzees pick up the rope and offer it to the new partner, or do anything to indicate what the other should do. Although the experienced chimpanzees knew how to perform the joint task, they seemed not to know that the inexperienced partner had intentions, or needed help to act cooperatively on the task.

Esther Hermann, Michael Tomasello, and colleagues devised a range of tasks to compare the abilities of chimpanzees, orangutans, and infant humans. There were 106 chimpanzees aged 3 to 21 years, 32 orangutans aged 3 to 10 years, and 105 human children aged two-and-a-half years. The tasks were separated into two sets. One set was of physical, tasks of the kind that Jean Piaget invented to see how infants understood the world in their sensory-motor stage. They included finding a reward when it had been hidden, discrimination of quantity, understanding causes of events, and use of tools to retrieve rewards. The second set was in the social domain, and included observing another individual solving a problem and then trying to solve it in the same way; understanding communicative cues that would indicate the position of a hidden reward; being able to choose a communicative gesture in relation to the attentional state of another individual to whom the gesture was made; following an individual's gaze toward a target; and understanding what an individual was trying to do when she or he was unsuccessful in completing a task.

In the physical tasks, chimpanzees and human infants were 69 percent correct, and did not differ from each other on average. Orangutans were less successful and scored 59 percent. On the social tasks, the human children scored 74 percent whereas chimpanzees and orangutans were correct only half as often, 33 percent and 36 percent. (The average chance scores on these tasks were above zero.) For the most part, the apes were unable to perform the social tasks.

So the ability of understanding one's own and others' intentions, of being able to do things jointly, is a human universal that emerges in human children by the age of two-and-a-half. This is the opening phase in a developmental pathway that includes perspective-taking and theory-of-mind. In the first phase, up to the age of two or so, babies come to know themselves and others as able to act in the world, capable of forming intentions to make changes to the world, and being able to cooperate with others.

This is a momentous leap: the basis of cultural activities of all kinds, including communication by means of language. In a later phase, at about age four, children come also to know both others and themselves as mental beings, capable of thinking and feeling. Cooperation, and the ability to know other minds and our own, are the most important principles we discuss in this book.

Altruism

It has often been said that what distinguishes us from the animals is that we have language. Even more profound is that members of our species can cooperate. Almost everything that is important to us—relating in love, family, friendship, society—is based on cooperation. Felix Warneken and Tomasello have shown that by the age of two, a young human child, on seeing that another person has a plan but cannot quite carry it out, will go to help that person, as depicted in figure 20.[2]

Chimpanzees can almost do this ... they can move something toward another chimpanzee, or human, when the other reaches for it. But they can't grasp the idea of another person as having

Figure 20. In a study by Felix Warneken and Michael Tomasello, a two-year-old opens a cupboard for a person whom the child sees as wanting to put some books in there, but cannot open the door because she is holding the books. *Source*: Warneken, F., & Tomasello, M. (2009). Varieties of altruism in children and chimpanzees. *Trends in Cognitive Sciences, 13,* 397–402. Photo by Sylvio Tuepke. Reproduced with permission of Felix Warneken, Anja Gampe, Jana Jurkat, and the staff of the Max Planck Institute of Evolutionary Anthropology.

a plan. They can't see when an intention has gone wrong, or do anything to help another person get the intention right.

Shared Intentionality

Unlike the apes, humans cooperate in caring for their children, they provide information that they think will be helpful to others, they teach others things they know will be helpful, they make group decisions, and they maintain social structures and norms.

Non-human primates do not collaborate in human-like ways because, although they have skills for carrying out intentions in an individualistic way, they don't have skills or motivations for shared intentions. Only humans are so social that they can conceive and carry out shared intentions.

In *A Natural History of Human Thinking*, Tomasello goes further. He proposes the shared intentionality hypothesis.

> Although humans' great ape ancestors were social beings, they lived mostly individualistic and competitive lives, and so their thinking was geared toward achieving individual goals. But early humans were at some point forced by ecological circumstances into more cooperative lifeways, and so their thinking became more directed toward figuring out ways to coordinate with others to achieve joint goals or even collective group goals. And this changed everything.[3]

To think in a human way involves not just language, or language-like features, but the cooperativity that supports language. Tomasello proposes that the principle of shared intentionality evolved in two stages.

He calls the first stage "joint intentionality." It probably emerged during foraging, when humans began to share the tasks of gathering food. Chimpanzees don't do this. They do travel in groups so that they are often together when they find a tree with fruit on it. But when they find some fruit, they take enough for themselves, then take it to one side and eat it on their own. When they have caught a monkey or piglet in a hunt, the joint activity often becomes a squabble over dominance.[4] Human foragers, by contrast, seek and produce most of their food in collaboration with others. It was when this stage was reached, Tomasello imagines, perhaps 400,000 years ago, that the human activity of pointing began. Over there is a place we can perhaps get food, and this may have been accompanied by emotionally based sounds: "Emmm." Or over there I see a wild animal: "Ohhhh." This kind of cooperation involves people taking on joint goals, "We" goals, and promoting them to make them more important than individual goals. Then, with such goals, joint plans are arranged, and these often involve separate roles. You pull out these roots, and I'll hold this animal skin (as a bag) so that we can put them in there, and take them back so that everyone in our group can eat them. Human beings have been adept at taking on such roles.

The taking on of "We" goals, rather than mere "I" goals, in children, was studied by Katharina Hamann along with Warneken and Tomasello. They had pairs of children work on a task together to get rewards. As they worked on the joint task, for every pair an arrangement was made so that one of the children was surprised to get her or his reward early. When this happened to two-and-a-half-year-olds, they were surprised to get a reward before the joint task was finished; they took the reward for themselves, and played no further part in the joint activity. The three-and-a-half-year-old children to whom this happened were different. When the surprise of an early reward came to them, they continued to work eagerly on the problem together with their partner until the other child also got the reward. For these older children, the joint goal—of both being able to complete the task together—became more important than the individual goal of getting a reward.

In adulthood, joint intentions and plans continue to be important. Laurette Larocque and I found that on average people made about ten new joint plans a day. We also asked participants to keep diaries of what happened when a joint plan went wrong. Usually this occurred not because of individuality, or selfishness, but because two people thought that what they knew and what the other person knew about the joint goal and plan were the same, but this was not so. Here is an example:

A participant was late in meeting her husband for a Toronto Blue Jays baseball game because she was waiting for their daughter to finish her homework, a condition that had to be fulfilled for the girl to see the game. The husband had the tickets and waited for his wife and daughter outside the baseball ground. When they arrived, he was angry at having been kept from seeing the game so far. He then missed several more innings arguing with his wife, trying to convince her that it was her fault that she was late. In this meeting that did not go as planned, there were multiple goals, including the daughter's homework. Angry emotions occurred, and there was an argument. The most significant feature, in our view, was that the attempts at repair did not focus on the plan that had gone wrong. Our participant did not report that her husband said anything like: "Let's go in as quickly as we can now so we don't miss any more of the game."[5]

We found, in this way, that joint plans mostly occurred between people who had ongoing relationships and that the relationship (with its ongoing set of shared social arrangements, in marriage, friendship, and so on) was more important than any particular plan.[6]

A difficulty with the issue of joint intentions is that not everyone is good in activities with others, and not always good with other people. Although there is a whole philosophy of ethics, it is all very well to propose that people should be decent and helpful with each other, but as Martha Nussbaum showed, this ability is affected by the accidents of life.

Dillon Browne and colleagues studied 385 families, each with a mother, a father, and two siblings. The study involved mothers and siblings cooperating in pairs (mother with older sibling, mother with younger sibling, two siblings together) to build a cognitively challenging design from children's building blocks. The interactions were recorded and sensitivity of each individual was scored for mutuality, mind-reading, and communicative clarity. The abilities of mothers in these respects were due to individual differences, but the abilities of children were found to be diminished by adversities that had occurred within the family. These adversities included living in poverty, discord between the parents, parental mental or physical illness, and other kinds of stress. Such adversities get inside the family and spill over into interactions, not just for the parents, but also for the children. Over time, effects of this kind become part of children's individual abilities in being able to take part in plans and projects that are shared with others, and the adversities become risks for psychiatric problems in adulthood. In mental illness a person is likely to become self-involved—in depression, anxiety, or resentments—less able to take part well in joint actions with others, or sometimes to take part in anything much in the social world.

A further challenge to the idea of joint intentions is that people might not really promote joint goals to the position of being more important than their individual goals. They might only cooperate with others because of arrangements like, "I'll do this for you, if you'll do that for me": individual intentions of a reciprocal kind. We may sometimes observe or read about people who have a tendency to act in this way.

When marriages break down, there is an immediate reversion to individual intentions, and the only cooperative thing that many couples can agree on, when they separate, is to prioritize their children. Even this, however, might be thought of as individual, because, from a biological point of view it will be each individual's genes that are being passed on.

In his 2014 book, Tomasello has identified a second stage, which he calls "collective intentionality." Here he proposes that we don't just work together on joint goals and plans, but we also collaborate within a community. When humans started hunting or scavenging, they would bring food for the whole group. For humans, eating became a collective activity. We identify with our community so that in our interactions we are affected by group agreements, and contribute to what the whole group is doing. Group rituals and group norms become established. We eat dinner together at seven o'clock. Other group activities arose, and those who did not contribute were frowned upon: an early stage in morality. Each person must play her or his part, not take more than the fair share, not cheat. It's at this stage that the strong and raw emotions of shame and guilt began to occur. We experience these now when we do something that is against the interests of the group. Also at this stage, self-monitoring began to take place as people regulated their actions to fit in with those of the group.

Another kind of function at the collective stage is of interactions that have effects on the future. Parents instruct their children, who are able to learn from the instruction, not just by observation and imitation, but by taking on goals, skills, and knowledge that have been explained to them. Then, of course, those who have been taught can themselves pass on goals, and instruct others in skills and knowledge. In a study of this issue, Lewis Dean and colleagues designed a puzzle box that could be solved with three stages of difficulty, with greater rewards at each successive stage. Success at the third stage built on success at the second stage, which was based on success at the first stage. Working together, three- to four-year-old human children were successful in being able to reach the higher stages. Monkeys and chimpanzees were not. The children's success in reaching higher-stage solutions was based on cooperative processes that included verbal instruction of each other and helping each other.

In *A Natural History of Human Morality*, Tomasello extends his proposals. He suggests that the first stage he outlines, of joint intentionality, ensures that both partners in joint enterprises have developed cognitive skills to assign roles, and to share results of joint activities. Rather than "me and that other one," or "me versus that other one," humans have become able to engage with each other, commit to each other, to be no longer just individuals but "We." In the second stage, of collective intentionality, distinct cultural groups have emerged, with morality based on loyalty, conformity, and cultural identity. The "We" becomes "Us," who are obliged, morally, to observe standards of the community as a whole, standards such as justice, and fairness.

Among the benefits of teaching and learning are technologies. Flint tools started to be made more than three million years ago. It seems likely that skills of making them were at first passed on by observing others, and imitating them. As Frederick Coolidge and Thomas Wynn explain, the earlier flint tools, mostly scrapers, remained the same for hundreds of thousands of years. Only between about 100,000 and 50,000 years ago did rapid changes, in the form of improvements in tool-making, begin to be seen, with the production of knives, arrows, and so on. At the same time, we can imagine technologies of clothing, cooking, and shelter underwent development. More recently still, technologies of transport and, of course, most recently, of the digital world have emerged. All require discussion, planning, and sharing. Agreements and shared conventions are established. It is only on the basis of such conventions—for instance of words as having certain agreed meanings—that language became possible.

Conversation

Language occurs in all societies, but how did conversation arise? An answer is proposed by Robin Dunbar in *The Human Story*.[7] It is that conversation arose as the principal means by which humans create and maintain relationships.

Primates live in social groups, and for each species the group has a maximum size. For lemurs it is about 9, for cebus monkeys it is about 18, for chimpanzees it is about 50, and for human beings it is about 150. For humans, this is the number of people with whom one maintains social relationships, and knows something of their history, their relations with others, their personality. The relative size of the cortex in primates is closely related to the size of their social group. In lemurs, the cortex is 1.2 times the rest of the brain. In cebus monkeys, it's 2.4 times. In chimpanzees, it's 3.2 times. In humans, it's 4.1 times. If one plots group size against brain size, the result is a straight line. In other words, the larger the group size, the larger the cortex. Dunbar's suggestion is that the more individuals there are in the social group, the more cortex must be devoted to maintaining mental models of them.

Chimpanzees maintain their relationships by grooming. They sit with those with whom they are close, cuddle a bit, and go through the other's fur, removing twigs and insects. It's a relaxed and affectionate activity. Chimpanzees spend about 20 percent of their time doing this, and they need to do it with all the individuals in their group with whom they have close relationships. Dunbar has proposed that as group size and brain size kept increasing, as primates evolved, so did the time necessary for maintaining relationships in the social group. As this increase continued, Dunbar has calculated that in our forebears, such as *homo erectus* and *homo habilis*, a point was reached when they needed to spend 30 percent of their time grooming. Beyond this point, there just was not enough time to do everything else. It was at this point that conversation emerged. Based on Dunbar's analyses, this seems to have occurred some 200,000 years ago.

From Dunbar's findings we learn that conversation is verbal grooming. When we start a relationship, we tell the other about our self, and we learn from the other about who she or he is. Conversation is also the way in which we maintain our relationships. In conversation, we don't just talk about ourselves, we gossip: and in this way we develop our understandings of others whom we know.

Starting at the point at which infants begin to put words together, we are fascinated by the actions and the effects of actions, and interactions, of ourselves and others. Dunbar, with Anna Marriot and N. D. Duncan, recorded topics of conversation, and the amount of time people spent on different topics, in university cafeterias and places such as bars and trains. They found 70 percent of females' speaking time and some 60 percent of males' speaking time were occupied by issues of social relevance: by relationships ("personal relationships arising from social events, social relationships and actual behavior in social situations and the emotional experiences involved"), by personal experiences ("factual experiences, events and circumstances as experienced by the speaker or third party including emotional response to these"), and by future social activity.[8] Sport and similar topics accounted for 8.7 percent of speaking time. Work-related and academic topics accounted for 13.5 percent.

Equipped with what Michael Tomasello and Hannes Rakoczy call "the real thing" of knowing that we and others can act in the world, and can do things with others, we become fascinated by the doings of ourselves and others, and the effects of such doings.

Maxims and Expectations

Paul Grice has proposed that conversation is based on four maxims. The first is that when you take your turn in a conversation, you should say the right amount: not too little and not too much. Next is truthfulness: don't say anything false and don't say anything for which you lack any basis. Third is relevance: what you say should relate to what's going on in the conversation. Fourth is to be clear and orderly: avoid obscurity, organize what you say appropriately, be immediate, and be brief.

Grice points out that these principles apply to other cooperative activities. Imagine you are helping someone cook dinner. This person asks you to pass a saucepan. The maxim of the right amount enables the cook to expect that you don't supply three saucepans. As to truthfulness, if the cook asks for salt, you shouldn't surreptitiously hand over sugar. For relevance, if the cook asks for olive oil, then you shouldn't offer an oven cloth. For clarity and orderliness, you should act with reasonable dispatch and not say, for instance, "Not now. I've got to go off for ten minutes to read a book."

Human cooperation is enabled by language. It's not just going about in a group like a shoal of fish, not just joining together as wolves do when hunting, not just foraging for food—some of which might be shared as happens also with chimpanzees. It's the making of cooperative arrangements with others to go out with a friend, to have families, to work together in jobs, to form societies. We do together what we cannot do on our own.

When one recalls some incident, or when one is in the process of constructing or repairing something, visual images can occur that are individual. But a great deal of our thinking, perhaps most of it, is verbal, or verbal-like. Language is based on social cooperation, so most thinking is socially based.

We humans experience ourselves and others as having a life of the mind, and this life is therefore based on cooperation. In a recent book, Charles Taylor has argued that although language has often been regarded in terms of information, and of naming things and concepts that we know, it does not merely describe. It brings a world into being, usually a social world. Conversational language is a way of constructing our experiences of ourselves with others.[9]

15

What Is It about Love?

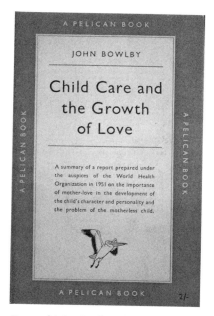

A PELICAN BOOK

JOHN BOWLBY

Child Care and the Growth of Love

A summary of a report prepared under the auspices of the World Health Organization in 1951 on the importance of mother-love in the development of the child's character and personality and the problem of the motherless child.

A PELICAN BOOK

2/-

Cover of John Bowlby's book of 1951, in which he studied effects of children being loved, and of them losing their parents.

John Bowlby and Mary Ainsworth studied how attachments of infants with primary caregivers are central to development. One-year-olds have three main styles of attachment that carry forward into adulthood. One is Securely Attached; people with this style are comfortable and trustful in their intimate relationships. Among those who are insecure are the Ambivalently Attached, who want to relate, but can be angry and rejecting. Those who are insecure with an Anxiously Attached style want to rely only on themselves. Donald Winnicott proposed that as infants grow, a space comes into being between infant and caregiver, a space-in-between. It is in this space that culture grows. Long-term romantic love can include attachment, but is a uniquely human mode. It's an important aspiration for many people, and can provide a strong sense of meaning in life.

Attachment and Beyond

Apart from the widespread acceptance that whatever our gender, ethnic group, or religious background, we all have basic human rights, another legacy of World War II was recognition of the sad state of many orphaned children.[1] In London, during the war Anna Freud (Sigmund Freud's daughter) and Dorothy Tiffany Burlingham (granddaughter of Charles Tiffany, the New York jeweler) set up the Hampstead War Nurseries, in response to the destruction of families during the blitz on London.[2]

With the loss of parents, children would tend first to protest, then perhaps look for them everywhere, then become sad. Often later, they would sink into apathy and despair. The World Health Organization commissioned John Bowlby to make a report on what children had experienced during the War, with air raids, losses, and evacuations. His book of 1951, *Child Care and the Growth of Love*, the cover of which appears at the opening of this chapter, derives from that report. In this book Bowlby wrote: "What is believed to be essential for mental health is that the infant and young child should experience a warm, intimate and continuous relationship with [a] mother (or permanent mother substitute . . .) in which both find satisfaction and enjoyment."[3]

The early relationship with a mother or other caregiver provides a foundation for later relationships, for what Michael Tomasello calls shared intentionality. Those who have experienced love as a child find it easier to love others when they are adults. Those who have been separated, or neglected, or ill-treated, find it more difficult to form trusting relationships in adulthood, and often they find it difficult to take part in society in ways that others find acceptable. Such unfortunate people can become mentally ill, perhaps act in criminal ways, or both. Bowlby's idea was that the foundation for being able to relate cooperatively with others—sexual partners, offspring, friends, colleagues, acquaintances—in adulthood is a continuous and affectionate relationship with a mother or mother substitute during the first three years of life.

Bowlby proposed the concept of attachment: a biologically based system, in which an infant keeps close to a caregiver, and in which the caregiver cares for and protects the infant during the period when the child is most vulnerable.[4] The opposite was "maternal deprivation," a term Bowlby used in the title of the second part of his 1951 book. There has been a great deal of research, now, on the subject, starting with, and being strongly influenced by, the work of Michael Rutter.

Think of it like this. Mammals are born live, with infants fitted by evolution to be nourished by mothers' milk. This is a physiological adaptation. Attachment is a parallel psychological adaptation. It is based on emotions of trustful security when the mother or other caregiver is present. It doesn't need to be the biological mother; it can be a father, or someone unrelated to the baby. This presence enables the baby to feel safe, and able to explore the world from the secure home base of the relationship. When the caregiver is absent, the infant tends to feel intense anxiety, and loses confidence.

John Bowlby was born in London into an upper-class family.[5] As a child he saw his mother for only an hour a day, after tea, though he saw her more in the summer. His own primary caregiver was a nanny with whom he was close. Bowlby became a doctor, and while still a medical student he started training in psychoanalysis. He became a psychiatrist with a special interest in children and their separations from parents. During World War II, he was a doctor in the army, but immediately afterward (drawing on work by Anna Freud, Dorothy Burlingham, and others) he focused again on problems of separation of children from their parents.

The concept of attachment came to Bowlby when biologist-friends introduced him to the works of Konrad Lorenz on imprinting, a phenomenon in which, after hatching, a gosling comes to recognize as its mother the first largish sound-making object that moves around. Lorenz sometimes arranged that this object was himself. You may have seen photos of him walking across a field, followed by a gaggle of goslings who think he is their mother-goose.

The idea of attachment as the mammalian equivalent of imprinting came to Bowlby—as Mary Ainsworth later related—in a flash of inspiration.[6] This idea of the foundational status of early relationships has been the important link between biology and psychoanalysis. More and more, Bowlby regarded children's difficulties as based on their real history in infancy, though many psychoanalysts emphasized their patients' fantasies. One result was that Bowlby was ostracized by many psychoanalysts in London.

In terms of empirical research, it is clear that infancy is indeed the main time for forming attachments, which become templates for later intimate relationships. Bowlby's idea, however, that there is a window of just the baby's first three years in which attachment can occur, is too narrow. Although difficulties of forming a first close relationship increase with age, it is now recognized that even with disturbed early experience, people can form decent relationships beyond infancy.

Styles of Attachment

Mary Ainsworth earned her PhD in Toronto, Canada, and during the War she, too, was in the army.[7] After the War, she moved with her husband to London, where he completed his PhD. She answered an advertisement in the *Times*, and got a job at the Ta-

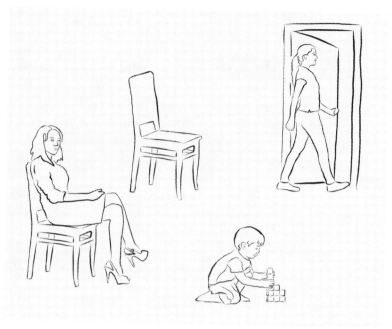

Figure 21. An infant's mother leaves the room in the Strange Situation Test, devised by Mary Ainsworth and colleagues. *Source:* © Susan Beattie, with permission.

vistock Clinic, working with Bowlby on children's separations from parents. She became Bowlby's principal colleague. Later, Mary Ainsworth's husband got a job in Uganda, so she moved with him, and studied mothers and babies there. She found that, while most characteristics were the same as in North America and England, there were some differences. After Uganda the couple moved to Baltimore, in the United States, and it was there, with Mary Blehar, Everett Waters, and Sally Wall, that Ainsworth devised the Strange Situation Test.

The Strange Situation was a room in Ainsworth's laboratory, with a couple of chairs and some toys: it is strange to the child. At first the child is in the room with her or his mother, who sits quietly. Then a stranger enters, and also sits quietly. Then the mother leaves the room. You can see a picture of this in figure 21.

Then the stranger tries to interact with the child. The mother then returns and the stranger leaves.

Ainsworth and her colleagues identified three styles of attachment. The first style is Secure. Infants with this style are distressed when their mother leaves the room, but when she returns they seek her out and allow themselves to be comforted by her. Then there are two styles of Insecure Attachment. Some infants are Insecurely Attached with a style called Ambivalent. They want to be near their mother when she returns, but they do not allow themselves to be comforted by her. Instead they show a great deal of anger. Infants who are Insecurely Attached in an Avoidant way seem barely to notice when the mother leaves and they make no attempt to interact with her when she returns. They appear to be unconcerned.

Working Models from Infancy to Adulthood

Since the work of Bowlby and Ainsworth, attachment and its effects in adolescence and adulthood have become the largest topics of research in social development. Attachment is based on an idea of Sigmund Freud, that love in infancy—feeling loved by a parent and being able to love that parent—forms a template for later intimate relationships.[8] Bowlby proposed that the child forms an internal working model of relating.[9] This model is a set of inner beliefs about what to expect in relationships, for instance about whether the other person is to be trusted. These beliefs develop too early to be verbalized, but if put into words, for a Secure person, they would include something like this. "This person is there for me. If I am frightened, I know this person will protect me." For an Avoidant infant, the beliefs are something like this. "When anything seems threatening, don't trust anyone. I will be wary, and rely only on myself." Ideas of these kinds form foundations for subsequent intimate relationships. You may hear someone announce that "We live alone and we die alone." Although this person may think this is a deep truth, it's more likely to be an externalization of an internal working model of relating formed in the person's early years.[10]

Critical tests of the idea of internal working models as seen in different attachment styles have been made in research on whether styles of attachment carry through into adulthood. Carol George, Nancy Kaplan, and Mary Main developed the Adult Attachment Interview: an hour-long semi-structured interview in which people are asked to talk about past relationships with parents or caregivers. They are asked, for instance, to list five adjectives to describe these relationships with parents, to talk about what they would do when they were upset in childhood, and about whether they ever felt rejected. The interviewer also asks people to talk about their current relationships, so that researchers can understand their participants' internal working model in their adult forms.

Main and her colleagues concluded that, based on the Adult Attachment Interview, there were three styles. They called one style Secure/Autonomous. People with this style talked about their early relationships with objectivity and balance. They gave a coherent account of their childhood experiences, including both the good and the bad. In a second style, the people were called Preoccupied. The account they gave was incoherent. Some of their experiences from childhood were traumatic and still overwhelming for them. A third style was Dismissing. They gave brief and distanced accounts of their childhood. They didn't remember many events, and showed no emotion when talking about them.

In a 1991 study, Peter Fonagy and colleagues gave the Adult Attachment Interview to mothers and the Ainsworth's Strange Situation Test to their one-year-old infants. They found that 75 percent of the women who were securely attached had babies who were also securely attached, and 73 percent of women who were Preoccupied or Dismissing had infants who were Ambivalent or Avoidant.

Everett Waters and his colleagues followed up with people from a Strange Situation Test that they had been given when they were one year old to an Adult Attachment Interview when they were aged twenty-one. In three groups of people, different results were found. One group consisted of sixty white middle-class people. For them, 72 percent maintained their style of Secure or Insecure attachment.[11] For those whose style changed, the switch was associated with a negative life event, such as childhood abuse, loss of a parent, or parental divorce. A second group was of thirty people in a research project on alternative lifestyles: twelve of them were from conventional families with parents who were married, while the other eighteen were from unconventional families, with single parents, or unmarried parents, or parents who lived in a commune or in an unattached way.[12] The stability of those from unconventional backgrounds was similar to that of people from conventional backgrounds. Overall in this study 77 percent of people maintained their Secure as compared with Insecure status. In a third study, there were fifty-seven people from a background of poverty and developmental risk.[13] For these people, continuity of attachment status was not found. People in this group had, however, suffered high rates of severe life events, such as childhood abuse, as well as high rates of depression in their mothers, and family malfunctioning. Any of these might have been responsible for changes of attachment style. In an even longer follow-up, Robert Waldinger and Marc Schulz have found that men who came from families with warm relationships as children had greater intimacy with spouses when they reached their seventies and eighties.

So, people's abilities to take part in activities that involve shared intentions are affected. We can even see mental illness as born partly of genetic temperament, but partly, too, from experience in relationships in which intentions were not shared, in which there was disappointment, or fear, or loss.

Attachment is just one aspect of the relationship with parents. It is based on protection from harm.[14] One can see its importance in evolution. Just as important, however, is how sensitive parents are to their children. Attachment and sensitivity both involve joint intentions. In attachment, when it works well, if the child is worried or sad and the caregiver is there, the child is comforted. For sensitivity, when the child wants to engage, the caregiver does so, takes part in whatever the little one wants.

In a study of maternal sensitivity, Vivian Zayas and colleagues found that the greater the sensitivity of mothers when their toddlers were eighteen months old, the less avoidant the people were seen to be with friends and in romantic relationships when they were twenty-two-year-old adults. In contrast, when their mothers had been more controlling, as adults they were more avoidant of friends, as well as showing more avoidance and more anxiety in relation to romantic partners.

Falling in Love

In the West, falling in love was depicted in the medieval poem *The Romance of the Rose*, by Guillaume de Lorris and Jean de Meun. It starts with a young man who dreams that he strolls beside the river of life, then enters the garden of courtly love, in which he sees a beautiful lady. The young man's consciousness is represented as a succession of characters: Hope, Sweet Thought, Reason, and so on. The lady, too, appears as a succession of characters: Bielacoil (her conversational self), Status (her sense of her aristocratic position), and Pity. When the young man makes a false step, these characters disappear, to be replaced by the character Fear, or Shame. As the young man reaches toward the Rose at the center of the garden, the god of Love fires an arrow at him, and makes him Love's servant.

Elaine Hatfield and Richard Rapson (married as they are) define passionate love like this:

A state of intense longing for union with another. Passionate love is a complex functional whole including appraisals or appreciations, subjective feelings, expressions, patterned physiological processes, action tendencies, and instrumental behaviors. Reciprocated love (union with the other) is associated with fulfillment and ecstasy.[15]

Falling in love seems to occur worldwide. In 1992, William Jankowiak and Edward Fischer surveyed ethnographic accounts of love mostly by anthropologists from 166 societies and found that in 147 of them at least one of the following could be recognized: (a) personal anguish or longing, (b) love songs and the like, (c) elopements, (d) indigenous accounts of passionate love, (e) the anthropologist's assertion that love occurred. In another survey made at about the same time, Susan Sprecher and colleagues interviewed 1,667 people in the United States, Russia, and Japan. Among college students, 59 percent of Americans, 67 percent of Russians, and 53 percent of Japanese said they were in love.

Love Is Love

Randolph Nesse has said that the best gift of evolution is our human ability to love. We can love our children, our sexual partners, our friends, sometimes we can even love our parents. But what is this love? Many psychologists have argued that love isn't love, that really it's something else.

One argument is that love is attachment.[16] Another argument, almost as popular, is that we humans are unusual among mammalian species in our pair-bonding. The arrangement came about, proposed Owen Lovejoy, when the human line branched off from that which led to chimpanzees, who do not know who their fathers are. In the human line, our male ancestors started to focus on a single female, so that in return for her exclusive and compliant partnership in sex, they would provide food and other input to her and her offspring. Thereby he would help promote the survival of the genes of both of them, and children would come to know both their mothers and their fathers. A third kind of proposal is based on social exchange. Thus, John Gottman has proposed that successful partners make positive statements to each other as reinforcements and that, to maintain a loving relationship, there need to be at least five positive statements for each negative one.

Despite ideas that love isn't love, but is attachment, or pair-bonding, or mutual reinforcement, the idea of love as love remains a strong one. Perhaps instead of the archives of scientific research we should look to Margery Williams's 1922 book for children, *The Velveteen Rabbit*, about a rabbit given as a present to a young boy. Although the Velveteen Rabbit was a favorite, for a long time it lived in the toy cupboard, or on the nursery floor. It was looked down upon by the mechanical toys. The Rabbit was naturally shy, and the only one who was kind to him was the Skin Horse. One day Rabbit asks Skin Horse, "What is REAL?"

"Real isn't how you are made," said the Skin Horse. "It's a thing that happens to you. When a child loves you for a long, long time, not just to play with, but REALLY loves you, then you become Real."[17]

The Space-in-Between

Donald Winnicott wrote about how, to start with, when a baby wants something, its mother is likely to respond so that what's in the baby's mind, the object of the baby's desire, is met and satisfied by something that then appears in the outer world.[18] A baby who is hungry cries, and a breast full of milk is presented. But after the first few months of life, the wish and the world begin to separate. A space appears—a space in between—and it is from here, says Winnicott, that all language and all culture grow. However elaborate they become, each individual's language and personal culture never lose this connection with the earliest relationship, with parents or other caregivers. They grow in the space-in-between.

The first material object to appear in this space is often what Winnicott called a transitional object, a soft toy or something similar. It's cuddled and caressed, and must never be changed. It stands in for the mother and is loved as she is.

As development proceeds, says Winnicott, transitional phenomena "spread out over the whole intermediate territory between 'inner psychic reality' and 'the external world as perceived by two persons in common' that is to say, over the whole cultural field."[19]

From the sensitivity of the mother or other caregiver, there can arise joint intentionality, and later collective intentionality. Winnicott doesn't mention *The Velveteen Rabbit* in his discussion of transitional objects, although perhaps he might have done. Later in his work he does, however, take up the Rabbit's problem of becoming Real, and of how, from being loved, a child may experience becoming real, a sense of having a true self. An alternative is that a child may internalize a set of expectations, typically from a parent, and attempt to enact them in order to be loved.[20] Such enactments can lead to the construction of what Winnicott called a false self, so that the person who takes them on may inside forever feel empty and unlovable. It's a continuation of the idea proposed by Karen Horney, discussed in chapter 1.

It's when a caregiver can engage jointly with a baby in a sensitive way, not just to impose expectations, that love can grow. And this love, emerging from Winnicott's space-in-between, can become the basis for relationships with others that are cooperative, with a basis of mutuality, as a person grows up. In turn, such relationships can become bases for shared intentions of whole societies.

16

Culture

Margaret Mead, who caused consternation with her report of easy-going sex lives of adolescent women in Samoa.

Practices and beliefs of different societies profoundly affect who we are and how we feel about others. In Samoa, Margaret Mead found that adolescent women had many lovers, and enjoyed a life that was largely free of anxiety. On the Pacific Island of Ifaluk, Catherine Lutz found that happiness was not valued as it is in America, because it can make people too pleased with themselves. Although on Ifaluk people are generally cheerful, their most valued emotion is anxiety about whether everyone in the social group is alright. In the precarious life of Inuit people, in the Arctic, Jean Briggs found the main principle in adult life was to accept others, and never to be angry.

Margaret Mead and Samoa

A society is a group of people who live in a particular place and time. A culture is the set of customs and beliefs of a society that its members take in for themselves, that brings them together ... holds them together. Cultures are ways of life of specific social worlds, ways of collective intentions. The social science of understanding them is cultural anthropology.

Margaret Mead (see a photo from 1948, at the head of this chapter) became the world's most famous cultural anthropologist. She went to live in Samoa to study the experience of adolescent women and, in 1928, she wrote *Coming of Age in Samoa*. She brought back a perspective that challenged the ideas of her own middle-class America. During her life, Mead made a number of field trips to other societies. Rather than confining herself to the academy, she engaged in public debates about different cultures and what we could learn about them that would be of relevance to life in the West.[1]

Mead was born in 1901 to a mother who was a sociologist and a father who was a professor of finance.[2] Although her father urged her to go into nursing, she didn't want to do that and in 1923 she earned her bachelor's degree in psychology at Barnard College, in New York. It was in New York that she met Franz Boas, a professor at Columbia University, a leading anthropologist of his day. (It was one of Boas's collected stories that Frederic Bartlett used in his study of remembering, discussed in chapter 7.) With Boas as her advisor, Mead went on to earn her PhD at Columbia in 1929.

In the foreword to *Coming of Age in Samoa*, Boas wrote:

> Courtesy, modesty, good manners, conformity to definite ethical standards are universal, but what constitutes courtesy, modesty, very good manners, and definite ethical standards

is not universal. It is instructive to know that standards differ in the most unexpected ways ... We feel, therefore, grateful to Miss Mead for having undertaken to identify herself so completely with Samoan youth that she gives us a lucid and clear picture of the joys and difficulties encountered by the individual in a culture so entirely different from our own.[3]

Mead learned the language of the people she went to visit. They lived in three contiguous villages along a shore of the island of Taū, in Samoa. The villages had a combined population of about 600. Mead wrote that she spent "six months accumulating an intimate and detailed knowledge of all the adolescent girls in this community, 68 in number."[4] As well as living with them, conversing with them, taking part in their activities, she administered intelligence tests, and took meticulous field notes.

Mead described childcare as more distributed than that of the Western nuclear family, with relatives and other village members joining in so that children had close relationships with several adults. The world of childhood and adolescence was kept fairly separate from the world of adulthood. Mead characterized the lives of the young women when they entered adolescence as not only stress-free and unproblematic, but enlivened by sexual relationships that tended not to last very long. The relationships were usually either with boys of their own age, or with young men in the village.

Although people's sexual relationships were topics of conversation in Samoan society, for the most part adolescent young women had sex with whomever they chose, without adverse criticism. Their way of life continued until they became adults and entered into marriage arrangements on largely economic grounds, at which time they began to bring up children of their own. Mead said that with the exception of a few cases (that she discussed in detail), adolescence represented no period of crisis or stress, but was instead an orderly developing of a set of slowly maturing interests and activities. The girls' minds were perplexed by no conflicts, troubled by no philosophical queries, beset by no remote ambitions. To live as a girl with many lovers as long as possible and then to marry in one's own village, near one's own relatives and to have many children, these were uniform and satisfying ambitions.[5]

Mead's book was both popular and controversial. Her finding that adolescent girls had pleasant and casual sexual relationships before they married and that later they might have sex outside marriage, would have been challenge enough to the social norms and moral beliefs of those who read her book in the late 1920s and early 1930s. But to combine this, as Mead did, with blunt criticism of the intense turmoil about identity, about sexual prohibitions, about aspiration, and about disappointment, that she described as characteristic of young women's adolescence in America, multiplied the shock.

After Mead died in 1978, an anthropologist named Derek Freeman published a book in which he maintained that Mead had had her leg pulled by her chief informant in Samoa. He said this person had invented the material Mead later published as a kind of joke. Mead, however, kept meticulous field notes, and from these it is clear that she reached her main conclusions before she met this informant who, by the time Freeman met her, had converted to Christianity. The American Anthropological Association dismissed Freeman's book as unscientific and misleading. The incident shows that becoming a popular figure can make a researcher a target for unwarranted attacks, perhaps based on envy. At the same time, the need has arisen in psychology to know, more clearly, what findings are reliable, and this has led to a new movement in which findings that are controversial can be replicated.[6]

Vygotsky and Internalization of the Social World

Whereas Jean Piaget concentrated on innate stages of development, Lev Vygotsky emphasized the cultural. When a child acquires language, the resources of an individual child are augmented by the resources of family and society. The mind becomes, according to Vygotsky, an internalization of the social world. But it's not a container into which objects are put, so that they become mental objects. The mind becomes a means of imagining, conceptualizing, planning, a means of talking with oneself, and of talking with others within oneself. It becomes an internal social world of its own, able to inform interactions in the outside social world.

Here is an example from Vygotsky's colleague, Roza Levina, who studied how a four-and-a-half-year-old girl would retrieve some candy from a cupboard when given a stool and a stick. The child talks to herself in the way that she has been talked to by parents. She keeps up a running commentary, then makes suggestions to herself in the form of plans:

"No, that doesn't get it," the girl says. "I could use the stick." She takes the stick and knocks at the candy. "It will move now," she says, then reflects on the situation and analyzes what she has done. "It moved. I couldn't get it with the stool, but the stick worked."[7]

Here is the mind at work: a physical and social world within which is a model of the world outside, which makes plans so that the world outside comes to mirror the world within.

Vygotsky considered the importance of private speech: a transition from talking to others in the world into being able to think in verbal terms, which become terms of meaning. A revolution occurs when the kinds of thought of Piaget's sensory-motor stage come together with language to create a new kind of mental functioning, which we can experience for ourselves as adults when we reflect on what we are thinking or what we are planning.

Michael Tomasello and his colleagues showed that children know that they and others are able to act in the world. He has gone on to show that, as children develop language, actions become symbolized as verbs, and verb islands, which were discussed in chapter 6, become the mental means by which symbolic actions are connected to people, to their desires, and to things in the world. This kind of view, based on studies of how children begin to speak, is coming to replace the idea of specific languages being assimilated into a universal grammar of the kind proposed by Chomsky.[8]

Verb-symbols are used in communications to make what John Searle has called "speech acts": to call attention to something, to make a request, agree to do something, and so on. So an infant might say "Get more juice" as a request to a mother, knowing that she can act, by getting (verb) the juice, to fulfill the request. Such utterances are among the beginnings of explicit cooperation with others. They are based on knowledge translated into words, knowledge that can be used to call attention, to request, to agree, and so on.

At the end of chapter 6, we looked at an example of the language of a twenty-one-month-old child called Emily, whose parents Katherine Nelson asked to put a tape recorder by her bed, to record what she said to herself before she went to sleep. Here is Emily, continuing to talk before she goes to sleep, at the age of two years and eight months.

> Tomorrow when we wake up from bed, first me and Daddy and Mommy, you, eat breakfast like we usually do, and then we're going to p-l-a-y, and then soon as Daddy comes, Carl's going to come over, and then we're going to play a little while. And then Carl and Emily are both going down the car with somebody, and we're going to ride to nursery school,

and then we when we get there, we're all going to get out of the car, go into nursery school, and Daddy's going to give us kisses, then go, and then say and then we will say goodbye, then he's going to work and we're going to play at nursery school.[9]

Here we see the beginnings of narrative structure, the making of meaningful sense of the world in terms of agents who persist through time, and encounter incidents. Nelson proposes that here we see the kind of thinking that functions to comprehend and construct a whole world. Emily is rather precocious but, based on her mental models of the world, she affords us a privileged glimpse: an externalized version of thought as it takes place online.

Thus, language opens up not only a world of cooperation with others, but a world of self-reflective consciousness. As development proceeds, this will enable people to share with others their accounts of emotions they have experienced.

At the same time, in Emily's pre-sleep reflections, we see a person taking in a culture: with a nuclear family that has a mommy and a daddy, one that values play for children, one that involves cars and nursery schools, one in which parents kiss their children, and the father goes off to a place called "work." Here, too, are distinctive elements of a middle-class life. In other societies such as those of Samoa, and the one discussed in the next section, families are extended, play is not emphasized, and there are no cars.

The Island of Ifaluk

For nine months Catherine Lutz lived on the Micronesian island of Ifaluk, which had a population of about 430 people. On the basis of previous research, Lutz knew that on Ifaluk, "gender relations were more egalitarian than in American society."[10] She wanted to see how it might be possible for people to organize their lives in such a way as "to avoid problems that seemed to diminish American culture, in particular its pervasive inequality, of both gender and class, and its violence."

Lutz's research focused on emotions. As well as being close in spirit to Mead's, it enables us to continue to think about human universals such as those of cooperation and shared intentions. The title of Lutz's book, *Unnatural Emotions*—the cover of which appears in figure 22—gives a hint of her findings. The emotions she discovered on Ifaluk were not those proposed by Darwin as biologically based. When Lutz says that emotions on Ifaluk are "unnatural," she doesn't mean they are weird—she makes them very comprehensible—but that they are created and sustained by culture rather than nature.

Anthropologists know that from visits of six months or a year they cannot become full member of societies different from their own. If one emigrates, it may take five years, or ten, or more, to become fully part of one's new society. So anthropologists' intentions are not to attain this kind of experience. Instead, they bring us news of two kinds. One kind is of a world of cousins in faraway societies. The other kind is about ourselves, dwellers in industrialized societies. Lutz does this by juxtaposing Ifaluk's ideas and practices with Western ideas and practices. Her role was to offer herself as someone with whom we could identify as she took part in life on a Pacific atoll.

Here is an example of the kind of juxtaposition she makes. In the United States, people are brought up to believe that it is a self-evident truth that they have a "right to the pursuit of happiness." Indeed, happiness is very important in American society. Do people think in the same way on Ifaluk? There is a word that translates as "happiness": *ker*. But though Ifalukians often smile in a way that has been found to be recognizable worldwide, they don't think they have a right to *ker*. They are rather suspicious of it, because it can lead to over-excitement, or to showing off, or even to being rowdy, all types of behavior that are thoroughly disapproved of. The proper way to behave on Ifaluk is

Figure 22. Cover of Catherine Lutz's book about the culture of the atoll of Ifaluk. *Source:* Front cover of Lutz, C. A. (1988). *Unnatural emotions: Everyday sentiments on a Micronesian atoll and their challenge to Western theory.* Chicago: University of Chicago Press, paperback edition. © 1988 University of Chicago Press.

to be *maluwelu,* meaning "gentle, calm, and quiet."[11] This state is important because you need to be what the Ifalukians think of as socially intelligent, to see that everyone in your group is alright.

At its highest, the atoll of Ifaluk is only five meters above sea level. Typhoons can wipe out the taro gardens that the women cultivate, and deplete the lagoons of fish that the men catch. Women and men live fairly separate lives and it was one of Lutz's regrets that she was not able to gain much insight into Ifaluk's world of men. Women tended the infants and kept their brothers supplied with vegetables. Men supervised the toddlers while they were making rope or mending nets, and kept their sisters supplied with fish. Lutz proposes that the Ifalukians value interdependence because of the precariousness of their existence. By contrast, Westerners tend to value independence, and we like to feel secure in our powers.

Had Lutz been a clan sister, visiting from another atoll, she would have slept in the main residence of her family, with a dozen other women and infants, so that everyone's sleeping mat touched the mats of others. In that way nobody feels lonely. When Lutz arrived on the island, her adoptive father, who had some experience of American Peace Corps workers, knew that Americans were exotic beings who have strange ideas such as a preference for sleeping alone. Over two or three days a solution was reached, in which a cooking hut was converted and moved to just a few feet from a women's residence so that Lutz could sleep in it. In this way, her peculiar predilection for aloneness could be satisfied without departing from the island's good sense of being close to other people.

If any emotional state is valued on Ifaluk in the way happiness is in America, it is *metagu* (fear/anxiety). Here is an incident that illustrates it. Lutz found that on Ifaluk, as Margaret Mead had found on Samoa, sexual relationships were often relatively casual, and couples would go off into the interior for sexual meetings. But such encounters occurred only at night. Meetings in public, in the daytime, that had any sexual component did not occur.

One night, sleeping quietly, Lutz was woken by a man "entering [her] doorless house. The danger I saw in that instant led me to scream out, using unreflectively the sense I had brought from home that strange men entering your house at night intend violent harm of any number of kinds."[12]

The man ran away quickly and Lutz's adoptive mother and family, sleeping just a few feet away, were with her immediately. When they heard that Lutz had been afraid they found it hilarious. Although they knew that men could sometimes be frightening, particularly in public places if they were drunk or if they seemed to be about to fight, they knew that a man coming privately at night could only mean one thing. It was to suggest a sexual tryst: the very opposite of anything that, on Ifaluk, a woman would be frightened of.

Lutz said that afterward, although for the Ifalukians the reason for her display of *metagu* seemed wonderfully strange, she found that when her adoptive mother subsequently talked about the incident, she did so with some satisfaction because her adopted daughter, rather than being utterly peculiar, had shown herself sensible enough to be capable of feeling and showing this important emotion.

English is a language in which it seems people are rather passive in relation to emotions. Terms for emotions tend to be adjectives: he is sad, she was angry, and so on. This usage implies that emotions happen to a person. On Ifaluk, emotion is not distinguished from thought, so that the word *nunuwan* means "emotion/thought," and it is not individual but social. It's a connection that people make with each other. And on Ifaluk, emotions don't just happen. People do them. Something similar happens in the Russian language, in which one doesn't say and feel the equivalent of "I am angry," but something closer to "I contend," with the expectation that in an interaction with the other person the matter will be resolved.[13] We do have the more active kind of emotion in English with the idea of love, an emotion we do, which forms a relation with someone else, but English speakers seem often to receive emotions rather than perform them.

We are left with puzzles. Happiness is a state to which Americans have a right. But the corresponding idea in Ifaluk, *ker*, is suspect because to do it is to start to walk about on one's own, to become too self-centered and risk forgetting one's responsibilities to others. By contrast, anxiety in America is to be avoided, and replaced with security. On Ifaluk, *metagu* (anxiety) expresses human vulnerability. It is about others, and it relates people with each other. There is something universal about emotions. We can understand Ifalukian emotions and they can understand Western emotions, at least to some extent. At the same time, the differences are striking.

Other Societies, Other Minds

Many books and articles have now been written about societies very different from those of the industrialized West. Members of one society visited by Nelson Chagnon, the Yanomamö, call themselves the fierce people. They exist in a state of continuous warfare with neighboring groups of the same society. Because of this, among the Yanomamö a large proportion of young men suffer violent deaths. Then there are the Ik, displaced from their traditional hunter-gatherer way of life, and suffering devastating famines. Colin Turnbull lived with them for three years and described them as having become extremely individualistic. In contrast are the Inuit, in the Arctic, with whom Jean Briggs lived for a year and a half. They are barely individualistic at all. She found that among them anger was simply not part of adult life. The !Kung, visited by Elizabeth Marshall Thomas, continue a way of life as nomads in the Kalahari Desert which may be similar to that of nearly all of humankind over most of the last 200,000 years.

Katherine Nelson introduced us to the young Emily as she reflected on her life before falling asleep in a middle-class, two-parent, family in the United States. For an Ifalukian Emily, or an Inuit Emily, it would not just be that the people, things, and places that she brought to mind would be different. She would grow up to think and feel in a very different way.

A question for us humans is how to extend the love we have for a parent, for a sexual partner, or for a friend, beyond the immediate and particular society in which we live, to human society in general.

PART FIVE

Common Humanity

17

Imagination, Stories, Empathy

Two boys play together under a table; as described by Judy Dunn, such play draws on elaborate imagination, and develops intimacy.

As Judy Dunn has shown, children's play involves the making of model worlds. Among extensions of play are games, which are models of kinds of interaction which, as Erving Goffman has shown, give insight into the roles and modes of interaction of day-to-day life. Games and play are works of the imagination, which Paul Harris and his colleagues have shown also to be involved in abstract thinking. Fiction is another extension of childhood play into later life. It enables identification with literary characters, and engaging with circumstances of possible worlds. Engaging with fiction is associated with better empathy and understanding of others.

Children's Play

To imagine is to create a model world, a place and time to in-habit mentally. Or it's to think oneself into the world of another mind. In children's play we can see the making of such worlds. We see, too, the taking up of roles: the coming-to-be a firefighter, or a doctor, or a shopkeeper.

Here is a depiction by Judy Dunn of two four-year-old boys, friends in a nursery school for about a year, in a room that con-tains a table and some dress-up clothes. You can see two boys of this kind underneath a table in the picture at the head of this chapter.

> First they are pirates sailing on a search for treasure, then their ship is wrecked, and they are attacked by sharks; they reach the safety of an island, and build a house (under the table). What to eat and how to cook it are problems that are ingeniously solved. Their elaborate adventure, their quickly solved disputes (are they being attacked by sharks or by crocodiles?), their extended conversations about what happens next—all are captured by our video camera in the corner of the room.[1]

Dunn calls this the beginning of intimacy. In the roles the children are taking, they not only enact their own model-being of pirate, but they understand the other's role, the moves he makes, the things he says. They take on an elaborate shared in-tentionality. The reciprocity of children's play can be seen in hide-and-seek. To enjoy the game, when you are in the role of the person who is hiding, you have to imagine yourself into the role of the seeker. Play seems to be one of the ways in which, in childhood, we discover how to model others, to understand and coordinate with them.

Not content with writing one of the best books of history on the Middle Ages, Johan Huizinga followed it up with a book on play: *Homo Ludens: The Play Element in Culture*. Huizinga suggests it isn't that our species is particularly wise (*sapiens*). Rather, as a species we play or interact together imaginatively and cooperatively to create something that was not there before.

Fun in Games

It is sometimes thought that we play when we are children and stop when we grow up. But play doesn't stop. It becomes transformed. Among its transformations are games and sports.

Rather than being unstructured, as was the play of the boys who were being pirates, games and sports specify roles, specify how to engage in these roles, let us know what actions are available, what rules are to be obeyed. They are enactive models of modes of life, for instance of competition and skill. The sociologist Erving Goffman sketched the outline of a theory on this. In each game, he says, there is:

> a matrix of possible events and a cast of roles through whose enactment the events occur constitute together a field for fateful dramatic action, a plane of being, an engine of meaning, a world in itself.[2]

With a few exceptions such as Sudoku, games and sports are social events, cooperative encounters, even when their mode is competitive. And, says Goffman:

> there seems to be no agent more effective than another person in bringing a world for oneself alive or, by a glance, a gesture, or a remark, shriveling up the reality in which one is lodged.[3]

Many games and sports reflect social structures, so chess is based on medieval warfare, Monopoly is based on real estate speculation, Snakes and Ladders is based on downs and ups in our journey through life. The metaphor works in the other direction: forms of work can be spoken of as games or sports, the banking game, the writing game, and a person may say, "It came out of left field." In addition to such instances, Goffman explains how games enable us to reflect on the way in which, for each kind of interaction in life, we pass through a kind of semi-permeable membrane, into the interior of a certain way of life ("a world in itself") to participate, to accept the rules, to enact a role. In a restaurant, one doesn't order anything one can't pay for, and one doesn't take one's shirt off as one would in the changing room of a swimming pool. As one enters one's workplace one passes through another membrane. Within the workplace are rules of etiquette, modes of interaction, uses of time, which are different from within the membrane of home. And more than that: in real life as in games, as Goffman emphasizes, it makes all the difference how engaged we are in each role we adopt. If we are disengaged, or even not fully engaged, all is not well. And, as he also points out, in both real life and games, jokers and psychotics know how to cause disruption by breaking the rules.

Fun at the Movies

Play has also become transformed into plays, into novels, into films, into television series.

The film that is said to have been the most successful of all time in France is *Bienvenu aux Ch'tis* (in English, *Welcome to the Sticks*). It is about a post office manager, Philippe, who lives in Provence. His wife is grumpy and dissatisfied, and wants him to get himself moved to the Côte d'Azur. To obtain such a favorable transfer he would need to be disabled, but when he buys a wheelchair in order to present himself in this way he is found out and sent to a post office in Bergues near the English Channel which, for those who live in the south of France, is like being exiled to the North Pole. There, he finds that though the weather is not so good, his post office staff are friendly. They do, however, speak with a strange accent. Even the English subtitles are witty.

The humor of the early scenes in Bergues derives in part from interchanges in which the local dialect, Ch'ti, is at first almost incomprehensible to Philippe.[4] In Ch'ti, s-sounds are pronounced "sh," and "a" is pronounced "o." On Philippe's first day, the post office workers take him to lunch at the French Fry Shack on the town square, where he joins the others in having fricadelle (a local delicacy) and fries. He finds the fricadelle surprisingly good, and asks what's in it. "Can't ask whatsh in it," says a post office counter clerk. The ingredients are secret. "Like Americansh and Coco-Colo."

The staff of his post office make Philippe feel welcome, but on the phone to his wife, he tells her that it's even worse than they had imagined. As a result she stops being grumpy and becomes understanding, so that when he goes back to Provence every other weekend, his marriage is better than it has ever been, just as his job has become better than it has ever been.

Henri Bergson asked why people laugh, and said that among the reasons is that it's completely human; we don't laugh at landscapes or lampposts. We do laugh at people when, although they are human, they behave in a not-quite-human way, in a machine-like way. And generally we only laugh when we are with others: laughter needs a social echo. It may well have been an aspect of an evolutionary process of building group solidarity.

One reason *Welcome to the Sticks* is so good, so laugh-out-loud funny, is that rather than being about laughing at people who slip on banana peels or do other such silly things, it is about laughing with people. Philippe and his staff laugh together, and we in the audience laugh with them.

Imagination and Reasoning

With the spread of education, the question arose as to whether learning to read and write would improve people's ability to think. Does it, for instance, enable them to think in more abstract ways, as Jean Piaget would say, to reason logically? And might such changes affect whole societies?

Eric Havelock put the difference between oral and written information like this:

> Oral information is likely to be unfriendly to such a statement as, "The angles of a triangle are equal to two right angles." If however you said, "The triangle stood firm in battle, astride and posed on its equal legs, fighting resolutely to protect its two right angles against the attack of the enemy," you would be casting Euclid backwards into Homeric dress, you would be giving him preliterate form.[5]

What does learning to read and write do for our thinking? It was partly to answer this question that in 1931 and 1932 Alexander Luria traveled to Uzbekistan to study the effects of literacy programs that the USSR had begun. Among his tests was whether people who had attended such programs could reason from syllogisms, as conceived by Aristotle in *Prior Analytics*. In a syllogism, a person is given a proposition in the form of a general statement, then a particular statement that relates to it, and asked to make an inference. Here's an example:

All men are mortal.
Socrates is a man.
Inference: Therefore Socrates is mortal.

Here is a transcript from a person whom Luria interviewed: Abdurakhm, aged thirty-seven, who had not attended a literacy program.

INTERVIEWER: In the Far North, where there is snow, all bears are white. Novaya Zemlya is in the Far North. What color are the bears there?[6]

ABDURAKHM: I don't know; I've seen a black bear, I've never seen any others ...

INTERVIEWER: But what do my words imply? (The syllogism is repeated.)

ABDURAKHM: If a man was sixty or eighty and had seen a white bear ... he could be believed, but I've never seen one, and hence I can't say. That's my last word. Those who saw can tell, and those who didn't see can't say anything.

Abdurakhm seems on the edge of irritation with these silly questions, but at this point a young man who had attended literacy classes joined in. "From your words," he says, "it means that bears there are white." Luria reported that in a sample of fifteen people who had attended a literacy program, all of them could solve syllogisms of this kind, whereas from fifteen who had not attended a literacy program only four could solve syllogisms of this kind.[7]

A next step was taken by Sylvia Scribner and Michael Cole, who went to Liberia to see whether Luria's findings would be found there. One group of their participants was illiterate; the people in it had never been to school. In a second group, people were literate; they had been to school and could read and write English. In a third group, people had not been to school, and could not read or write English but they could write in a local indigenous script that was used for personal correspondence and commerce. Would the ability to read and write, which members of this third group had, enable these people to reason with syllogisms? Scribner and Cole found that it wasn't being able to read and write that made the difference. People who could read and write their indigenous script were not able to solve syllogisms. Only those who had been to school could do so.

Children's Imagination and Implications
for Thinking

Paul Harris reasoned that the literacy programs that people had started to take in Uzbekistan were very elementary, and that for Luria's finding perhaps something much more basic was involved than becoming literate. Perhaps, in these programs, and in schools in Liberia, he thought, people had been introduced to the idea that, by thinking, they could imagine possible worlds. They could do this, perhaps, because they had been able to think imaginatively in play when they were children.

With Maria Dias and Antonio Roazzi, Harris thought they would see how this idea might work with illiterate people in Recife, in Brazil. They tested twenty-four people who had attended literacy classes two or three times a week for two years, and twenty-four who were unschooled and illiterate. They constructed a set of syllogisms with premises that would be unfamiliar to their participants, such as "All leucocytes are white," and a set with premises that would be familiar: "All blood is red." Then half the participants were tested in the way that Luria had tested his informants. To these people the researchers said, "I am going to read you some little stories about things that will sound funny. But let's pretend that everything in the stories is true. Okay, now I'm going to tell you the first story."[8] The other half of the participants were invited to use their imagination. The researchers asked them to imagine being on another planet. To these people they said: "I am going to read you some little stories about things that will sound funny. But let's pretend that I am telling you all about another planet. Everything in that planet is different. Okay, now I'm going to tell you the first story about that planet."

With the first group of participants, Dias and her colleagues found that people responded in much the same way as Luria's respondents had. They tended not to be able to solve the syllogisms. Instead they drew only on their own experience. In contrast, those who were asked to imagine being on another planet—both those who had received some literacy instruction and those who had not—were able to do significantly better on syllogisms with both unfamiliar and familiar content.

The coming of language, perhaps 200,000 years ago, changed the mind from its previous ape-like state, into a hybrid. At this time in human evolution our ancestors would have been able to make individual mental associations, such as those of conditioned avoidance of the kind discovered by John Watson and Rosalie Rayner. At the same time, they would have taken part in shared plans with individuals, offspring, sexual partners, friends. They would also have taken on characteristics of their own local group culture. But now, in addition, they would have started to use a processor that worked in a new way, and could understand and generate language.

Andy Clark has proposed that a property of this new processor is that thoughts can themselves become objects of thought. As Philip Johnson-Laird has shown, this new processor is computationally more powerful than that of mental associations. It depends, too, on a new kind of memory that can work with language. This is short-term memory, of the kind discussed by George Miller in his paper on the magical number seven, plus or minus two.

So, some 200,000 years ago, the human mind became a hybrid with two kinds of processors that Keith Stanovich calls System 1 and System 2. System 1 is the older processor: associative and intuitive. Its memory is long-term and capacious, based mainly on direct experience. Then there is the newer processor, System 2, computationally more powerful, able to generate and understand language, able to direct and organize itself, but with a memory that is short-term and limited in capacity. In *Thinking, Fast and Slow*, Daniel Kahneman writes about how thinking fast draws on System 1, while thinking slow draws on System 2 and enables us to go step-by-step through a problem to become more accurate.[9]

More recently, a further mental development has occurred: the coming of imagination. It's this that explains how one can not only use thoughts to work on thoughts, but to think about things beyond the immediate and beyond the realm of remembered experience. This includes play, and being able to reason in abstract terms. It's what Dias, Roazzi, and Harris found with their participants in Brazil, who were asked to imagine what it might be like on another planet.

Imagination seems to have required a suite of six abilities to operate in the brain, some of long standing, others more recently acquired.[10] All of them emerge, in modern children, in the first four years of life. They are as follows.

- *Imitation.* Andrew Meltzoff and M. Keith Moore have reported that babies' abilities to imitate others' facial actions start when they are just a few weeks old. Imitation develops into abilities to learn how to do things if one is shown how.
- *Empathy and altruism.* The idea of empathy, defined as the ability to feel what someone else is feeling, goes back to the beginning of the twentieth century, when it was separated from the idea of sympathy. It is reviewed by Marty Hoffman and by Nancy Eisenberg. Empathy emerges in babies between twelve and eighteen months of age. It seems to grow from emotional engagement, and it can give rise to motivation to help others altruistically.
- *Knowledge of one's abilities to act in the world.* Michael Tomasello and Hannes Rakoczy say that an important faculty that differentiates us from apes is that by about the age of eighteen months human children know that both they and others are able to act in the world.
- *Symbolic play and role-based play.* Alan Leslie has discussed how a two-year-old may take a banana and use it as a telephone to talk to her friend. Hide-and-seek is an early kind of role-based play.

- *Understanding models.* Judy DeLoache found that three-year-olds, though not younger children, could find a toy hidden in a room if they had been shown a miniature toy being hidden in a dollhouse model of this room. Children also become able to understand pictures as representations.
- *Theory-of-mind, perspective-taking.* Heinz Wimmer and Josef Perner discovered that four-year-olds were able to know what someone else knows even when this is not the same as what they themselves believe.

It doesn't seem as if these abilities depend on each other. For instance, being able to take part in roles during play does not predict the development of theory-of-mind. It does, however, seem that these abilities matter for our modern human minds. They matter for our joint plans and for our development and maintenance of cultural worlds. They matter for our ability to imagine what it is like to live in circumstances other than our own: being in a minority ethnic group, beset by starvation, or made a victim of war. They are also essential for being able to think in abstractions, as well as understanding possible futures such as consequences of climate change, of rates of income inequality, and of international conflict.

Art Appears in the Human Record

More than 100,000 years ago a new human mode began, the mode of art. It's not directly practical, like the technology of stone tools, the earliest of which are more than three million years old. But in some ways this mode is comparable because it involves externalization, the sharing of mind. This earliest-discovered form of art was of shells, drilled to make beads, which seem to have been used for necklaces.[11] Whereas tools are used in the outer world, necklaces had other purposes. Did they perhaps work in the same kind of way as clothes, which may already have started by that time? Did they help people to fashion their identities, to transform themselves partly in the social world but also within?

Later, other kinds of art began to appear. Dating from 40,000 years ago, burial mounds have been found.[12] The earliest cave paintings were discovered at Chauvet. They date back 31,000 years.[13]

Personal ornaments and art mean that a mental connection is being made between the mind of the artist and the mind of another person who engages with it. Steven Mithen calls this metaphor: a "this" is a "that." Burial mounds imply that a "this" (a person who is dead) is a "that" (this person who is alive on another plane, or in our memories). A set of marks on a rock (a "this") in the earliest cave painting is a rhinoceros (a "that"), and a mental connection to them is offered to another person who sees it.

Early written stories include the *Epic of Gilgamesh*,[14] Homer's *Iliad*, and stories of the Bible.[15] Although later it was written down, the *Iliad* is thought to have been composed, first, by someone who recited it orally, to groups of people who would gather and listen.[16] The same kind of storytelling still occurs in some parts of the world. We can think of all such narrative stories, oral and written, as fiction.

The idea of fact as compared to fiction is not very helpful for psychological understanding. Of course, we know what is meant. In a court of law, or in a newspaper, or in science, we want to know the facts. A better word for fiction might be imaginative stories which, with the wider development of literacy, became imaginative literature.

We can say that generally (in plays, novels, movies) fictional stories take a narrative form, and their subject matter is about human beings interacting with each other. Stories based on happenings and anecdote must have arisen from conversation, our human means of cultivating and maintaining our relationships with each other. In fiction, imagined worlds of the kind that children share with friends in interactive play are transformed into imagined worlds that authors share with readers, and that readers share with each other in reading groups.

The adult love of fiction can be seen as entering model worlds to encounter characters (model people) in whom we become interested, and whom we recognize in terms of traits and quirks that enable us to better understand the people we meet in day-to-day life.[17]

History of the Mind in Fiction

There are not many subject areas in which there is a book that everyone in the field thinks is indispensable. For Western literary fiction, there is one: *Mimesis: The Representation of Reality in Western Literature* by Erich Auerbach. He wrote it between 1936 and 1946 when he lived in Istanbul. The book has twenty chapters. The first includes discussion of an incident from Homer when Odysseus returns home from the Trojan War and is recognized by his former nurse, from a scar on his thigh, and the biblical story of Abraham being told to sacrifice his son Isaac. Then, in historical sequence, come chapters based on courtly romance, on Dante's *Inferno*, on Montaigne, on Proust, and on Virginia Woolf. With each one, there is a passage from a book and, as we start to read it, we find ourselves inside a society with its own meanings, and inside a mind of that time. It's a history of Western literature and it is also a history of the Western mind.

How do storytellers enable us to make a scene vivid? Gabriel Garcia Marquez said that it's no good writing, "There were butterflies," in a story. "I discovered," he said, "that if I didn't say the butterflies were yellow, people would not believe it."[18]

Jennifer Summerfield, Demis Hassabis, and Eleanor Maguire conducted an fMRI study that takes us closer to this issue. They studied what neuroscientists call the core network. It is involved in remembering events in our lives, making plans, imagining future possibilities. Summerfield and her colleagues say they managed to slow down the constructive process of imagination by presenting spoken phrases to their participants one at a time, in an fMRI machine. Among phrases they used were: "a dark blue carpet" . . . "a carved chest of drawers" . . . "an orange striped pencil." Participants were asked, as they heard each phrase, to imagine what it indicated, and when they heard each new phrase, to add it to the scene. They were also to report on how vivid the resulting scene was. As this was going on, the researchers looked to see which brain areas were activated.

Three brain areas of the core network were associated with imagination: the hippocampus (plus some other areas), the intraparietal sulcus (plus another area), and the lateral prefrontal cortex. When the first phrase was presented, the hippocampus and associated areas were activated; with the second phrase, activity of these areas increased; with the third phrase activity in these areas increased again, but phrases presented beyond the first three did not produce additional activation. In what they said of their experience of doing the task, participants confirmed that three elements were sufficient to construct a scene to its maximum vividness.

Here is an example from the work of Anton Chekhov, widely regarded as one of the world's greatest writers of short stories. His story "Gusev" is about a private soldier who has been in the East for five years, who has been discharged and is now on his way home. At the start of the story neither the readers not Gusev know that he is dying. On his journey he imagines his homeland.

> He pictures an enormous pond covered with snow . . . On one side of the pond, a porcelain factory, the color of brick, with a tall smokestack and clouds of black smoke: on the other side a village . . . Out of a yard, the fifth from the end, drives a sleigh with his brother Alexei in it (ellipsis points in the original).[19]

Chekhov offers us some suggestive phrases: a snow-covered pond, a factory with a tall smokestack, the village with a sleigh, with no more words than necessary, enough for the reader to imagine the scene. In the same year that he wrote "Gusev," in a letter to his mentor and friend Alexei Suvorin, Chekhov wrote that in his short stories he counted "on the assumption that [his readers] will add the subjective elements that are lacking in the story."[20]

When we look at the world and perceive it in terms of people and objects laid out in three-dimensional space, the brain uses cues from the retina to guide its constructions, to make mental models of how the world must be. Writers of fiction do much the same, but their cues are phrases on a page, or words heard on a stage. As Shakespeare put it at the beginning of *Henry V*:

> Think, when we talk of horses, that you see them,
> Printing their proud hoofs i' th' receiving earth:
> For 'tis your thoughts that now must deck our kings.[21]

Human Rights

Although we now think of human rights as universal and fundamental to society, it was not always so. In her book, *The Invention of Human Rights*, Lynn Hunt shows that the invention of rights began in the second half of the eighteenth century. In 1759, in his book *The Theory of Moral Sentiments*, Adam Smith wrote of sympathy for others as essential, and that indeed it is the glue that holds society together. Then, as Hunt explains, drafted by Thomas Jefferson, the American Declaration of Independence (of 1776) states:

> We hold these truths to be self-evident, that all men are created equal . . . with certain inalienable Rights, that among these are Life, Liberty and the Pursuit of Happiness.[22]

A photo of this Declaration is presented in figure 23. Hunt notes slyly that Jefferson did not explain these rights; to do so

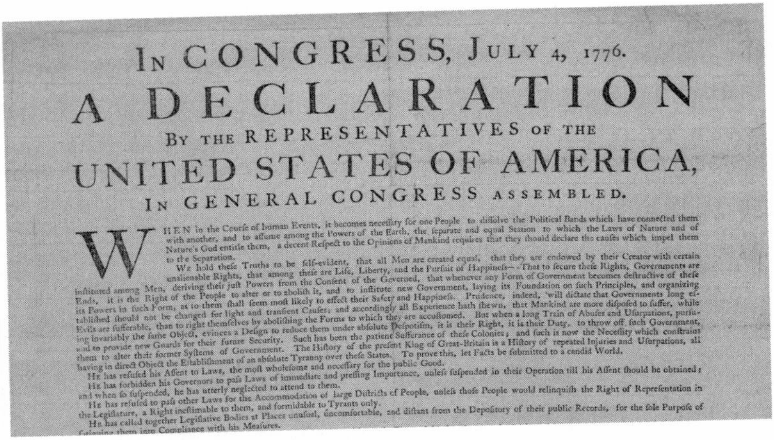

IN CONGRESS, JULY 4, 1776.

A DECLARATION

BY THE REPRESENTATIVES OF THE

UNITED STATES OF AMERICA,

IN GENERAL CONGRESS ASSEMBLED.

WHEN in the Course of human Events, it becomes necessary for one People to dissolve the Political Bands which have connected them with another, and to assume among the Powers of the Earth, the separate and equal Station to which the Laws of Nature and of Nature's God entitle them, a decent Respect to the Opinions of Mankind requires that they should declare the causes which impel them to the Separation.

We hold these Truths to be self-evident, that all Men are created equal, that they are endowed by their Creator with certain unalienable Rights, that among these are Life, Liberty, and the Pursuit of Happiness—That to secure these Rights, Governments are instituted among Men, deriving their just Powers from the Consent of the Governed, that whenever any Form of Government becomes destructive of these Ends, it is the Right of the People to alter or to abolish it, and to institute new Government, laying its Foundation on such Principles, and organizing its Powers in such Form, as to them shall seem most likely to effect their Safety and Happiness. Prudence, indeed, will dictate that Governments long established should not be changed for light and transient Causes; and accordingly all Experience hath shewn, that Mankind are more disposed to suffer, while Evils are sufferable, than to right themselves by abolishing the Forms to which they are accustomed. But when a long Train of Abuses and Usurpations, pursuing invariably the same Object, evinces a Design to reduce them under absolute Despotism, it is their Right, it is their Duty, to throw off such Government, and to provide new Guards for their future Security. Such has been the patient Sufferance of these Colonies; and such is now the Necessity which constrains them to alter their former Systems of Government. The History of the present King of Great-Britain is a History of repeated Injuries and Usurpations, all having in direct Object the Establishment of an absolute Tyranny over these States. To prove this, let Facts be submitted to a candid World.

He has refused his Assent to Laws, the most wholesome and necessary for the public Good.

He has forbidden his Governors to pass Laws of immediate and pressing Importance, unless suspended in their Operation till his Assent should be obtained; and when so suspended, he has utterly neglected to attend to them.

He has refused to pass other Laws for the Accommodation of large Districts of People, unless those People would relinquish the Right of Representation in the Legislature, a Right inestimable to them, and formidable to Tyrants only.

He has called together Legislative Bodies at Places unusual, uncomfortable, and distant from the Depository of their public Records, for the sole Purpose of fatiguing them into Compliance with his Measures.

Figure 23. United States Declaration of Independence. *Source:* Original Declaration of Independence as printed on July 4, 1776, top of page 1. This is the original printing sent to the states and the army. It differs from the "engrossed" copy that was made later. U.S. Library of Congress. https://commons.wikimedia.org/wiki/File:US-original-Declaration-1776.jpg.

would have meant they weren't self-evident. A decade later, in the French Declaration of Rights of Man and Citizen of 1789, influenced by Jefferson, the first article states: "Men are born and remain free and equal in rights." Hunt talks of invention, and how difficult it was; not everything was accomplished at once. Although in these early statements, "men" means "persons," it does not pass notice that Mary Wollstonecraft in 1792 would write *A Vindication of the Rights of Woman*. In 1948, a Universal Declaration of Human Rights was published, in which the first article is: "All human beings are born free and equal in dignity and rights."[23] In all these declarations Hunt argues that there are "three interlocking qualities: rights must be natural (inherent in all human beings), equal (the same for everyone), and universal (applicable everywhere)."[24]

To make a person a possession, by slavery or other means, is not to be tolerated. In many countries women and people who belong to ethnic minorities are equal before the law. Democracies enable everyone to vote. But we still have far to go. In the twenty-first century, in the name of war, politically based actions that kill civilians and destine millions to become refugees have been carried out for reasons in which human rights of all the people (naturally, and equally, and universally) have counted for little.

A principal means by which recognition of human rights began to occur was empathy. Hunt concludes that the growth of empathy, with its outcome of the recognition of human rights, is more important than any other social-political change in the last 5,000 years. This growth began some 300 years ago.

Hunt writes that empathy depends on "a biologically based ability to understand the subjectivity of other people and to be able to imagine that their inner experiences are like one's own."[25] She goes on to argue that among the processes by which this took place was fiction. "Reading novels," Hunt says, "created a sense of equality and empathy through passionate involvement in the narrative."[26] She describes Samuel Richardson's *Pamela* (1740) as encouraging empathy, by inviting the reader to identify with a servant woman. Hunt quotes from *Pamela* and includes this passage.

He kissed me two or three times, as if he would have eaten me.—At last I burst from him, and was getting out of the Summer-house; but he held me back, and shut the Door.

I would have given my Life for a Farthing. And he said, I'll do you no Harm, *Pamela*; don't be afraid of me. I said I won't stay! You won't, Hussy! Said he. Do you know who you speak to? I lost all Fear, and all Respect, and said Yes, I do Sir, too well!—Well may I forget that I am your Servant, when you forget what belongs to a Master.

I sobb'd and cry'd most sadly. What a foolish Hussy you are! said he: Have I done you any Harm?—Yes, Sir, said I, the greatest Harm in the World: You have taught me to forget myself, and what belongs to me.[27]

It was in the eighteenth and nineteenth centuries, when the technologies of reading and writing began to spread more widely in European and North American society, that novels began to flourish. *Pamela* was successful, and it enabled readers to enter the lives and minds of people different from themselves, and to feel empathetically toward them. So, writes Hunt, "Human rights grew out of the seedbed sowed by these feelings. Human rights could only flourish when people learned to think of others as their equals, as like them in some fundamental fashion."[28]

Literature was important in ending slavery in the West. A significant book was the 1789 autobiography of Olaudah Equiano, who was taken from Africa and shipped to the New World as a slave. He traveled widely, acquired a good education, bought his freedom, and settled in England. In fine literary prose, his autobiography is a moving story of how slaves were treated. His book became popular, and a powerful encouragement in Britain for the abolition of the slave trade. In the United States, Harriet Beecher Stowe's *Uncle Tom's Cabin* was credited with comparable effects in the abolition of slavery.

George Eliot wrote: "We are all born in moral stupidity, taking the world as an udder to feed our supreme selves."[29] So, despite our propensities for cooperation, we need to cultivate our understandings of others, of how they also are selves, and of how they are affected by our behavior.

Marcel Proust put it like this:

Only through art can we escape from our selves and know the perspective of another on the world, which is not the same as our own, and which contains views of landscapes that would otherwise have remained as unknown as any there may be on the moon.[30]

In 2006, Raymond Mar and others in our research group published a study in which we found that the more fiction people read, the better were their empathy and their understanding of others. Reading non-fiction didn't have this effect. We replicated the study with another group of participants and found that the effect was not due to people who were more empathetic preferring to read fiction rather than non-fiction. Nor was it due to any other individual differences; it seemed as if fiction itself had the effect. Subsequently, effects of this kind have been found experimentally. Short-term effects, of reading short stories followed by immediate testing, have been published, though some have become controversial and may be due to priming, a process in which exposure to something makes a certain kind of response more likely. But there have also been medium-term effects, which have been based on people reading whole books. Together with the longer term associations of the kind that Mar and colleagues have found, and with statistical analyses of groups of studies (meta-analyses) that have been performed, this kind of result is now fairly firmly established.[31]

Effects of this kind imply that fiction, particularly fiction about intentions of others, as in love stories and detective stories, and as in literary fiction, tends to focus on character and its complexities.[32] Fiction of these kinds, and some kinds of narrative non-fiction such as biography, can invite us mentally to create for ourselves the world of the story, and to think ourselves into the minds of its characters. In this way, it is a form of what Søren Kierkegaard called "indirect communication."[33] This kind of communication doesn't attempt to instruct, or persuade, let alone (as in propaganda) to coerce, but instead enables people to think for themselves, and also to think into the minds of others. Roland Barthes put it like this. To read in a way that involves creating and constructing the world of the story and its characters is to do very much what the writer does; it's writerly reading. To read passively, to do merely a readerly reading, he says, is to be "plunged into a kind of idleness."[34]

In *Ethics through Literature*, Brian Stock writes: "All Western reading, it would appear, has an ethical component, and the value placed on this component does not change much over time."[35] In 2015, a conversation was published in the *New York Review of Books* between U.S. president Barack Obama and novelist Marilynne Robinson. Obama is quoted as saying:

> The most important set of understandings that I bring to that position of citizen, the most important stuff I've learned I think I've learned from novels. It has to do with empathy. It has to do with being comfortable with the notion that the world is complicated and full of grays, but there's still truth there to be found, and that you have to strive for that and work for that. And the notion that it's possible to connect with some[one] else even though they're very different from you.[36]

Reflection, and learning, about morality, and what Tomasello calls group intentionality, in other words, can be prompted through reading fiction.

Reading fiction, going to movies, watching television series, and playing video games have been thought to be mere pastimes: entertainment. Effects of fiction on empathy have been found not just for reading, but with the better kinds of television series and video games, and thus point to something deeper.[37] Through engagement in certain kinds of fiction, we become better able to understand others by means of our imagination.

18

Authority and Morality

Apparatus devised by Stanley Milgram to enable his participants to suppose that they were delivering electric shocks of higher and higher voltage as punishments to a man who made mistakes in learning word associations.

Stanley Milgram asked male volunteers to give increasingly severe electric shocks to another man when he made mistakes in learning word associations. Most volunteers continued even when the machine they used indicated that the shocks were dangerous. In another study, Philip Zimbardo and colleagues studied prison guards and prisoners in a simulated prison. Christopher Browning found from interviews that most ordinary men recruited by the Nazis into the Order Police in World War II had been willing to kill civilians. Many of us, evidently, can be cruel under certain circumstances. Morality involves one of several kinds of intuition, such as authority, loyalty, and justice, which are accorded different degrees of importance by different cultures.

Doing What We Are Told

Stanley Milgram's study of obedience is one of the most publicly discussed pieces of research in psychology. In 1961 and 1962, Milgram placed newspaper advertisements and sent direct mail to invite men to come to his laboratory at Yale University to take part in an experiment on memory. They were each paid $4 to take on a role of teacher and told that, when a learner made mistakes they were to punish him by administering electric shocks.

Milgram was born in New York in 1933, and died of a heart attack at the age of fifty-one.[1] His parents were Jewish immigrants and in the later part of World War II, the young Stanley and his parents listened on the radio to news of the horrors of the Holocaust, which European Jews were suffering. He became fascinated by news, and described himself as a news addict. Milgram was a bright young man who earned a degree in political science, expecting to go into the American Foreign Service. But, on hearing him give a speech in his final year as an undergraduate, the dean of his college suggested that he might consider going into social psychology. It was something he hadn't considered. He became interested, and he applied to complete a PhD in psychology at Harvard, but was rejected because he had taken no psychology courses as an undergraduate. In an article she wrote about him, his widow Alexandra said he was never one to take No for an answer. During that summer, he took nine psychology courses at three different universities in New York. He was admitted to Harvard's PhD program. He did well and, in 1960, became an assistant professor of psychology at Yale. He devised his studies of obedience explicitly to pursue his early interest in the Holocaust which, he saw, could not have been the work of just a few people. He wondered how, in the civilized country of Germany—which had produced great musicians, philosophers, and writers—enough people could be found who were willing to hasten people to their deaths in concentration camps, and press levers to release the poisonous gases that would kill them.

Before performing his first experiment, Milgram described his experiment to forty Yale psychiatrists. He said he would test volunteers by asking them to administer increasingly severe shocks to a learner who made mistakes. The psychiatrists uniformly predicted that only a tiny number of the volunteers would deliver electric shocks at the level labeled as dangerous.

Milgram's first full experiment was published in 1963. In the paper, he described how men from unskilled, skilled, and professional backgrounds were recruited and came to his laboratory. Forty men took part. When they arrived, one at a time, each was greeted by a laboratory assistant who wore a grey technician's coat. He presented the volunteer with his $4 payment, and told him that the money was his whatever happened while he was there. Another man was present, whom participants assumed had also volunteered. He was a likeable man, a trained accomplice of the experimenter. Both the participant and the accomplice were told that the experiment was on effects of punishment on learning words, and that it might be important for education. The men were asked to draw one of two slips of paper to see who would be the learner and who the teacher. In fact both slips bore the word "teacher," so the real volunteer was cast into that role, and the accomplice said he had drawn the slip labeled "learner." The volunteer saw the learner being taken into a room and strapped into a chair, with electrodes on his arms, through which electric shocks could be delivered.

The teacher was then taken into an adjoining room. On a table was a large and impressive piece of apparatus, labeled "Shock generator," a photo of which you can see at the start of this chapter. It had a row of switches, a light above each, and labels beneath the switches that started at 15 volts, and ranged up to 450 volts in 15-volt intervals. At the left-hand end, 15 volts to 75 volts, the switches were labeled, in capital letters, "SLIGHT SHOCK." Extending rightward were switches labeled "MODERATE SHOCK," then "INTENSE SHOCK," up to "EXTREME INTENSITY SHOCK" and, at the top of the range, 375 to 420 volts, the "DANGER, SEVERE SHOCK, with two switches beyond this point (435 and 450 volts), labeled "XXX."

The volunteer was told his job was to sit at the table and, using a microphone, to read out lists of four pairs of words from a piece of paper. Then he would say one of the words from the list, and the learner had to indicate which other word it had been paired with. If the learner were correct, the teacher would move to the next list of words. When the learner made his first mistake, the teacher was to switch the left-most switch on the shock generator, announce the voltage, "15 volts," and then press a lever to deliver the shock. As the learner made more mistakes, the teacher delivered more severe shocks, in turn, each one higher than the last by 15 volts. With each shock a light above the switch came on, another light flashed, a galvanometer needle on a dial swung to the right, and a loud buzz sounded. As the 300-volt and 315-volt levels, labeled "EXTREME INTENSITY SHOCK," were reached, the learner was heard pounding on the wall. Beyond that point he made no more responses. The teacher was instructed by the laboratory assistant to treat non-response as a mistake, and continue with the experiment. At this point the volunteers tended to ask if it were alright to carry on. The assistant used a sequence of prods, such as, "It's absolutely essential that you continue."[2] Many participants became visibly agitated, and asked more questions. Fourteen participants (35%) refused to continue delivering shocks when they reached this point or just beyond it. But twenty-six of the forty participants—65 percent of them—agitated and upset though many of them were, did carry on right up the highest level of shock, 450 volts.

At the end of the experiment the learner reappeared, said he was none the worse for the experience, and a reconciliation took place between him and the volunteer. Milgram says in his paper that procedures were undertaken to assure that the volunteer would leave the laboratory in a state of well-being. Steve Reicher and Alex Haslam reported that, in all, Milgram did around forty pilot tests and ancillary studies for his experiment and found that, depending on the conditions, anywhere between zero and 100 percent of people complied with the experimental instructions. Many of these studies are described in Milgram's book *Obedience to Authority*. Because it is so controversial, Milgram's research has been the subject of the current debate in psychology about reproducibility of results.[3] Jerry Burger has replicated Milgram's experiment, and found that nearly fifty years after the original publication, the results still hold up. This research also raises the question of how research findings are to be interpreted.[4]

Psychological Experiment as Theater

Milgram's experiment was a piece of theater. In it, everyone but the volunteer had rehearsed his part. Rather than taking seats in the audience, the volunteers found themselves on stage, but without a script. Their actions derived from the social situation of doing what they were told, what was expected, as we human beings, social creatures as we are, very often do. As Michael Tomasello has pointed out, we have become not individuals, but members of social groups, "Us." Within such a group we tend to be loyal.

Augusto Boal invented what he called the Theatre of the Oppressed, in which audience members first watch a play about social oppression of a kind with which they were familiar, which then leads to a tragic outcome. Then, in a second performance that would follow it immediately, some members of the audience are invited onto the stage to take roles in the play, and explore how they might stand up to the coercive maneuvers of the other characters, and so achieve a different outcome. Milgram's theatrical piece can be thought of as a more radical version of Boal's idea. One difference was that it inserted people, without their knowledge, into an experience of a situation that they had never imagined.

If you are wondering what effect their performance had on the men who volunteered for Milgram's experiment, Lauren Slater, in her book of 2004 on ten great experiments of psychology, tried to track them down. She was able to find two of them.

The first man Slater interviewed seemed, to her, a fairly conventional person, who said that he refused to deliver shocks to the top of the scale. If he'd continued to the top of the scale, he said, he wouldn't be talking to her but to a psychiatrist.

The other man whom Slater interviewed said he had continued delivering shocks to the top of the scale. When he was later told of the actual purpose of the experiment, he had a stark recognition of what he had done. He said recognizing that he had conformed to what had been asked of him changed his life. He had been struggling, at the time, with being homosexual. He had been complying with societal constraints. His confrontation, in Milgram's experiment, with his own propensity to conform to a compelling social situation was a turning point. He decided to come out as homosexual. Slater recounts how, as compared with the man she interviewed who said he hadn't given shocks up to the top of the scale, this man seemed to be freer. Slater saw him as someone who was more alive, who had led a more satisfying life.

Milgram's experiment offers us an important glimpse of ourselves. As ordinary people, we think we are autonomous agents when, really, we are extremely responsive to social situations. Milgram's volunteers entered a reputable laboratory of Yale University. They trusted the experimenter. They did what they were asked. They did what they were paid to do.

A feature film has been made of Milgram, called *Experimenter*, which depicts his obedience experiments as well as the public reaction to them. The film also treats Milgram's close relationship with Alexandra, whom he met and married when he was at Yale. The film takes up the idea that the shocks that the volunteers thought they were administering weren't the only ones that occurred. As people heard about Milgram's studies, and started to think about their significance, further shocks—real ones this time—occurred, and they continue to occur.

The first shock is that, although Milgram was aiming to solve one of the most important ethical problems in recent history—how educated citizens of a civilized nation could be murderously cruel—many psychologists have reacted to Milgram's experiments by criticizing them as unethical.[5] People were tricked, they say, invited into a laboratory to do experiments on memory, when the experiments were not on memory at all but on how far obedience could go. They were tricked into thinking they were delivering shocks, when they weren't. Is it not unacceptable, they ask, for an assistant professor at a reputable university to inflict this kind of experience on unsuspecting members of the public for a payment of $4?

The next kind of shock, for each of us, might occur as we ask ourselves which group we would have been in: would we have been among the 65 percent who conformed, or the 35 percent who refused to conform?

The most profound shock is yet more radical. It's the realization that we all—you, me, our relatives and friends—may be capable of being cruel to others when a compelling social reason that arises from our cultural group is more important to us. From this perspective, it's no good thinking that we might have been among the inmates of concentration camps while those others—them—would have been camp guards and executioners. Because of our inherent sociability we all have it within ourselves to conform to social expectations, and to be cruel.

Amidst the controversy that Milgram's experiments have aroused, two issues are often neglected. The first important principle is that Milgram had the insight to bring the question of how we human beings engage in wars and other kinds of internecine conflict from history into the psychology of everyday life, and into the laboratory. Although for Milgram the everyday life with which he was concerned was that of World War II, the issue of cruelty

Figure 24. Hannah Arendt, from a mural. *Source*: By Bernd Schwabe in Hannover (own work) [CC BY-SA 3.0 (http://creativecommons.org/licenses/by-sa/3.0)], via Wikimedia Commons. https://commons.wikimedia.org/wiki/File%3A2014-08_Graffiti_Patrik_Wol ters_alias_BeneR1_im_Team_mit_Kevin_Lasner_alias_koarts%2C_Hannah_Arendt _Niemand_hat_das_Recht_zu_gehorchen%2C_Geburtshaus_Lindener_Marktplatz _2_Ecke_Falkenstra%C3%9Fe_in_Hannover-Linden-Mitte.jpg.

continues into peacetime. In 2011, in Norway, a man blew up a government building, killing eight people, then drove to an island on which a summer camp was being held for young people who belonged to a political party with which he did not agree.[6] There, he shot and killed 69 individuals and wounded 319 others.

The second important consideration is to treat Milgram's hypothesis as what it is: a psychological hypothesis. It's a hypothesis about the Holocaust that was shared, at least in part, by Hannah Arendt. You can see a picture of her from a mural in Hanover, Germany, in figure 24. In her book on the trial of Adolf Eichmann Arendt used the phrase, "the banality of evil." She saw Eichmann not so much as perverted, but as rather normal. She considered that he didn't think much about what he was doing. He just did it. She wrote that this kind of unthinking going-along-with-things-as-normal, with the rest of a group, thought of as "us," makes the Holocaust even more terrifying.

Is obedience to authority a good hypothesis to explain human genocidal actions? Augustine Brannigan and colleagues argue that although obedience may have been a factor, in Nazi Germany, people acted willingly, and consciously, for a cultural cause and thought they were doing the right thing. They propose that factors that prompted people toward cruel actions in those times, and their tolerance of others they saw performing similarly cruel acts, are more complex than simply being obedient.

Being Cruel

An experiment on a simulated prison extended some of the issues with which Milgram dealt, and was an even more explicit piece of theater. Craig Haney, Curtis Banks, and Philip Zimbardo carried out what has become known as the Stanford Prison Experiment. Men were recruited by newspaper advertisements, and from the population around the university, to take part in an experiment in a simulated prison. The volunteers were rigorously screened and all those with histories of drugs, crime, or psychiatric disorders were excluded. Twenty-four were chosen, all college students, as being the most psychologically stable of the original seventy-five volunteers. Half were randomly assigned to be guards, and the other half prisoners. When the experiment ran, there were eleven guards, who worked eight-hour shifts, and ten full-time prisoners.

Among the prisoners, loss of identity was frequent, as were depression and helplessness. Five of the ten were released early because the experimenters judged their reactions to be too severe. Among the eleven men assigned to be guards, nine acted as their roles required. Among these, four clearly enjoyed their power in this situation, and invented new forms of harassment of the prisoners. Only two of the eleven guards refused to go along with cruel treatment, and were kind to the prisoners. The experiment had been planned to last for fourteen days, but the researchers became so concerned with what was happening among some of the guards that they stopped the experiment after only six days. (Harassment of the kind that developed in this experiment is not a general feature of real prisons, where efforts are made to ensure that procedures are regulated.)

In a re-run of the Stanford Prison Experiment, sponsored in Britain by the British Broadcasting Corporation (BBC), Stephen Reicher and Alex Haslam allocated eight men to the role of guards and eight to the role of prisoners. The guards could not identify with their role. They did not impose their authority. They became disorganized and were overcome by the prisoners. Reicher and Haslam analyzed the circumstances in which people do and don't identify with groups, and suggested that tyranny can arise when cultural groups fail, when people are not able to feel themselves to be one of "Us." When people feel despairing and ineffective as a group, they become more easily able to respond to, and be identified with, a tyrant who offers hope.

As with Milgram's experiment, the volunteers in the Stanford Prison Experiment, and its re-run, found themselves in a piece of theater in which they did not know the script, but were led by small steps into roles that were unfamiliar to them. As with Milgram's study, part of the purpose of Zimbardo's experiment was to determine how ordinary people had been able to behave with cruelty under the Nazi regime. In World War II, between five and six million Jews, and several hundreds of thousands of others, including members of non-Nazi political parties, Gypsies, homosexuals, and mental patients, were killed under orders of the Nazis. All such people were thought to be undesirables. The idea of eugenics (discussed in chapter 4), proposed by Galton and promoted by some early intelligence testers, had taken on a new and terrifying form.

A study comparable to Zimbardo's prison experiment, but in many ways more convincing in its implications because it was based in direct historical evidence—judicial investigations of 125 men of the 486 members of Battalion 101 of the Nazi Order Police—was carried out after the war by Christopher Browning.

Some of the officers in Battalion 101 had education up to the level of high school. Most of the men were recruited from the skilled and unskilled workforce of Hamburg. Two years after recruitment their job was to round up and kill Jews in Poland. Browning compares his study with Zimbardo's. He found that between 10 percent and 20 percent of the members of Battalion 101 refused to take part in the shootings. He found, too, that those who refused to go along with their orders were not court-martialed.

Morality

As Michael Tomasello has argued, and in part demonstrated in experimental work, we humans are members of a species that is based on cooperation, and that seems to us a good thing. At the same time, studies such as those of Milgram, Zimbardo, and Browning show that we can cooperate for ends that are anything but good. We can be cruel, to the point of killing fellow members of our species.

Jane Jacobs, the influential writer on how we live cooperatively in cities, put the issue in her book, *Systems of Survival*. We exist in two quite different systems, which are present simultaneously in the Western industrialized world. Jacobs calls them "syndromes." Each has its own moral codes, within which we humans cooperate. One is what Jacobs calls the Guardian Syndrome; she takes the term from Plato's *Republic*. In this syndrome we adhere to tradition and respect hierarchy. In this syndrome deception is sometimes required. The deception is aimed at "Them," adversaries within and outside the group. In the Guardian Syndrome, something else is always more important than any individual, and the worst thing anyone can do is to be disloyal. In political systems we see, time and again, people come into power as leaders, alpha males (though some have been female) whose first demand to everyone is to be loyal to them.[7] In the other system, the Commercial Syndrome, Jacobs argues, people are open to inventiveness and novelty; they come to voluntary agreements with others. Here, we have to respect other individuals and be honest, otherwise the system breaks down. Among outcomes generated by the Guardian Syndrome can be tyranny and dictatorship. Among outcomes generated by the Commercial Syndrome can be pervasive social inequality, as people and organizations with more mental and physical resources strive to increase their own resources in competition with others.

There is a long-standing debate in philosophy about how we might become virtuous and moral beings.[8] Do we come to be in this way by means of our emotional make-up, or because of cultural promptings of society, or from individual reasoning? Only recently have psychologists started to investigate this issue.

Jonathan Haidt has proposed that our abilities to cooperate, in what we might call a moral way, are based on shared judgments, and on intuitions that derive from social, emotional, and cultural influences, rather than from step-by-step reasoning of the kind produced by what Keith Stanovich calls "System 2," and what Daniel Kahneman calls "thinking slow." Among these intuitions are: care for others as compared to infliction of harm, fairness as compared with cheating, liberty as compared with oppression, loyalty as compared with betrayal, authority as compared with subversion, and purity versus degradation. We can see the experiments of Milgram and Zimbardo, and the study by Browning, as pitting the intuition of care for others against the intuition that we should be loyal and obey authority.

Although we may think that wrongdoing is committed by people whom we label as criminals, who become those other people over there, "Them," this research suggests that it might be better to think of another group: "We."[9] Might philosophers, historians, psychologists, and lawyers work together to better understand the reasons why human beings harm each other, and what the legal and social implications might be? Might they work together to overcome some of the impediments to cooperation?

19

Creativity, Expertise, Grit

The Royal Pavilion, at Brighton in the south of England, was influenced at the end of the eighteenth century by Romanticism in which the East was seen as exotic; the building is a "stately pleasure dome," of the kind that Samuel Taylor Coleridge wrote about in "Kubla Khan."

Creativity was once thought to occur as inspiration to people who became famous artists and scientists. It is now clear that it is important for us all. Expertise, as studied by Anders Ericsson, is the ability to do something so well that others find it hard to understand how. Ericsson and colleagues say it requires about 10,000 hours of practice, which needs to include setting oneself problems one can't yet solve. We may be able increase our abilities, including our creative ones, and fulfill our aspirations, by what Angela Duckworth calls grit, making choices and following them with determination and persistence.

Creativity

Here are the first five lines of "Kubla Khan," one of the most famous poems in the English language.

> In Xanadu did Kubla Khan
> A stately pleasure dome decree:
> Where Alph, the sacred river, ran
> Through caverns measureless to man
>   Down to a sunless sea.

You can see an example of a stately pleasure dome of the kind referred to in the poem, at the opening of this chapter. When Samuel Taylor Coleridge published this poem in 1816, he accompanied it with an account of how he wrote it.

> In the summer of the year 1797, the Author then in ill health, had retired to a lonely farmhouse between Porlock and Linton ... The Author continued for about three hours in a profound sleep, at least of the external senses, during which time he has the most vivid confidence, that he could not have composed less than two to three hundred lines; if that indeed can be called composition in which all the images rose up before him as *things*, with a parallel production of the corresponding expressions, without any sensation or consciousness of effort. On awakening he appeared to himself to have a distinct recollection of the whole, and taking his pen, ink, and paper, instantly and eagerly wrote down the lines that are here preserved.

The poem is about art, the sacred river that runs through society, that fertilizes it, but that also provokes conflict. Here are its last lines, which are about the artist or, perhaps one should say, The Artist.

Weave a circle round him thrice,
And close your eyes with holy dread,
For he on honey dew hath fed,
And drunk the milk of Paradise.

For Coleridge, The Artist is a special person, a genius, set apart from society, in touch with the gods. His account, in the early part of the Romantic era, has been influential; it's partly due to him that we think of artists as inspired.

In psychology, a change has taken place to upset the idea of creativity as unusual, a characteristic of only a precious few. We are all creative. Donald Winnicott suggests that an important principle is that it's creativity

> more than anything else that makes the individual feel that life is worth living ... In a tantalizing way many individuals have experienced just enough of creative living to recognize that for most of their time they are living uncreatively, as if caught up in the creativity of someone else, or of a machine.[1]

Creativity takes place in what Winnicott called the space-in-between (discussed in chapter 15), which originates as the space between the baby and a mother or other caregiver. Taking up Coleridge's emphasis on art, it's in this space that the mind can expand without persuasion or coercion. It's in this space, with written art, that the reader can take up and turn over the words as she or he imagines the world the writer suggests, and in this way the imagined world becomes the reader's own. This kind of experience is a creative continuation of childhood play.

An influential researcher on creativity is Mihaly Csikszentmihalyi, who discovered a sense of flow in people as they engage themselves creatively in what they are doing. One of the people Csikszentmihalyi interviewed was Rico Medellin, who had been working for five years on an assembly line in a factory that made movie projectors. His task was to perform a certain operation on the projector as it arrived at his station, and to do it nearly 600 times a day. The operation was supposed to take 43 seconds. Rico had carefully thought about what he needed to do, and how to use his tools most efficiently. His best average over a day was 28 seconds per operation. Many people would find this job intolerable, but Rico had trained himself like an Olympic athlete and said, "It is better than anything else . . . It's a whole lot better than watching TV."[2] He told Csikszentmihalyi that he was taking evening courses in electronics, and when he received his diploma he would get a more complex job. One can imagine that he would approach it with the same enthusiasm.

Among Csikszentmihalyi's other interviewees was Pam Davis, a lawyer in a small partnership. She would spend hours in the library finding references, and outlining possible courses of action for her senior partners. Often she would be so involved that she would forget lunch and not even notice when it got dark. Even when she was frustrated, she would recognize what caused the frustration and think of it as an obstacle that she would discover how to overcome. Then there was a dancer: she said that when a performance went well, "Your concentration is very complete. Your mind isn't wandering, you are not thinking of something else."[3] A rock climber said: "You are so involved in what you are doing [that] you aren't thinking of yourself as separate from the immediate activity." A mother spoke of how she spent time with her daughter. "She reads to me and I read to her, and that's a time when I sort of lose touch with the rest of the world."

We can cultivate flow, says Csikszentmihalyi, by choosing to do what we are doing. It's a striking idea. It's not a matter of waiting for the world to present us with things. We can create for ourselves meaningful activity; even sometimes when in the course of our life we don't have much influence, we can nevertheless choose to do what we are doing.

If we have a chosen pursuit, as Coleridge did in poetry, we can set ourselves problems in it, take on goals that are sufficiently specific that we know whether they are being achieved, know how to work out the best ways of achieving them, and observe effects of our actions.

There's now a good deal of research to show that it's in this way that we can be creative. If we were to immerse ourselves in poetry, become engaged in it, write and develop many poems, it's possible we might even have a dream from which we would awake with a poem in mind. That wouldn't happen without deep interest in the subject, without working on the writing and improving of poems over many years, without full engagement. Without these activities, it wouldn't have happened to Coleridge.

Expertise

"Expertise" is a term for the state in which, in a particular activity—poetry, working on the manufacture of movie projectors, dancing—a person has become noticeably different, and far more proficient than novices. Over a long period, the expert has amassed a store of theoretical and practical knowledge in a particular domain. Expertise becomes a way of acting in the domain about which novices say, "I don't know how anyone could do that."

An early piece of research on expertise was by Adriaan de Groot, who played chess for the Netherlands in the 1930s, and was also a psychologist. His PhD thesis was translated into English as *Thought and Choice in Chess*. After a one-page preamble on the literature of chess, de Groot turns to discussing work by Alfred Binet (who, as we have discussed in chapter 4, with Théodore Simon, was the first to measure intelligence in children). Binet and Henneguy considered how some expert chess players are able to play and win games while blindfolded. They announce their moves, and the moves of their opponent are told to them. These people can remember chess positions, and the course of a game.

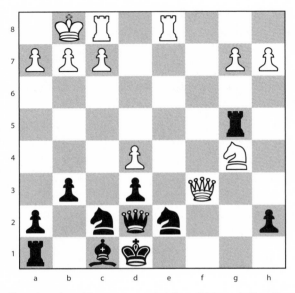

Figure 25. Chess board position reconstructed from Adriaan de Groot's experiment, from a game that had been published but was not well known, which chess players at different levels were asked to remember. *Source*: Position reconstructed by Keith Oatley, from de Groot, A. (1978). *Thought and choice in chess.* The Hague: Mouton, p. 326.

De Groot performed a startling experiment. He asked people who were at different levels in chess, including a grand master, a master, a person who was fairly good, and a person who was a novice, to look for five seconds at a board position that you can see in figure 25 (from a game that had been played, and published in an obscure place). Then the people were asked to reconstruct the position they had seen. Each person was given a score out of 22 (the number of pieces in the original position), with one point for each piece correctly placed. The grand master scored 22. He placed all the pieces correctly. The master scored 21 (an extra white pawn had been inserted). The good player scored 16, and the novice scored, guess what? Nine—George Miller's magical number: 7 + 2.[4]

One hypothesis might be that whereas most of us are stuck in our short-term memory with the magic number of seven plus or minus two slots, some unusual people, who have the ability to become chess masters and grand masters, have a short-term memory that is three times as capacious.

The real answer is different. Expert chess players have thought so much about chess, played so many games, read so many chess books, and analyzed so many positions that when they look at a board position from a game that has been played, and are asked to remember it, instead of filling each slot in short-term memory with a single piece on a single square, they can see how a game has gone, see how it's developing, and operate with whole patterns of pieces: meaningful groupings of a kind that might occur in a game. William Chase and Herbert Simon replicated de Groot's findings, and call these groupings "chunks." In figure 25, the pieces in the board's top-left hand corner are a chunk, recognizable as "white-castled-on-the-Queen's-side." When master chess players are asked to memorize random positions, not derived from games that have been played, they are no better than novices.

Another result based on memory was found by Virpi Kalakoski and Pertti Saariluoma for taxi drivers in Helsinki. The taxi drivers' memories for street names on real routes was far better than that of novices, but on randomly organized lists of street names they were no better than novices. Eleanor Maguire and colleagues found that taxi drivers in London had the hippocampus area of their brains (a part involved with the making of mental maps) enlarged as compared with non–taxi drivers, and this size was associated with the number of years spent taxi driving.

When we learn a new skill, we are conscious of much of what we do. We think through moves deliberately. We might remember doing this when we learned to drive a car, or play a musical instrument, or use our mobile phone. When we reach an expert level of performance in that skill, we no longer have to think through moves, one by one. We have formed schemas that assimilate necessary features of the particular world, and orchestrate necessary skills. We have achieved intuitions about what to notice, and what to do. We simply seem to know.

Anders Ericsson has argued that in many domains—chess, professions such as science, the arts, athletics—people typically work for ten years before they achieve expertise.[5] In more recent research it has been found that to reach excellence in most domains, one needs to put in 10,000 hours of practice. That comes out to three hours a day for ten years, comparable to the amount of time spent doing academic work in grade school, or ten hours a day for three years, about the amount needed to achieve a PhD. It isn't just a matter of putting in the time. It is a matter of setting oneself problems that one doesn't know how to solve, learning from mistakes, receiving tutoring and training, and committing oneself to understand and improve everything one can in the domain.

Here is what Ericsson, Raif Krampe, and Clemens Tesch-Römer say:

> High levels of deliberate practice are necessary to attain expert level performance. Our theoretical framework can also provide a sufficient account of the major facts about the nature and scarcity of expert performance. Our account does not depend on scarcity of innate ability (talent) . . . individual differences in ultimate performance can largely be accounted for by differential amounts of past and current levels of practice.[6]

"Expert level performance" echoes the rhetoric of advertising. It's far more important to understand how to be ordinary than to think the extraordinary is all that matters. Nonetheless, expertise is a matter of psychological interest. One reason is that if we want to become better in the skills essential to a project or activity that is close to our heart, the principle of deliberate practice seems to be common across domains. Another reason is that when we read a book, or listen to a piece of music, or watch a football game, we may just want to relax, but often we want to improve our minds. To do this, we are likely to get the most improvement by taking in the best.

Ericsson's theory has been influential, but it has become controversial. There are now many studies in which the relation of practice to expertise has been measured. There is evidence that practice changes the structure of the brain.[7] At the same time the associations between amounts of deliberate practice and expertise in a domain are not large. Brooke Macnamara and her colleagues have shown in a large meta-analysis of 111 independent samples, that involved 11,135 participants, that for professions the amount of variance explained by deliberate practice was 1 percent, for education 4 percent, for sports 18 percent, for music 21 percent, and for games 26 percent.

Why are these associations relatively small? It isn't that deliberate practice is unimportant. One could not become a master chess player, a brain surgeon, a concert violinist, or an Olympic athlete without a great deal of practice. One reason the associations are smaller than one might expect is that those who aren't at the top but who aspire to it, all put in about the same amounts of deliberate practice.

Fredric Ullén and his colleagues present evidence that to attain expertise, not just practice is involved. Other factors include our genetic talents, the physiology of our brains and bodies, people we meet, motivation, encouragements from families, facilities for training. These researchers propose a multi-factor theory: a gene-times-environment interaction theory, which provides a more complete explanation for understanding expertise, and for conducting research on the topic. Ericsson has of course replied to criticisms of his theory and his critics have replied to him.[8]

The conclusion is that if you want to become really good at something, you do need to practice a lot, but there are also physical and mental prerequisites. You are unlikely to make it as an Olympic high jumper if as an adult you are five feet tall. To become a poet, you need some verbal fluency, and you need to be very interested in poetry.

Creative Thinking and Evolution

Howard Gardner has written an engaging book of psychological biographies of creative people, who include Albert Einstein, Pablo Picasso, Martha Graham, and Mahatma Gandhi. Another such book on the psychology of creativity is *The Mind's Best Work* by David Perkins. In it he talks the reader through many of the ideas that have developed on creativity and the psychological research that has taken place. He discusses Coleridge's theory of inspiration, Arthur Koestler's hypothesis that creativity involves seeing an association between two previously unrelated ideas, Edward de Bono's programs for lateral thinking, and he relates Marie Curie's discovery of radioactivity.[9]

Perhaps most central to understanding creativity is Charles Darwin's theory of evolution by natural selection. According to this, Nature has generated all the forms of plant and animal life, including our selves, and enabled them to thrive, each one in its ecological niche. In this Nature has been extraordinarily creative: think of a whale and a hummingbird, think of an orchid, think of how the human eye works. To do this, evolution has first produced different possibilities. Darwin called this Variation. Second, it produced more individuals than were needed for replacement. Darwin called this Superabundance. Then it enabled some characteristics to go forward while other characteristics became extinct. Darwin called this Selection.

Donald Campbell proposed that human creative thought is based on essentially the same processes. In creativity, he argues there is production of wide and frequent variation of ideas; then comes selection among the ideas. He stresses that, as in evolution, variation is blind, without direction. Maja Djikic and I reviewed this idea and offered evidence that in creative writing, variation is not blind.[10] Creative writers read what they have written, and use this to guide the variations they next generate.

Artists of other kinds—painters, sculptors, musicians—do the same thing. Mihaly Csikszentmilalyi and Jacob Getsels studied students at art school and gave them a set of objects that they were asked to arrange and then paint as a still life picture. They found that the more a student artist manipulated the objects, the more arrangements she or he tried out, and the more they thought that further change would be possible to their painting, the better artists they became seven years later.

Both the artist and the scientist explore and, depending on what they discover, they generate new possibilities in the course of further exploration. Part of the exploration is to determine what to ask. Albert Einstein and Léopold Infeld put it like this:

> The formulation of a problem is far more often essential than its solution ... To raise new questions, new possibilities, to regard old problems from a new angle requires creative imagination.[11]

Creativity and Emotion

In what may be the best theory of art that has been produced in recent times, Robin Collingwood proposes that art properly so called does not involve having a finished product in mind, in the way that in cooking one may follow a recipe to produce a known dish: porridge or coq au vin. Rather, the artist takes some state, usually an emotion-based state, that she or he does not understand, and externalizes it in a language—of words, or paint, or dance, or a jazz solo—in order to explore and understand it better. To get a sense of the artist, he says, imagine a man as follows:

At first he is conscious of having an emotion, but not conscious of what this emotion is. All he is conscious of is a perturbation or excitement, which he feels going on within him, but of whose nature he is ignorant. While in this state, all he can say about his emotion is: "I feel ... I don't know how I feel." From this helpless and oppressed condition he extricates himself by doing something which we call expressing himself. This is an activity which has something to do with the thing we call language: he expresses himself by speaking. It also has something to with consciousness: the emotion expressed is the emotion of whose nature the person who feels it is no longer unconscious.[12]

In written, visual, and musical art, the artist puts something out there to pass it on to someone who will become engaged with the art. But prior to this, and equally important, is that the work in progress can be passed on to oneself, so that the generation of new possibilities is not blind, but guided. Darwin himself was an example: he undertook the exploratory voyage on the *Beagle*, which lasted nearly five years, and then spent much of the period after he had returned in 1836 making notes and reading them, exploring possibilities, reading, discussing, thinking things through, in order to conceive and write (in a first private draft of 1842) his evolutionary theory of the origin of species.[13]

Incubation

In 1908, Henri Poincaré wrote:

The genesis of mathematical creation is a problem which should intensely interest the psychologist. For fifteen days I strove to prove that there could not be any functions like those I have since called Fuchsian functions ... every day I seated myself at my work table, stayed an hour or two, tried

a great number of combinations and reached no results ...
Just at this time I left Caen ... The changes of travel made
me forget my mathematical work ... At the moment when
I put my foot on the step [of an omnibus] the idea came
to me, without anything in my former thoughts seeming
to have paved the way for it, that the transformations I had
used to define the Fuchsian functions were identical with
those of non-Euclidian geometry.[14]

Based on Poincaré's account, Graham Wallas published *The Art of Thought*, in which he proposed that creative thought has four phases. First comes Preparation. You must work on a problem, work on it a lot, think about it deeply. Then you must put it aside, as Poincaré did when he went on his travels. During this period, which Wallas calls Incubation, the unconscious can be at work in ways that the conscious mind doesn't know about. Then comes Illumination, when the unconscious tells our conscious self of a possible solution. Last comes Verification, when one compares the new insight to the world to see whether it will really work. In an experimental study, Catherine Patrick tested Wallas's theory in an experiment in which she asked poets and non-poets to look at a picture, and write a poem about it. The non-poets wrote about the picture itself, and what it suggested. The poets wrote in a way that was recognizable as their usual published work, and they put more imagination and meaning into their poem. Patrick found some evidence for incubation in that when a person had an idea, then after exploring other approaches, this person would often come back to it.

Grit

An idea that became popular two hundred years ago in Europe, in the early stages of what became known as the Romantic Era, was of Nature: somewhere to visit, something for artists to depict, something a person could express of themselves without artificiality. If someone did something really well, this person might be called "a natural." The Romantic idea is that ability as an artist, as a scientist, as an athlete, comes as a gift. As an idea of how a person who is interested in producing something worthwhile—perhaps a novel, perhaps a best time in a marathon, perhaps a good plan for city transportation, perhaps a beautiful garden—the idea of being a natural is not so helpful. As the literature on expertise shows, the ability to do such things doesn't just fall out of the air. It requires committing oneself to a project, with effort over a period of years. It requires putting in time and practice. Grit is the motivation, the passion, the determination, to keep at it.

The idea of grit has been developed by Angela Lee Duckworth, who completed her Bachelor of Arts degree in neurobiology at Harvard and earned a Master of Science degree in neuroscience at Oxford. She took a highly paid job as a management consultant, then gave it up to teach seventh-grade mathematics at the Learning Project, an alternative public school in New York, and then at another school in San Francisco. After teaching, she pursued a PhD and now she is a professor of psychology at the University of Pennsylvania. Her book, *Grit: The Power of Passion and Perseverance*, became a *New York Times* bestseller.

In 2007, with colleagues, Duckworth published a study in which the researchers found that success in Ivy League universities, and at West Point Military Academy, did not relate to IQ, but was predicted by the Big Five personality trait of Conscientiousness. In addition, a measure called Grit, of perseverance in long-term goals, which has a large component of Conscientiousness, contributed further to predictions of success.

In another study, Duckworth (with colleagues who included Ericsson) conducted research to see what it took for people to do well at the United States National Spelling Bee. The researchers looked to see which of three activities predicted success: deliberate practice (studying words and memorizing them alone), doing practice quizzes given by others, and reading for pleasure.

The results were that although deliberate practice was the most effortful and least enjoyable of these methods, it was the best preparation for doing well in spelling bees. Grit is the trait of passionate determination to engage in an activity, and it was the grittiest people who did more deliberate practice and succeeded in spelling bees.

Early in her book, Duckworth cites a principle that William James suggested in a paper of 1907, which he published in *Science*, then and now the world's foremost scientific journal. In the article James writes:

> Compared with what we ought to be, we are only half awake. Our fires are damped, our drafts are checked. We are making use of only a small part of our possible mental re-sources . . . men the world over possess amounts of resource, which only exceptional individuals push to their extremes of use.[15]

We can make more of these resources, says Duckworth, by grit. We can make our lives meaningful, by discovering something in which we are interested, be it gardening, friendship, or science. Perhaps we find, unexpectedly, that we have a talent, and exercis-ing it is satisfying. We can come to know that, for our selves, it is important to do a certain kind of thing in life, perhaps raise a family, perhaps work in a refugee camp. Then we get more deeply into it, immerse ourselves in it, find ourselves engaged in it, find ourselves being creative, becoming more expert.

In part, what is involved is interest, perhaps genetic, perhaps due to some accident of the environment. How intensely, how satisfyingly, we pursue a project that has become meaningful to us will depend in part on perseverance, grit.

20

Consciousness and Free Will

An ancient Greek water vase with an image of a seated woman reading from a book scroll, while companions stand nearby.

Roy Baumeister and E. J. Masicampo propose that consciousness is a simulation in which past memories, understandings of the current social situation, and plans for the future are related to each other. It has effects on action, but usually over a period of reflection, and discussion with others. Nico Frijda argued that coming to be the kind of person we have decided to be involves free will, and conscious consideration. This kind of will can be an important principle in how we think about our interactions with others, and how we become ourselves with these others.

Greek Poetry

"Know yourself." That was the injunction of the oracle at Delphi. How is it possible? What is it to be conscious? Earlier in this book we have assumed that we each have a mind and we've asked how we can understand it in others and ourselves. In his book of 1948, Bruno Snell proposed that mind was not just there. It needed to be discovered.

Snell cites the incident near the beginning of Homer's *Iliad*, on which the story turns. Agamemnon, commander-in-chief of the Greek army in their attack on Troy, has had to restore to her father, who is a priest of Apollo, a girl who was awarded to him as a prize of battle. Agamemnon says he prefers this girl to his wife. Now that he has lost her, he threatens to confiscate from Achilles his prize, "the beautiful Briseis." Homer says that anger came upon Achilles, and caused in him the intention to kill Agamemnon.[1] As he starts to draw his sword, the goddess Athene appears to Achilles, and says, "I have come from heaven to stop your fury, if you will obey me." Here, says Snell, we see that for Homer, human beings do not regard themselves "as the source of [their] decisions."[2]

Snell does not put it this way, but it's as if Homeric man is a stimulus-response machine. At first, Achilles responds to the stimulus of Agamemnon's threat to confiscate Briseis. Then another stimulus occurs: Athene.[3] She promises a greater reinforcement. She describes it in exactly these terms. She says, "three times these splendid gifts will be laid before you."

If we were in the situation of Achilles, we might think of self-control as a mental problem. But, says Snell, this idea had yet to occur in Greek culture. Words that Homer uses, which we might think of as mental, were not mental. *Psyche* meant "livingness."

It's what leaves the body when you are killed. *Noos* referred to seeing, visually. *Thumos* is an agitation that helps propel a person toward certain behavior.

Not until the lyric poets, 200 years after Homer, does mind begin to be discovered. Sappho is one of its inventors, perhaps its principal inventor. It's almost as if the idea of mind and selfhood begins, wonderfully, to emerge in Sappho's consciousness.[4] At the beginning of the chapter you can see an ancient Greek water vase on which is pictured a woman, whom some think is Sappho, reading a book scroll, as three companions stand nearby.

It is Sappho who, most clearly, starts to write in a modern way: "Once again Love loosens my limbs and turns me giddy, bitter-sweet creature, irresistible."[5] Sappho's word, "bitter-sweet" is *glucopicron*. In English, the order of the two senses is changed; "bitter-sweet" seems smoother than the Greek order "sweet-bitter." Sappho's idea of two opposing senses has continued in European thought for more than 2,500 years, bringing to mind for us, and hinting at, an essence: love as both anguish and joy. From Sappho comes the idea that love moves us in ways that prompt us toward action, but now, as with "bitter-sweet," we may experience ambivalence, perhaps even ambiguity, which invites reflection within us, as we wonder about the influence that love can have on us. It's no longer a matter of stimuli, but a matter of the person, and of choice. Sappho writes, for instance: "Some say an army of horsemen is the fairest thing on the black earth, others an army of footsoldiers, others a navy of ships—but I say the fairest thing is the one I love."[6]

Snell writes that the lyric poets introduced not just new language, but new ways of thinking. They were the first, he says:

> to voice this new idea, that intellectual and spiritual matters have "depth." Archaic poetry [of lyric writers such as Sappho] contains . . . concepts like "deep knowledge," "deep thinking," "deep pondering," as well as "deep pain" . . . In these expressions, the symbol of depth always points to the

infinity of the intellectual and spiritual, which differentiates it from the physical.[7]

In Snell's use of the term "physical," here, he refers to Homeric
terms such as *psyche, noos,* and *thumos* as happenings, caused by
something outside the self. The "new ideas" about which he writes
are those of the movement depicted by the lyric poets, in which
psyche comes to mean mind as consciousness, a world within. *Noos*
comes to mean understanding, or conscious mind. *Thumos* becomes emotion which, although it can move and shake one, and
although it functions to give priority to a concern and action of a
particular kind, has about it an element of choice, of free will.

In his book of 2016, Brian Stock shows how, in the West, influenced by Plato and some early Christian thinkers, it was thought
that the self was in two parts: body and soul, which have different roles in life. So, for some, the body was the prison of the soul.
Stock proposes that it was Augustine who realized, and wrote
about, how the self is integrated, so that body and soul, body
and mind, are interdependent. From there we can move forward
via the case of Phineas Gage, whose emotional and interpersonal
self became disordered from his brain damage, to Nico Frijda's
proposal that emotions, which affect mind, body, and action, are
about events that affect our inner concerns, our selfhood.

A strong strain in research on emotions is that of regulation
of emotions, of being able to moderate them rather than letting
them just take us over, or letting them drive us into actions that
might be destructive to people we care about, or that we might
regret. An important paper on this by Batja Mesquita and Nico
Frijda is "An emotion perspective on emotion regulation." In it
they say:

> Emotional events in real life have the potential of eliciting
> several emotions . . . at the same time. We are happy as well
> as embarrassed when our guests sing the "Happy Birthday"

song at our birthday party. The same event is relevant to multiple concerns, and evokes ... happiness and embarrassment simultaneously.[8]

Consciousness

Consciousness seems to be the means by which, rather than just being propelled by reinforcements or buffeted by circumstance, we can choose to act. But a finding by Benjamin Libet suggests that this may not be so. He used ElectroEncephaloGraphy (EEG) and asked people to flex their fingers within a certain time period, and to notice the point a spot had reached on a revolving wheel when they decided to move their fingers. He found that electrical activation of the motor areas in the brain that controlled the fingers occurred a third of a second before people were conscious of their intention to act.

This result shocked the neuroscientific community because it seemed to imply that processes in the brain initiate action, and that consciousness has no role in this.[9] Controversy has arisen. In *Consciousness Explained*, Daniel Dennett argues that the brain determines behavior, and that consciousness is an extra. The brain computes what it needs to compute; neurons and muscle fibers are recruited to determine behavior. Consciousness has no causal effects. Every aspect of human behavior, says Dennett, could occur without it. Consciousness is a small, and not particularly significant, summary, largely in narrative form, of what the brain has already done in the way of determining decisions and actions.

The function of consciousness, continues Dennett, is to put a good face on what we have done. Rather than having any causal influence, it's like an industrial company's public relations office. Or, using another metaphor, Dennett says each of us has a self, a kind of novelist, who makes what happens and what we have done about it into a single good story, our autobiography.

Dennett and people who are known as hard determinists say that what we do is explained by our DNA having structured our brain so that our neurons and other physiological mechanisms, together with learned and immediate input from the physical and social world, determine what we do on a moment-by-moment basis. Unconsciously these determinists seem to provide a strong argument for discounting what they say. If they were correct, then their argument could not be meaningful. It would be empty, just a scattering of marks on a page that results from a mechanical process such as the pattern of leaves on a tree, or a noise like the clattering of a water wheel in a mill.

Or, if we don't like the idea of a clattering water wheel, but were to take up Dennett's proposal that consciousness is just the brain's public relations office, then by his admission he hasn't explained consciousness at all. All he has done is to say: "Look, see: I have written a book with all these words, less than $30 for more than 500 pages."

Consciousness and Decisions

If consciousness seems not to have an immediate effect on action, perhaps it can act over a longer period. Silvia Galdi and her colleagues completed an ingenious experiment to take this idea further. In the Italian city of Vincenza, they studied conscious and unconscious processes of 129 residents in their thinking about a controversial proposal to enlarge a U.S. military base in the city. The residents' decisions about the proposal were assessed by a single question: whether they were for or against it or were undecided. Their conscious beliefs were assessed by a ten-item questionnaire on environmental, social, and economic consequences they thought the enlargement might have. Unconscious associations to the proposal were measured by a test in which people had to make categorizations such as "good" or "bad" by pressing separate buttons in response to positive and negative words, and then pressing these same buttons when shown pictures of the base.[10] These tests were run on a first occasion, and then again a week later.

For people who were decided—for or against the base's enlargement—their conscious thoughts about the base predicted both their decision at the time and their unconscious associations one week later. In contrast, among people who were undecided on the first occasion of testing, their conscious thoughts at that time did not predict the decision they would make a week later. For these people, however, their unconscious associations on the first occasion of testing did predict both their decision and their conscious beliefs a week later.

Figure 26. What is this young person thinking? Is she on the edge of consciousness? *Source:* Photo by Josie Holt, with permission.

Our conscious thoughts are affected by processes of which we are not always consciously aware—including the processes that produce our emotions—and rather than conscious thoughts being in synchrony with the processes that control our decisions they can, instead, work over a longer term to affect the structure of our minds, for instance as we think about an issue, become aware of our emotions about it, and discuss it with others. Figure 26 depicts a young person looking upwards. At what age do you imagine she might become conscious of her thoughts and emotions so as to recognize them in herself and discuss them with others?

Consciousness as Simulation

Roy Baumeister and E. J. Masicampo were influenced by the experiments of Libet, and of Galdi and her colleagues. They suggest that the function of consciousness is not to initiate actions. Instead, it works over a longer period to relate our general knowledge (stored in long-term memory) and remembrances of specific incidents (stored as episodic memories) to our understandings of our selves in our current social situation, and to our plans. It's a process of simulation. It is the means by which we explain ourselves to ourselves, by which we explain ourselves to others, by which we reflect on ourselves and others, as Sappho does. It's a means, too, by which we use our theory-of-mind to understand those with whom we might interact in our plans and arrangements, and for creatively exploring options in complex situations.

Baumeister and Masicampo offer this example of how consciousness can work in planning:

When one has a plane to catch tomorrow, one typically engages in a simulation that calculates backward from the plane's takeoff time, allowing for airport procedures, the trip to the airport, and perhaps the hotel checkout before that, so one knows at what time to commence the sequence of acts. All the information used for this simulation is already in the mind, so conducting the simulation does not bring in new information from the environment . . . These simulations work remarkably well in enabling people to be on time for their flights without having to spend many extra hours at the airport.[11]

The implication of the experiments of Galdi and her colleagues is that consciousness helps us, literally, to make up our minds. It enables us to compose our mental associations so that when it comes to making decisions, these associations, including those necessary for taking actions, are ready, having set up the conditions for making an action. Baumeister and Masicampo say this:

> The influence of conscious thought on behavior can be vitally helpful but is mostly indirect. Conscious simulation processes are useful for understanding the perspectives of social interaction partners, for exploring options in complex decisions, for replaying past events (both literally and counterfactually) so as to learn, and for facilitating participation in culture in other ways.[12]

When something pressing happens and we don't know what to do about it, or when we are moved by an emotion that doesn't seem appropriate, the everyday advice is to "Sleep on it." It's an idea that resonates with the extended functioning of consciousness. The idea resonates with the proposal by Henri Poincaré and Graham Wallas of incubation, that in a creative endeavor, we can work intensely for a period without reaching a solution. Then a way forward, or a solution, may come, after a period during which we have not been thinking about the problem consciously.

Free Will

Thomas Webb and Paschal Sheeran have found, in a meta-analysis of experimental tests, that the formation of conscious intentions to act in a particular way has a causal effect on implementing these actions; this indicates that the will is important.[13] Nico Frijda, thought by many to be the twentieth century's principal researcher on emotions, has also considered this issue. In an article of 2013, he proposed that although some people sneer at the idea, free will is important in psychology. Among examples he relates are how, during World War II, non-Jewish people resisted Nazi threats and coercion to shelter Jewish people. In his article on this issue he does not mention that he had been harbored in this way.

Frijda discusses how, more recently, in the genocidal conflict in Rwanda, as described by Gerard Prunier, some women who were members of the Hutu ethnic group sheltered Tutsi children. These people were acting freely to protect others rather than simply giving priority to their own self-interest. They were able not just to withstand the fear for their own lives, to be merely members of the "Us" group of their ethnicity. They were not just obedient, in the way Stanley Milgram argued. They were able to mobilize their empathy. They chose to become "We" with the children of the Tutsis, to do what was important, rather than to do what was expedient, what the social situation seemed to coerce them into.

Should we hope that we would be among the number of those Hutu women? Should we think of ourselves as among those who usually conform? Or can we learn from the lessons of the genocides of the last century?

If there is to be hope for the human experiment, we need not think that we are on the right side against those on the wrong side. Perhaps instead we might learn to think not in terms of Us-versus-Them, but in terms of Us-and-Them: black people and white people, Jews and Muslims, Westerners and Asians, Conservatives and Liberals, women and men, we who live now and those who will live in the future. "Us-versus-Them" continues to be a scourge of humankind, one that threatens to destroy us all, perhaps in the not-too-distant future. Perhaps we might consider not just "Us-versus-Them," but "We."

The whole idea of law in society depends on free will: A person who commits a crime is said to do so because of a personal intention. If the act is committed because of a compulsion of a mental illness, it is not a crime. There may be paradoxes here. Azim Shariff and colleagues did a set of studies in which people who were less sure about whether free will existed, were less retributive in their attitudes toward punishing criminals. They showed too that people who had learned some neuroscience, about how the brain works, also reduced their support for retributive punishment.

In our day-to-day lives we see people we know caught up in actions and emotions in which they don't seem to have any free will. Such people may be psychotic, or obsessive-compulsive. They may be caught up in an addiction. In anxiety states, they are unable to free themselves from fear. In oppositional states, they seem only able to act in resentment and aggression. In depression, they can become self-absorbed and despairing, without the will to act in the world or relate to others.

We can think of free will as an opposite of compulsion and coercion. It's being able to choose, to make plans, to relate to others in cooperation and in kindness, even when self-interest or social pressures might prompt us otherwise. It is being able to discuss actions with others, and to choose how to act responsibly to realize our values, although we are not always conscious of what really motivates us.[14] Sometimes it is choosing to do what we are doing, even when we may not want to. In *The Myth of Sisyphus*, Albert Camus writes of this state. Sisyphus was an ancient Greek king of Corinth, who was condemned by the gods to roll a boulder up a hill and, at the top, watch it roll down. Then he had to go down and roll the boulder up again. For Camus the allegory is of Sisyphus being able to choose, and he does so. We may be reminded of Rico Medellin, interviewed by Mihaly Csikszentmihalyi in his study of flow, working on a production line as a modern Sisyphus. To roll the bolder up the hill, and to go back down and do it again, is Sisyphus's task in life. He is not one of the gods (whoever or whatever they may be). He is not a rock. He is a human being and as such, Camus says, in the last line of his essay: "One must imagine Sisyphus happy."

Perhaps we can choose freely in only 5 percent of our actions. Part of the project of humankind, in that case, might be to create societies in which the ecological niche enables us more frequently to act freely, perhaps in 6 percent or 7 percent of our actions, perhaps for instance to promote joint goals, "We" goals, rather than just egotistical goals. It's up to us to create such societies. Cities are recent habitats, and new observations indicate that animals and birds that have come to live in cities have started to produce genetically transmissible adaptations to city dwelling much more quickly than had previously been imagined, perhaps in less than a thousand years.[15]

We may know some people who don't seem to have much free will, who react to events always in much the same way, who interact with others in a monotonous fashion. We may notice such tendencies in ourselves. Perhaps we human beings, having left the ranks of those animals who survive because they are fitted to their physical environment, are still adapting to the cooperative life which means being open to others, which means changefulness and creativity. Perhaps as a species, we humans have not yet had much time to cultivate, in societies and in ourselves, the ecological niches that might best enable both cooperation and free will.

The cognitive psychology of the meaningful mind suggests that whether or not the physical world has meaning, we humans make meaning for ourselves and those with whom we interact. We construct worlds of shared meaning. If we can choose in relation to the meaningful, we act not just as a mechanism, but because of what we consider to be the better thing to do, not just for our own benefit but also for others. As George Eliot put it in *Middlemarch*, "What do we live for, if not to make life less difficult for each other?"[16]

Epilogue

The *New York Times* is among media outlets that now feature announcements of psychological findings, and discuss the psychology of events in the news.

Coming to know more about the mind may help us improve our understanding of others and ourselves, and help to build societies in which people of different abilities, and from different backgrounds, find it worthwhile to live.

A Glimpse of the Future

Only recently has psychology entered everyday conversation and understanding. Newspapers now carry reports of psychological research. For instance, the *New York Times*, pictured at the head of this epilogue, has a Sunday Review section in which there is a column called "Grey Matter," that is devoted to psychology. Developments like these mean that psychology is becoming more open. This provides us with means that enable all of us to think about ourselves and those we know.

On May 27, 2016, the Grey Matter column was about why, when researchers try to replicate them, some psychological studies fail to reproduce the same results as those reported by the original researchers. One reason is that psychologists have not always been scrupulous. Some have published only findings that agreed with their own theory.[1] This may have overcome the scientific obligation to look for evidence that might refute one's theory. Another answer suggested by the writer of this article, Jay van Bavel, is that many findings depend on culture. Some processes, such as basic operations of perception, are shared by all humankind. For other processes, including some of the most critical, such as how we feel about each other, and how we treat each other, findings in one society may not replicate in another. Therapeutic properties of psychoanalysis have been found in Sweden. Perhaps they are similar in the United States. But what about in Nigeria, or Japan? A new movement is taking place in psychology, to see how far research findings can be replicated, and to show which findings are reliable.[2]

As much as any other field of research, in conjunction with research in history, in sociology, in anthropology, in computer science, in medicine, psychology is making itself available to us, to offer us knowledge, some directions for education, psychiatry, town planning, and even perhaps in government. We still live in times where much of life is peaceful and cooperative, but life can also be dangerous. There are still enough nuclear weapons to end the human species. Not enough notice is devoted to human rights either of our contemporaries, or of those who will be our descendants.

Psychology has tended to be the psychology of the individual— one-person psychology—but a shift is taking place toward the psychology of what goes on between us and among us—two-person and many-person psychology. There is also a growing movement in psychology of how to live well, not in terms of individual rewards, but well in terms of our contributions to others and society. Joar Vitterso has taken from Aristotle the term "eudaimonia"—the psychology of how to live well—and published a handbook on it. Printing was a technology that enabled us, by means of reading, to understand each other better, and to enable empathy to grow for people in circumstances different from our own. Perhaps newer technologies will enable us to make group decisions better, and to live better with each other. One start on this has been by John Richardson, with his program Ethelo, in which people on their computers or phones join together to discuss a social issue that concerns them. People can offer considerations for discussion, and others join in by making inputs. At the same time, they rate their degree of agreement with different proposals. In this way, not only is a range of concerns and options generated, but the amount of agreement on various choices goes forward, is registered, and is enabled to change. Though the Greeks invented democracy, it may need something of this kind to implement it in the modern world.

Plato was exaggerating when he said that our ordinary perception was like being shackled in a cave, able to see only shadows. The interpretations that the mind makes of the world around us are not direct, but they are good enough for human purposes. We don't need to struggle out from a cave of illusion. The shadow idea, however, is useful, because there is something between us and the world. That something is a set of constructed models within our minds. The model-based perceptual world is generally used not so much for recognizing eternal truths like those of mathematics, but for purposes that are, for the most part, dependable enough for interacting with each other, and for providing the wherewithal for our lives.

At the beginning of the 1300s, Dante wrote about a world in which everything had been arranged by God except for human free will. In the *Inferno*, Dante meets the father of his best friend, Cavalcanti. Ignoring the flames of Hell, this man rises from his tomb to ask Dante whether his son is alright. Here, perhaps, Dante is asking whether this life on Earth, this life of families and friends, may not have more meaning than the seemingly unattainable world of the ideal about which Plato wrote, and which Christianity adopted.

Since the time of Hermann Helmholtz, psychology has established itself as exploration of the mind. Psychology is different from the physical and biological sciences in that what we discover can affect the objects of study: ourselves. In this book, I suggest, too, that psychology is better not kept as a separate science, but rather that it needs to be integrated with other disciplines: not just neuroscience and biology but also philosophy, history, sociology, anthropology, psychiatry, linguistics, computer science, and literary studies. Psychology has the capacity to make a difference to us in our relationships with each other and within ourselves. It is not likely to be effective in sudden and sweeping ways, as occurred with the discovery that electricity could light our houses. But as members of society we can take it in, perhaps a little at a time, and reflect on its meanings.

NOTES

Sources of citations and evidence on which the text is based are mostly clear from the References. Where this is not so, these notes indicate sources, and further thoughts.

Prologue

1. This picture is of my eldest granddaughter. Photographs not unlike this are employed in Baron-Cohen et al.'s (2001) Mind in the Eyes Test, a widely used measure of empathy and understanding others.
2. Semir Zeki said this in a talk entitled "Neuroaesthetics" at a 2011 symposium entitled "Reading mediated minds: Empathy with persons and characters in media and art works," at the University of Amsterdam's Centre for Creation, Content and Technology.

Chapter 1. Conscious and Unconscious

1. Plato's metaphor of the cave comes from *The Republic*. His book on how we are unconscious of mathematical truths, and how they can be led out of us, is *Meno*, in which a slave boy solves Pythagoras's theorem about the square on the hypotenuse of a right-angled triangle being equal to the sum of squares on the other two sides.
2. Plato's *Protagoras*.
3. Whitehead (1979), p. 39.
4. See for instance Ellenberger (1970).
5. Biographies of Freud: Clark (1980), Gay (1988).
6. Oatley (1990).
7. Decker (1991).
8. Freud (1905), p. 146.
9. Freud (1905), p. 150.

10. Clark (1980), p. 285.

11. For a while, if psychology were mentioned, people would think psychoanalysis was being referred to. It even became a theme in Hollywood, for instance with Alfred Hitchcock's *Spellbound*, in which a man played by Gregory Peck has a guilt complex, thinking he has murdered someone. He is tended by an analyst, played by Ingrid Bergman, who falls in love with him. Among principal current "Freud debunkers" (citation in online blurb) is Crews (2017).

12. Freud & Breuer (1895), p. 231.

13. It's been found that children who have been treated negatively, and less favorably than a sibling, are at greater risk for both psychological and physical illness: Jenkins, McGown, & Knafo-Noam (2016).

14. Hafiz (circa 1380): "With that moon language." These are the first seven lines of a translation by Daniel Ladinsky, from *The Gift* (1999), cited with the permission of Daniel Ladinsky.

15. Morton Hunt (2007), p. 142.

16. Biographies of Helmholtz: Koenigsberger (1906), Hall (1912).

17. Helmholtz was not only eminent in physiology; he was the founder of the science of perception, and he also became influential in physics. One outcome of his studies of muscle actions was a paper he published in 1847 on the law of conservation of energy: that energy can be transformed, but neither created nor destroyed. This was seen as a crucial advance in understanding the universe.

18. Helmholtz (1866), p. 11.

19. Oatley, Sullivan, & Hogg (1988). See also Gregory (1997).

20. See Oatley (2013a). *The Great Train Robbery* was written and directed by Edwin Porter (1903).

21. My translation, emphasis in original; Taine (1882), p. 13.

22. Martinez-Conde et al. (2013).

23. The finding by Arnold et al. (2007) that young cows show the same reaction as human infants implies that the pattern of the visual cliff and the response of avoiding it are evolutionarily acquired. For people who are persuaded by this kind of argument, no inferences are made, and no inferences are needed. In chapter 5 we will come to further versions of this argument by the behaviorists.

Chapter 2. The Sad Case of Phineas Gage

1. Randerson (2012). See also Azevedo, Herculano-Houzel, et al. (2009), Herculano-Houzel (2016).
2. Biography of John Harlow: Macmillan (2001).
3. Harlow (1868/1993), p. 281.
4. Harlow (1868/1993), p. 277.
5. Macmillan (2001).
6. Cannon (1931) argued that emotions arise in lower regions of the brain, and can be inhibited by higher regions, that is to say the cortex. MacLean (e.g., 1993) proposed that the principal seat of emotions is the lower region that he calls the limbic system, whereas rationality arises in the cortex. In this book a different idea is developed: of humans as inherently social, and that rather than being regarded as primitive, emotions manage what is most important to us: our relationships with other people. See chapters 3, 14, and 18.
7. McCabe and Castel (2007) discovered that people found that reasoning about a neuroscientific issue was more convincing when it was accompanied by a picture of a brain than when it was not.
8. Panksepp (1998), p. 309.
9. Preston has gone on to investigate the relation between empathy and altruism; see, e.g., Buchanan & Preston (2016).

Chapter 3. Understanding Our Ancestors, Understanding Our Emotions

1. Biography of Darwin: Bowlby (1991).
2. In their fascinating book, Gruber & Barrett (1974) have transcribed and commented on Darwin's notebooks entitled "Transmutation" and "Mind and Materialism."
3. Leakey & Lewin (1991), p. 16.
4. Bowlby (1991), p. 411.
5. Darwin's *Expression of the Emotions*, second edition of 1890, p. 13.
6. Gribbin & Cherfas (2001); White et al. (2009).

7. Hublin et al. (2017). Later emerging human universals include language (see chapter 6), cooperation (see chapter 14), and art (see chapter 17).

8. Darwin's *Expression of the Emotions*, second edition of 1890, p. 18.

9. A comprehensive book on facial expressions, which includes both Ekman's proposals and analyses by dissenting researchers, is Fernández-Dols and Russell (2017).

10. Ekman (1992).

11. Ekman & Friesen (1978).

12. Bartlett & Whitehill (2010); Lewinski et al. (2014). These systems, however, are likely soon to be superseded by a method devised by Kang Lee (2016) which uses normal video recording and, by a method called transdermal optical imaging, detects blood flows beneath the skin of the face. These images indicate much more accurately than visible muscle movements what emotions a person is experiencing. See also Zanette et al. (2016).

13. Ekman (2009).

14. Baum (2009). The series aired from January 21, 2009 to January 31, 2011. Not on currently.

15. In 2014, a year before he died, Frijda attended the International Summer School in Affective Sciences, in Geneva, at which Andrea Scarantino said: "We are all neo-Frijdians now." An extension of the paper Frijda gave in Geneva is Fridja (2016), and Scarantino's comment is on p. 209.

16. Oatley & Johnson-Laird (2014).

17. Oatley & Duncan (1994).

18. Oatley (2009); Oatley & Johnson-Laird (2011).

19. The interpersonal nature of much of our emotional life is discussed in *Ethics*, by Spinoza (1661–1675), and by Reid (1818), who wrote of emotions that they involve "principles of actions in man, which have persons for their immediate object, and imply, in their very nature, our being well or ill affected to some person." More recent work on shared emotions is found in Krebbs (2011).

20. This and the subsequent quotation are from Erasmus (1508), p. 29. It is likely that Shakespeare wrote *A Midsummer Night's Dream* after reading *Praise of Folly*; in his play, an emotion is induced by Puck dripping the juice of a "little western flower" into a sleeper's eyes.

When the person wakes, she or he falls in love with the first person she or he sees, and finds words appropriate to the emotion (see Oatley 2001).

21. See also van Kleef (2016).

Chapter 4. Individual Differences and Development

1. Wolf (1969).
2. The term Intelligence Quotient (IQ) and the concept of its measurement were invented by William Stern (1914).
3. Biography of Binet: Fancher (2009).
4. Recounted in English by Flavell (1963).
5. Biography of Piaget: Evans (1973).
6. Kamin (1974); Fancher (1985).
7. Kamin (1974), p. 27.
8. Cited by Kamin (1974), pp. 23–24.
9. Kamin (1974), p. 27.
10. Terman & Merrill (1937), p. 34.
11. The title of Herrnstein and Murray's book comes from the Gaussian distribution, which has the shape of a bell. It's the most common distribution of naturally occurring characteristics, e.g., people's heights, or temperature on a certain day of the year in a particular place, and it is fundamental to the science of statistics.
12. Selzam et al. (2017).

Chapter 5. Stimulus and Response

1. Pavlov biography: Todes (2014).
2. Cohen (1979) and Boakes (1984).
3. Watson (1925), p. 15.
4. Cohen (1979), p. 175.
5. Cohen (1975), p. 185.
6. Cohen (1975), p. 185.
7. Bjork (1997); Skinner (1938, 1976).
8. Slater (2004).

Chapter 6. Language

1. Chomsky (1959).
2. As one might expect, there are people now who want to argue that Chomsky had it entirely wrong. In 2016, Tom Wolfe, famous for his 1975 essay on the New Journalism, has proposed that not only was Chomsky completely wrong, but so was Darwin. Also in 2016, Paul Ibbotson and Michael Tomasello published a better-informed article that is critical of Chomsky's idea of an inborn language acquisition device.
3. Tomasello (2008).

Chapter 7. Mental Models

1. Bartlett (1932), p. 65.
2. Bartlett (1932), p. 75.
3. The term "schema" was also used for implicit theory by Jean Piaget. See Flavell (1963).
4. Bartlett (1932), p. 201.
5. Bartlett (1932), p. 213.
6. Memory analogies are discussed by Roediger (1980).
7. Loftus & Doyle (1987).
8. Bartlett (1932), p. 20. Now, also, a movement is beginning in psychology to understand people's sense of meaning in life; see for instance, King et al. (2016).
9. Bartlett (1946), p. 109.
10. Johnson-Laird (1983, 2006).
11. See Johnson-Laird (1983, 2006), Friston et al. (2016).
12. Zangwill (1980), p. 12.
13. Dunbar (2004), p. 162.

Chapter 8. The Digital World

1. Hodges (1983) and Copeland (2012) are both good biographies of Turing and his work.
2. Wittgenstein (1922), *Tractatus* (4.01).

3. Hodges (1983); Johnson-Laird (2006).
4. Turing (1950) pp. 434–435.
5. Hsu (2002).
6. Gardner (1985), p. 17.
7. Gardner (1985), p. 28.
8. Gardner (1985), p. 29.
9. An important computationally based theory was given by Marr (1982); see also Oatley, Sullivan, & Hogg (1988).
10. The most important conversational program from early years of artificial intelligence was by Winograd; see, for example, Winograd (1983).
11. LeCun, Bengio, & Hinton (2015); Hinton (2015).
12. See Lewis-Kraus (2016) for a non-technical history of the development of Google Translate; also see Schuster et al. (2016).
13. Stephen Hawking (2014).
14. Bacon (1605).
15. Mendelson (2016), p. 34.
16. This issue is taken further in the epilogue.

Chapter 9. You Need Your Head Examined

1. Parssinen (1974); van Wyhe (2004).
2. Boring (1950), p. 56.
3. McCrea & John (1992).
4. Ormel et al. (2013); Smillie (2013).
5. There have also been at least 15 studies of people keeping diaries of what they do over periods of days and weeks, and these agree quite well with the personality traits that derive from questionnaire measures; see Fleeson & Gallagher (2009).
6. Costa & McCrea (1996), p. 369.
7. Henry James (1884), p. 405. A recent book on the philosophy and psychology of the idea of character is Fileva (2017).
8. Keith (1988).
9. Shostrom (1966).
10. Magai and Haviland-Jones (2002), p. 57.
11. Magai and Haviland-Jones (2002), p. 90.
12. Proust (1919), p. 470, my translation.

13. Hassabis et al. (2014). In a study of inferences in the opposite direction, Küfner et al. (2010) found that it was possible to infer personality characteristics of people from stories they wrote.

14. Browne et al. (2016).

Chapter 10. Mental Illness, Psychosomatic Illness

1. Scull (2015), p. 562.
2. Scull (2015), pp. 425–426.
3. Kreitman et al. (1961).
4. Scull (2015), p. 381.
5. Angell (2008), p. 1069.
6. Kirsh (2009b), p. 80.
7. In those days, the work could not find a publisher, and its authors were vulnerable. Jahoda and Lazarsfeld published their book anonymously in 1933. The 1971 version is an English translation.
8. Meta-analysis is a method in which a range of studies is grouped together, and a statistical analysis is performed to find the mean and variance of all the results.
9. As well as studies by Sandell and his group, two studies by Huber et al. 2013a, 2013b) show positive effects of psychoanalytic therapy as compared with other forms of therapy. Also Leichsenring and Rabung (2008, 2011) have found in meta-analyses of randomized controlled trials that longer-term psychoanalytic therapy afforded better outcomes than shorter therapies. In another meta-analysis, however, Smit et al. (2012) found that although it did better than no therapy, psychoanalytic therapy was no better than some other forms of therapy.
10. Gloaguen et al. (1998).
11. There is now a large literature on the positive effects of mindfulness meditation on its own, or in conjunction with other forms of therapy, for depression, anxiety, and psychosomatic stress. See for instance Segal et al. (2002); Gu et al. (2015); Gotink et al. (2016). Kok & Singer (2016) have found that different kinds of mindfulness meditation have different effects.
12. The study by van Niel et al. (2014) found that people who had four or more adverse childhood experiences "were twice as likely

to be smokers, 12 times more likely to have attempted suicide, 7 times more likely to be alcoholic, and 10 times more likely to have injected street drugs," p. 549.

13. Marucha, Kiecolt-Glaser, & Favagehi (1998).
14. E.g., Gouin et al. (2012).
15. Pennebaker, Zech, & Rimé (2001).

Chapter 11. fMRI and Brain Bases of Experience

1. Starr (2015), p. 14.
2. Starr (2015), p. 23.
3. Starr (2015), p. 82.
4. Bartels & Zeki (2004), p. 1164.
5. See also Chatterjee & Vartanian (2016), and Kandel (2012).
6. Zeki (2004), p. 189.
7. Vessel et al. (2013), first sentence of the second paragraph in the section headed "Intense aesthetic experience."

Chapter 12. Feeling within the Self, Feeling for Others

1. Piccolino (1998).
2. The study of neurons sensitive to orientation of line segments was by Hubel and Wiesel (1962). In a recent study of single neurons and visual recognition in monkeys, Chang and Tsao (2017) have discovered neurons involved in the recognition of faces. They fire with displacements from average face shapes, in different orientations, from points such as the tip of the nose, the corner of the lips, and so on.
3. Singer (2015). Tania Singer is Professor and Managing Director of the Max Planck Institute for Cognitive and Brain Sciences in Leipzig.
4. There is evidence that studying economics may encourage self-centeredness and discourage cooperation; Frank et al. (1993).
5. Singer (2015).
6. Beckes et al. (2013), p. 676.
7. This study can be seen as part of a movement to understand empathy in a positive way. But the movement is becoming controversial. Paul Bloom has written *Against empathy*, in which he argues

that empathy can sometimes be harmful; instead we should enter a state of compassion. The idea of compassion is important, but we can imagine Bloom writing his next book called *Against action*, because sometimes what we do is wrong.

8. Controversies about the implications of mirror neurons are discussed by Ocampo and Kritikos (2011). A book-length argument against mirror neurons as having a role in explaining language and social cognition is by Hickok (2015), who fell in love with mirror-neurons and then fell out of love with them. See also Arbib (2015).

9. Sato & Yoshikawa (2007).

10. Donald (1991). The human proclivity for dancing is a further indication of the social importance of mirror-based mimicry.

11. The 1949 film was directed by Carol Reed, and written by Graham Greene.

Chapter 13. In Affection and Conflict

1. Gruber & Barrett (1974), p. 289.
2. Goodall (1986), p. 594.
3. Weisfeld (1980).
4. Nishida et al. (1992).
5. Goodall (1986), p. 144.
6. Boesch et al. (2007).
7. Sherif & Sherif (1953), p. 252.
8. Sherif & Sherif (1953), p. 257.
9. See Bergman Blix (forthcoming).
10. Sibley & Alquist (1984).
11. Green et al. (2010).

Chapter 14. Cooperation

1. Franco et al. (2009).
2. Warneken & Tomasello (2009). If you Google "Warneken Tomasello videos" you can see several examples of babies' altruism in recognizing others' plans, and helping the others to complete them.
3. Tomasello (2014), pp. 4–5.

4. Tomasello (2011).
5. Larocque & Oatley (2006), pp. 255–256.
6. Further evidence of this, including cultural differences in Canada and Italy, was found by Grazzani-Gavazzi & Oatley (1999).
7. The original paper from which Dunbar developed his work on the social brain hypothesis is Aiello & Dunbar (1993). Data and proposals in the paragraphs that follow this one are from the work of Dunbar (2003; 2004; 2014).
8. Dunbar, Marriot, & Duncan (1997), p. 235.
9. Zeldin (1998).

Chapter 15. What Is It about Love?

1. Lynn Hunt (2007).
2. Anna Freud and Dorothy Burlingham became life-long partners. Among their books is Freud and & Burlingham (1943); see also Midgley (2007).
3. Bowlby (1951), p. 11.
4. Bowlby (1969).
5. Holmes (1993).
6. Ainsworth (1992).
7. Bretherton (2000).
8. See, for example, Freud & Breuer (1895).
9. Bretherton (1990).
10. A striking version of this kind of truth was told to me by a famous research psychologist who, when he was six or seven, was picked up and stood, by his father, on top of a tall chest of drawers and told to jump into his father's arms. "No," said the boy, "I don't want to." But his father persuaded him. The boy jumped and the father let him fall to the ground. "There," said the father. "Don't ever trust anyone. Ever."
11. Waters, Merrick, Treboux, et al. 2000.
12. Hamilton (2000).
13. Weinfield et al. (2000).
14. Goldberg, Grusec, & Jenkins (1999).
15. Hatfield & Rapson (2006), p. 227.
16. Hazan & Shaver (1987).

17. Williams (1922), pdf version, p. 3. (http://www.deborahward.co.uk /pdfs/velveteenrabbit.pdf)
18. Winnicott's book, in which he discusses this issue, is *Playing and reality* (1971).
19. Winnicott (1953), p. 90.
20. Winnicott (1965). This issue was raised in chapter 1, in the discussion of Karen Horney's case of her patient, Clare.

Chapter 16. Culture

1. Geertz (1989).
2. Biography by Bowman-Kruhm (2011).
3. From the foreword of Mead (1928), pp. xiv–xv.
4. Mead (1928), p. 260.
5. Mead (1928), p. 157.
6. See Munafò et al. (2017).
7. Vygotsky (1930), p. 25.
8. Ibbotson & Tomasello (2016).
9. Nelson (2015), p. 173.
10. Lutz (1988), pp. 16–17.
11. Lutz (1988), p. 112.
12. Lutz (1988), p. 200.
13. Pavlenko (2005).

Chapter 17. Imagination, Stories, Empathy

1. Dunn (2004), p. 1.
2. Goffman (1961), p. 26.
3. Goffman (1961), p. 41.
4. Oatley (2009).
5. Havelock (1978), pp. 42–43.
6. Luria (1976), pp. 108–109.
7. Luria (1976), p. 116, table 8. See Olson (1994) for a general introduction to the psychological effects of literacy.
8. Dias et al. (2005), p. 552.

9. A book called *The Undoing Project*, about Kahneman and his friend Tversky and their research, is Lewis (2016).

10. Oatley (2013b).

11. Vanhaeren et al. (2006).

12. Bowler et al. (2003).

13. Chauvet et al. (1996).

14. Anonymous (1700 BCE).

15. The earliest parts of the Bible are translated and discussed by Rosenberg & Bloom (1990).

16. See the account of Lord (2000), who describes twentieth-century oral telling of tales, and of Powell (2002), who suggests that the first written language with both vowels and consonants, Greek, came into being to take dictation from the *Iliad.*

17. Mar & Oatley (2008); Oatley (2016).

18. Garcia Marquez (1981), p. 324.

19. Chekhov (1890).

20. Yarmolinsky (1973), p. 395.

21. Shakespeare (1623), p. 1455.

22. Hunt, L. (2007), p. 216.

23. Hunt, L. (2007), p. 224.

24. Hunt, L. (2007), p. 20.

25. Hunt, L. (2007), p. 39.

26. Hunt, L. (2007), p. 39.

27. Richardson (1740), p. 23.

28. Hunt, L. (2007), p. 58.

29. Eliot (1871–1872), p. 243.

30. Proust (1927), pp. 257–258, my translation.

31. Non-replications of short-term experimental effects of improving empathy by reading short stories, published by Kidd & Castano (2013), have been reported by Dijkstra et al. (2015) and Panero et al. (2016). Overall, results that include those over shorter, medium, and longer terms have shown increases of empathy and theory-of-mind with reading fiction. These have been reviewed by Oatley (2016) and Oatley & Djikic (2017). Meta-analyses of associational effects have been performed by Mumper & Gerrig (2017), and of experimental effects by another group (as yet unpublished).

Both meta-analyses show small, but significant, effects of reading fiction on improved empathy and theory-of-mind.

32. Fong, Mullin, & Mar (2013).
33. Kierkegaard (1846), pp. 246–247.
34. Barthes (1975), p. 4.
35. Stock (2007), p. 136. A psychological hypothesis offered by Zillmann (1996) is that we are disposed to like fictional characters who act well, and to dislike those who act immorally.
36. Obama & Robinson (2015), p. 6.
37. Black & Barnes (2015); Bormann & Greitemeyer (2015).

Chapter 18. Authority and Morality

1. Biography: Blass (2009).
2. Milgram (1963), p. 374.
3. See Munafò (2017).
4. Haslam et al. (2016).
5. Among those who have denounced Milgram's experiments on ethical grounds has been Perry (2013). More balanced is Carol Tavris in her 2013 review of Perry's book. Tavris concludes that the subject and conclusions of Milgram's experiments are still important psychological findings, and important for us to think about.
6. The story of this outrage is told by Åsne Seierstad (2015).
7. See, for instance, Browning (2017).
8. See, for instance, Nussbaum (1986) and Sherman (1997).
9. Also developing, now, is a psychology of the law, and how legal judgments are made; see, e.g., Moroney (2011).

Chapter 19. Creativity, Expertise, Grit

1. Winnicott (1971), p. 65.
2. Csikszentmihalyi (1990), pp. 39–40.
3. This and other quotations in the same paragraph are from Csikszentmihalyi (1990), p. 53.
4. Miller (1956).

5. Ericsson has published many articles on expertise, for example Ericsson (1996), Ericsson & Lehmann (1999).
6. Ericsson, Krampe, & Tesch-Römer (1993), p. 392.
7. Scholz et al. (2009).
8. Ericsson (2016); Macnamara, Moreau, & Hambrick (2016).
9. See also the biography of Curie by Goldsmith (2005).
10. Oatley & Djikic (2016).
11. Einstein & Infeld (1938), p. 95.
12. Collingwood (1938), pp. 109–110.
13. Darwin's voyage on the *Beagle*, Darwin (1839); Darwin's note-making, Gruber & Barrett (1974).
14. Poincaré (1908), p. 33 and pp. 36–37.
15. James (1907), pp. 322–323.

Chapter 20. Consciousness and Free Will

1. Homer (762 BCE), p. 55.
2. Snell (1948), p. 31. A psychological exploration of these issues is by Jaynes (1976).
3. Homer (762 BCE), p. 55.
4. Williamson (1995).
5. Page (1955), p. 136.
6. Snell (1953), p. 47.
7. Snell (1953), pp. 17–18.
8. Mesquita & Frijda (2011), pp. 782–783.
9. Glannon (2015).
10. This kind of measurement relies on priming, a process that has become controversial because results are not always replicable; Yong (2012).
11. Baumeister & Masicampo (2010), p. 955.
12. Baumeister & Masicampo (2010), p. 945.
13. Various factors can, however, militate against carrying out intentions. Sheeran & Webb (2016).
14. Doris (2015).
15. Donihue & Lambert (2015).
16. Eliot (1871–1872), p. 781.

Epilogue

1. Popper (1962) has rightly insisted that looking for evidence that might refute a hypothesis is more important than looking for evidence to confirm it.
2. See Munafò et al. (2017).

REFERENCES

Acevedo, B. P., Aron, A., Fisher, H. F., & Brown, L. (2012). Neural correlates of long-term intense romantic love. *Social Cognitive and Affective Neuroscience, 7*, 145–159.

Aiello, L. C., & Dunbar, R.I.M. (1993). Neocortex size, group size, and the evolution of language. *Current Anthropology, 34*, 184–193.

Ainsworth, M.D.S. (1992). Obituary: John Bowlby (1907–1990). *American Psychologist, 47*, 668.

Ainsworth, M.D.S., Blehar, M. C., Waters, E., & Wall, S. (1978). *Patterns of attachment: A psychological study of the strange situation*. Hillsdale, NJ: Erlbaum.

Almereyda, M. (Director). (2015). *Experimenter* (Film). USA.

Angell, M. (2008). Industry-sponsored clinical research: A broken system. *Journal of the American Medical Association, 300*, 1069–1071.

Angell, M. (2011, June 23). The epidemic of mental illness: Why? *New York Review of Books*.

Anonymous. (1700 BCE). *The epic of Gilgamesh: The Babylonian Epic Poem and other texts in Akkadian and Sumerian* (A. George, Trans.). London: Penguin (current edition 2000).

Arbib, M. A. (2015). The myth of "the myth of mirror neurons." *PsycCRITIQUES, 60*(9).

Arendt, H. (1963). *Eichmann in Jerusalem: A report on the banality of evil*. New York: Viking.

Aristotle. (circa 330 BCE). Prior analytics. In J. Barnes (Ed.), *The complete works of Artistotle: The revised Oxford translation* (Vol. 2, pp. 39–113). Oxford: Oxford University Press (current publication 1984).

Arnold, N. A., Ng, K. T., Jongman, E. C., & Emsworth, P. H. (2007). Responses of dairy heifers to the visual cliff formed by a herringbone milking pit: Evidence of fear of heights in cows (Bos taurus). *Journal of Comparative Psychology, 121*, 440–446.

Asimov, I. (1950). *I Robot*. New York: Gnome Press.

Auden, W. H. "In memory of Sigmund Freud." In *From another time.* New York: Random House.

Azevedo, F.A.C., Herculano-Houzel, S., et al. (2009). Equal numbers of neuronal and nonneuronal cells make up the human brain as an isometrically scaled-up primate brain. *Journal of Comparative Neurology, 513,* 532–541.

Bacon, F. (1605). *The advancement of learning.* Oxford: Oxford University Press (current edition 1974).

Baron-Cohen, S., Wheelwright, S., Hill, J., Raste, Y., & Plumb, I. (2001). The "Reading the Mind in the Eyes" Test Revised version: A study with normal adults, and adults with Asperger's syndrome or high-functioning autism. *Journal of Child Psychology and Psychiatry, 42,* 241–251.

Barrett, L. F. (2017). *How emotions are made: The secret life of the brain.* Boston: Houghton Mifflin Harcourt.

Barrett, L. F., Mesquita, B., & Gendron, M. (2011). Context in emotion perception. *Current Directions in Psychological Science, 20,* 286–290.

Bartels, A., & Zeki, S. (2000). The neural basis of romantic love. *NeuroReport, 17,* 3829–3834.

Bartels, A., & Zeki, S. (2004). The neural correlates of maternal and romantic love. *NeuroImage, 21,* 1155–1166.

Barthes, R. (1975). *S / Z* (R. Miller, Trans.). London: Cape.

Bartlett, F. C. (1932). *Remembering: A study in experimental and social psychology.* Cambridge: Cambridge University Press.

Bartlett, F. C. (1946). Obituary notice: Kenneth J. W. Craik, 1914–1945. *British Journal of Psychology (General Section), 36* (3), 109–116.

Bartlett, M. S., & Whitehill, J. (2010). Automated facial expression measurement: Recent applications to basic research in human behavior, learning, and education. In A. Calder, G. Rhodes, J. V. Haxby, & M. H. Johnson (Eds.), *Handbook of face perception* (pp. 489–513). Oxford, UK: Oxford University Press.

Baum, S. (2009). *Lie to me* (Television series). USA.

Baumeister, R. F., & Masicampo, E. J. (2010). Conscious thought is for facilitating social and cultural interactions: How mental simulations serve the animal-culture interface. *Psychological Review, 117,* 945–971.

Beckes, L., Coan, J. A., & Hasselmo, K. (2013). Familiarity promotes the blurring of self and other in the neural representation of threat. *Social Cognitive and Affective Neuroscience, 8,* 670–677.

Bergman Blix, S. (forthcoming). Perspective-taking in empathy: stage actors and judges as polar cases. In R. Patulny et al. (Eds.), *Interdisciplinary approaches to emotion: in conversation with sociology*. London: Routledge.

Bergson, H. (1911). *Laughter: An essay on the meaning of the comic* (C. Brereton & F. Rothwell, Trans.). New York: Macmillan (original publication 1900).

Binet, A. (1903). *L'étude experimentale de l'intelligence*. Paris: Schleicher.

Binet, A., & Henneguy, L. (1894). *Psychologie des grands calculateurs et joueurs d'échec*. Paris: Hachette.

Binet, A., & Simon, T. (1908). The development of intelligence in the child. In H. H. Goddard (Ed.), *The development of intelligence in children*. Baltimore: Williams and Wilkins (current edition 1916).

Bjork, D. W. (1997). *B.F. Skinner: A life*. Washington, DC: American Psychological Association.

Black, J. E., & Barnes, J. L. (2015). Fiction and social cognition: The effect of viewing award-winning television dramas on theory of mind. *Psychology of Aesthetics, Creativity, and the Arts, 9*, 423–429.

Blass, T. (2009). *The man who shocked the world: The life and legacy of Stanley Milgram*. New York: Basic Books.

Bloom, P. (2016). *Against empathy: The case for rational compassion*. New York: Ecco.

Boakes, R. (1984). *From Darwin to behaviourism*. Cambridge: Cambridge University Press.

Boal, A. (1997). The theatre of the oppressed. *UNESCO Courier* (November).

Boesch, C., Head, J., Tagg, N., et al. (2007). Fatal chimpanzee attack in Loango National Park, Gabon. *International Journal of Primatology, 28*, 1025–1034.

Boon, D. (Director). (2008). *Welcome to the Sticks* (Film). (Original French title *Bienvenue chez les Ch'tis*) (Film). France.

Boring, E. G. (1950). *A history of experimental psychology, second edition*. New York: Appleton-Century-Crofts.

Bormann, D., & Greitemeyer, T. (2015). Immersed in virtual worlds and minds: Effects of in-game storytelling in immersion, need satisfaction, and affective theory of mind. *Social Psychological Personality Science, 6*, 646–652.

Bowlby, J. (1951). *Child care and the growth of love.* Harmondsworth: Penguin.

Bowlby, J. (1969). *Attachment and loss, Volume 1. Attachment.* London: Hogarth Press (reprinted by Penguin, 1978).

Bowlby, J. (1991). *Charles Darwin: A new life.* New York: Norton.

Bowler, J. M., et al. (2003). New ages for human occupation and climatic change at Lake Mungo, Australia. *Nature, 421,* 837–840.

Bowman-Kruhm, M. (2011). *Margaret Mead: A biography.* New York: Prometheus.

Brannigan, A., Nicholson, I., Cherry, F., & Mastroianni, G. R. (2015). Obedience in perspective: Psychology and the holocaust. *Theory and Psychology, 25,* 657–669.

Bretherton, I. (2000). Mary Dinsmore Salter Ainsworth (1913–1999) obituary. *American Psychologist, 55,* 1148–1149.

Briggs, J. L. (1970). *Never in anger: Portrait of an Eskimo family.* Cambridge, MA: Harvard University Press.

Brown, G. W., & Harris, T. O. (1978). *Social origins of depression: A study of psychiatric disorder in women.* London: Tavistock.

Browne, D. T., Leckie, G., Prime, H., Perlman, M., & Jenkins, J. M. (2016). Observed sensitivity during family interactions and cumulative risk: A study of multiple dyads per family. *Developmental Psychology, 52,* 1128–1138.

Browning, C. (1992). *Ordinary men: Reserve Police Battalion 101 and the final solution in Poland.* New York: HarperCollins.

Browning, C. (2017, 20 April). Lessons from Hitler's rise. *New York Review of Books, 94,* 10–14.

Buccino, G., Riggio, L., Melli, G., Binkofski, F., Gallese, V., & Rizzolati, G. (2005). Listening to action-related sentences modulates the activity of the motor system: A combined TMS and behavioral study. *Cognitive Brain Research, 24,* 355–363.

Buchanan, T. W., & Preston, S. (2016). When feeling and doing diverge: Neural and physiological correlates of the empathy–altruism divide. In J. Green, I. Morrison, & M.E.P. Seligman (eds.), *Positive neuroscience* (pp. 89–103). New York: Oxford University Press.

Burger, J. M. (2009). Replicating Milgram: Would people still comply today? *American Psychologist, 64,* 1–11.

Campbell, D. T. (1960). Blind variation and selective retentions in creative thought as in other knowledge processes. *Psychological Review, 67,* 380–400.

Camus, A. (1961). *The myth of Sisyphus* (J. O'Brien, Trans.). New York: Knopf.

Cannon, W. B. (1931). Again the James-Lange and the thalamic theories of emotion. *Psychological Review, 38,* 281–295.

Caspi, A., Sugden, K., Moffitt, T., E., Taylor, A., Craig, I. W., Taylor, A., . . . Poulton, R. (2003). Influence on life stress on depression: moderation by a polymorphism in the 5-HTT gene. *Science, 301,* 386–389.

Chagnon, N. A. (1968). *Yanomamö: The fierce people.* New York: Holt Rinehart & Winston.

Chang, L., & Tsao, D. Y. (2017). The code for facial identity in the primate brain. *Cell, 169,* 1013–1028.

Chase, W. G., & Simon, H. A. (1973). Perception in chess. *Cognitive Psychology, 4,* 55–81.

Chatterjee, A., & Vartanian, O. (2016). Neuroscience of aesthetics. *Annals of the New York Academy of Sciences, 1369,* 172–194.

Chauvet, J.-M., Deschamps, E., B., & Hillaire, C. (1996). *Dawn of art: The Chauvet cave.* New York: Abrams.

Chekhov, A. (1890). "Gusev" (R. Pevear & L. Volokhonsky, Trans.). *Anton Chekhov Stories.* New York: Bantam (current edition 2000), pp. 109–121.

Chomsky, N. (1957). *Syntactic structures.* The Hague: Mouton.

Chomsky, N. (1959). A review of B. F. Skinner's "Verbal Behavior." *Language, 35,* 26–58.

Clark, A. (2006). Material symbols. *Philosophical Psychology, 19,* 291–307.

Clark, R. W. (1980). *Freud: The man and the cause.* London: Cape, Weidenfeld & Nicholson.

Cohen, D. (1979). *J. B. Watson: The founder of behaviourism.* London: Routledge & Kegan Paul.

Coleridge, S. T. (1816). Kubla Khan. In *The portable Coleridge* (pp. 157–158, with explanatory note on writing the poem, pp. 156–157). Harmondsworth: Penguin (current edition 1977).

Collingwood, R. G. (1938). *The principles of art.* Oxford: Oxford University Press.

Collobert, R., & Weston, J. (2008). *A unified architecture for natural language processing: deep neural networks with multitask learning.* Paper presented at the ICML '08 Proceedings of the 25th international conference on machine learning, Helsinki, pp. 160–167.

Coolidge, F. L., & Wynn, T. (2016). An introduction to cognitive archaeology. *Current Directions in Psychological Science, 25,* 386–392.

Copeland, B. J. (2012). *Turing: Pioneer of the information age.* Oxford: Oxford University Press.

Costa, P. T., Jr. & McCrae, R. R. (1985). *The NEO Personality Inventory manual.* Odessa, FL: Psychological Assessment Resources.

Costa, P. T., & McCrae, R. R. (1988). Personality in adulthood: A six-year longitudinal study of self-reports and spouse ratings on the NEO Personality Inventory. *Journal of Personality and Social Psychology, 54,* 853–863.

Costa, P. T., & McCrae, R. R. (1996). Mood and personality in adulthood. In C. Magai & S. H. McFadden (Eds.), *Handbook of emotion, adult development, and aging* (pp. 369–383). San Diego: Academic Press.

Craik, K.J.W. (1943). *The nature of explanation.* Cambridge: Cambridge University Press.

Crews, F. (2017). *Freud: The making of an illusion.* London: Profile Books.

Csikszentmihalyi, M. (1990). *Flow: The psychology of optimal experience.* New York: Harper Collins.

Csikszentmihalyi, M., & Getsels, J. W. (1970). Concern for discovery: An attitudinal component of creative production. *Journal of Personality, 38,* 91–105.

Daly, M., & Wilson, M. (1990). Killing the competition: Female/female and male/male homicide. *Human Nature, 1,* 81–106.

Damasio, A. R. (1994). *Descartes' error.* New York: Putnam.

Damasio, H., Grabowski, T., Frank, R., Galaburda, A. M., & Damasio, A. R. (1994). The return of Phineas Gage: The skull of a famous patient yields clues about the brain. *Science, 264,* 1102–1105.

Dante Alighieri. (1307–1321). *La divina commedia (The divine comedy).* (M. Musa, Trans.). London: Penguin (1984).

Darwin, C. (1839). *The voyage of the* Beagle. London: Dent (current edition 1906).

Darwin, C. (1859). *On the origin of species by means of natural selection.* London: Murray.

Darwin, C. (1872). *The expression of the emotions in man and animals*. London: Murray; and second edition, of 1890, edited by Charles Darwin's son, Francis.

Darwin, C. (1877). A biographical sketch of an infant. *Mind, 2*, 285–294.

Dawkins, R. (1976). *The selfish gene*. Oxford: Oxford University Press.

De Lorris, G., & De Meun, J. (1237–1277). *The romance of the rose* (H. W. Robbins, Trans.). New York: Dutton (current edition 1962).

Dean, L. G., Kendal, R. L., Schapiro, S. J., Thierry, B., & Laland, K. N. (2012). Identification of the social and cognitive processes underlying human cumulative culture. *Science, 335*, 1114–1118.

Decker, H. S. (1991). *Freud, Dora, and Vienna 1900*. New York: Free Press.

DeLoache, J. (1987). Rapid change in symbolic functioning in young children. *Science, 238*, 1556–1557.

Dennett, D. C. (1991). *Consciousness explained*. Boston: Little, Brown & Co.

Dennett, D. (1995). *Darwin's dangerous idea: Evolution and the meaning of life*. New York: Simon & Schuster.

Descartes, R. (1648). *Treatise of man (Traité de l'homme)* (T. S. Hall, Trans.). New York: Prometheus (current edition 2003).

Descartes, R. (1649). Passions of the soul. In E. L. Haldane & G. R. Ross (Eds.), *The philosophical works of Descartes*. New York: Dover (current edition 1911).

DeYoung, C. G., Quilty, L. C., & Peterson, J. B. (2007). Between facets and domains: Ten aspects of the Big Five. *Journal of Personality and Social Psychology, 93*, 880–896.

Dias, M., Roazzi, A., & Harris, P. L. (2005). Reasoning from unfamiliar premises: A study with unschooled adults. *Psychological Science, 16*, 550–554.

Dijkstra, K., Verkoeijen, P., Van Kulik, L., Yee-Chow, S., Bakker, A., & Zwann, R. (2015). Leidt het lezen van literaire fictie tot meer empathie? Een replicatiestudie (Does reading literary fiction lead to more empathy? A replication study). *De Psycholoog, 50*, 10–21.

Doll, R., & Hill, A. B. (1954). The mortality of doctors in relation to their smoking habits: A preliminary report. *British Medical Journal, 328*, 1529–1533.

Donald, M. (1991). *Origins of the modern mind*. Cambridge, MA: Harvard University Press.

Donihue, C. M., & Lambert, M. R. (2015). Adaptive evolution in urban ecosystems. *Ambio, 44*, 194–203.

Doris, J. M. (2015). *Talking to our selves: Reflection, ignorance, and agency.* New York: Oxford University Press.

Duckworth, A. L. (2016). *Grit: The power of passion and perseverance.* Toronto: Collins.

Duckworth, A. L., Kirby, T. A., Tsukayama, E., Berstein, H., & Ericsson, K. A. (2010). Deliberate practice spells success: Why grittier competitors triumph at the National Spelling Bee. *Social Psychological Personality Science, 2*, 174–181.

Duckworth, A. L., Peterson, C., Matthews, M., & Kelly, D. R. (2007). Grit: Perseverance and passion for long-term goals. *Personality Processes and Individual Differences, 92*, 1087–1101.

Dunbar, R. I. M. (2003). The social brain: mind, language, and society in evolutionary perspective. *Annual Review of Anthropology, 32*, 163–181.

Dunbar, R.I.M. (2004). *The human story: A new history of mankind's evolution.* London: Faber.

Dunbar, R.I.M. (2014). The social brain: Psychological underpinnings and implications for the structure of organizations. *Current Directions in Psychological Science, 23*, 109–114.

Dunbar, R.I.M., Marriott, A., & Duncan, N.D.C. (1997). Human conversational behavior *Human Nature, 8*, 231–246.

Dunn, J. (2004). *Children's friendships: The beginnings of intimacy.* Oxford: Blackwell.

Einstein, A., & Infeld, L. (1938). *Evolution of physics.* New York: Simon & Schuster.

Eisenberg, N. (2000). Empathy and sympathy. In M. Lewis & J. M. Haviland-Jones (Eds.), *Handbook of emotions, second edition* (pp. 677–691). New York: Guilford.

Ekman, P. (1992). An argument for basic emotions. *Cognition and Emotion, 6*, 169–200.

Ekman, P. (2009). *Telling lies: Clues to deceit, in the marketplace, politics, and marriage.* New York: Norton.

Ekman, P., & Friesen, W. V. (1978). *Facial action coding system: a technique for the measurement of facial movement.* Palo Alto, CA: Consulting Psychologists Press.

Ekman, P., Sorenson, E. R., & Friesen, W. V. (1969). Pan-cultural elements in the facial displays of emotions. *Science, 164,* 86–88.

Elias, N. (1978). *The civilizing process, The history of manners* (E. Jephcott, Trans.). New York: Urizon Books (original publication, 1939).

Eliot, G. (1871–1872). *Middlemarch: A study of provincial life.* London: Penguin (current edition 1965).

Ellenberger, H. F. (1970). *The discovery of the unconscious: The history and evolution of dynamic psychiatry.* New York: Basic Books.

Equiano, O. (1789). *The interesting narrative of the life of Oludah Equano or Gustavus Vassa, the African, written by himself.* New York: Norton (current edition 2001).

Erasmus, D. (1508). *Praise of folly* (Ed. & trans. R. M. Adams). New York: Norton (current edition, 1989).

Ericsson, K. A. (1996). The acquisition of expert performance: An introduction to some of the issues. In K. A. Ericsson (Ed.), *The road to excellence: The acquisition of expert performance in the arts and sciences, sports, and games* (pp. 1–60). Mahwah, NJ: Erlbaum.

Ericsson, K. A. (2016). Summing up hours of any type of practice versus identifying optimal practice activities: Commentary on Macnamara, Moreau, & Hambrick (2016). *Perspectives on Psychological Science, 11,* 351–354.

Ericsson, K. A., Krampe, R. T., & Tesch-Römer, C. (1993). The role of deliberate practice in the acquisition of expert performance. *Psychological Review, 100,* 363–406.

Ericsson, K. A., & Lehmann, A. C. (1999). Expertise. In M. A. Runco & S. R. Pritzker (Eds.), *Encyclopaedia of Creativity, Volume 1* (pp. 695–706). San Diego: Academic Press.

Evans, R. I. (1973). *Jean Piaget: The man and his ideas.* New York: Dutton.

Eysenck, M. (Ed.). (1990). *The Blackwell dictionary of cognitive psychology.* Oxford: Blackwell.

Fancher, R. (1985). *The intelligence men: Makers of the IQ controversy.* New York: Norton.

Fancher, R. (2009). Alfred Binet: General psychologist. In G. A. Kimble & M. Wertheimer (Eds.), *Portraits of Pioneers in Psychology, Volume III* (pp. 67–84). Washington, DC: American Psychological Association.

Fast, E., McGrath, W., Rajpurkar, P., & Bernstein, M. S. (2016). Augur: Mining human behaviors from fiction to power interactive systems.

Association for Computing Machinery CHI 16. doi: org/10.1145/2858 036.2858528.

Felitti, V. J., Anda, R. F., Nordenberg, D., Williamson, D. F., et al. (1998). Relationship of childhood abuse and household dysfunction to many of the leading causes of death in adults: The Adverse Childhood Experiences (ACE) Study. *American Journal of Preventative Medicine, 14,* 245–258.

Fernández-Dols, J.-M., & Russell, J. (Eds.). (2017). *The science of facial expression*. Oxford: Oxford University Press.

Fileva, I. (Ed.). (2017). *Questions of character*. New York: Oxford University Press.

Fillmore, C. J. (1968). The case for case. In E. Bach & R. T. Harms (Eds.), *Universals in linguistic theory* (pp. 1–88). New York: Holt, Rinehart & Winston.

Flavell, J. H. (1963). *The developmental psychology of Jean Piaget*. Princeton, NJ: Van Nostrand.

Fleeson, W., & Gallagher, P. (2009). The implications of Big Five standing for the distribution of trait manifestation in behavior: Fifteen experience-sampling studies and a meta-analysis. *Journal of Personality and Social Psychology, 97,* 1097–1114.

Fonagy, P., Steele, H., & Steele, M. (1991). Maternal representations of attachment during pregnancy predict the organization of infant-mother attachment at one year of age. *Child Development, 62,* 891–905.

Fong, K., Mullin, J., & Mar, R. (2013). What you read matters: The role of fiction genres in predicting interpersonal sensitivity. *Psychology of Aesthetics, Creativity, and the Arts, 7,* 370–376.

Forman, M. (Director). (1975). *One flew over the cuckoo's nest* (Film). USA.

Franco, F., Perucchini, P., & March, B. (2009). Is infant initiation of joint attention by pointing affected by type of interaction? *Social Development, 18,* 51–76.

Frank, R. H., Gilovich, T., & Regan, D. (1993). Does studying economics inhibit cooperation? *Journal of Economic Perspectives, 7*(2), 159–171.

Fraser, J. (1908). A new visual illusion of direction. *British Journal of Psychology, 2,* 307–320.

Freedman, J. L. (1978). *Happy people: What happiness is, who has it and why*. New York: Harcourt Brace Jovanovich.

Freeman, D. (1983). *Margaret Mead and Samoa: The making and unmaking of an anthropological myth*. Cambridge, MA: Harvard University Press.

Freud, A., & Burlingham, D. T. (1943). *War and children*. New York: Medical War Books.

Freud, S. (1905). Fragment of an analysis of a case of hysteria (Dora) (A. Tyson, Trans.). In J. Strachey & A. Richards (Eds.), *The Pelican Freud Library, Vol 8: Case histories, II* (Vol. 8, 29–164). London: Penguin (current edition 1979).

Freud, S., & Breuer, J. (1895). *Studies on hysteria. The Pelican Freud Library, Vol. 3* (Eds. J. Strachey, A. Strachey, & A. Richards). London: Penguin (current edition 1974).

Frijda, N. H. (2007). *The laws of emotion*. Mahwah, NJ: Erlbaum.

Frijda, N. (2013). Emotion regulation and free will. In A. Clark, J. Kiverstein, & T. Vierkant (Eds.), *Decomposing the will* (pp. 199–220). New York: Oxford University Press.

Frijda, N. H. (2016). The evolutionary emergence of what we call "emotions." *Cognition and Emotion, 30*, 609–620.

Friston, K., FitzGerald, T., Rigoli, F., Schwartenbeck, P., O'Doherty, J., & Pezzulo, G. (2016). Active inference and learning. *Neuroscience and Biobehavioral Reviews, 68*, 862–879.

Galdi, S., Arcuri, L., & Gawronski, B. (2008). Automatic mental associations predict future choices of undecided decision-makers. *Science, 321*, 1100–1102.

Gall, F. J. (1835). *On the functions of the brain and of each of its parts: With observations on the possibility of determining the instincts, propensities, and talents, or the moral and intellectual dispositions of men and animals, by the configuration of the brain and head* (in English). Boston: Marsh, Capen & Lyon.

Gallese, V., Keysers, C., & Rizzolatti, G. (2004). A unifying view of the basis of social cognition. *Trends in Cognitive Sciences, 8*, 396–403.

Galton, F. (1884). *Anthropometric laboratory*. London: William Clowes.

García Márquez, G. (1981). Interview with Peter Stone. In G. Plimpton (Ed.), *Writers at Work: The Paris Review Interviews, 6* (pp. 315–339). London: Penguin, 1985.

Gardner, H. (1985). *The mind's new science: A history of the cognitive revolution*. New York: Basic Books.

Gardner, H. (1993). *Creating minds: An anatomy of creativity seen through the lives of Freud, Einstein, Picasso, Stravinsky, Eliot, Graham, and Gandhi.* New York: Basic Books.

Garland, A. (Writer and Director). (2015). *Ex machina* (film). USA.

Gay, P. (1988). *Freud: A life for our time.* London: Dent.

Geertz, C. (1989). *Biographical Memoirs: Margaret Mead 1901–1978* (pp. 329–354). Washington, DC: National Academy of Science.

George, C., Kaplan, N., & Main, M. (1985). The Berkeley Adult Attachment Interview. *Unpublished protocol.* Department of Psychology, University of California, Berkeley.

Gibson, E. J., & Walk, R. D. (1960). The visual cliff. *Scientific American, 202* (April).

Gibson, J. J. (1950). *The perception of the visual world.* Boston: Houghton Mifflin.

Gillham, N. W. (2001). Sir Francis Galton and the birth of eugenics. *Annual Review of Genetics, 35,* 83–101.

Glannon, W. (2015). Free will in light of neuroscience. In W. Glannon (Ed.), *Free will and the brain: Neuroscientific, philosophical and legal perspectives* (pp. 3–23). Cambridge: Cambridge University Press.

Gloaguen, V., Cottraux, J., Cucherat, M., & Blackburn, I. (1998). A meta-analysis of the effects of cognitive therapy in depressed patients. *Journal of Affective Disorders, 49,* 59–72.

Goffman, E. (1961). Fun in games. In *Encounters: Two studies in the sociology of interaction* (pp. 15–81). Indianapolis, IN: Bobbs-Merrill.

Goldberg, S., Grusec, J. E., & Jenkins, J. M. (1999). Confidence in protection: Arguments for a narrow definition of attachment. *Journal of Family Psychology, 13,* 475–483.

Goldsmith, B. (2005). *Obsessive genius: The inner world of Marie Curie.* New York: Norton.

Goodall, J. (1986). *The chimpanzees of Gombe: Patterns of behavior.* Cambridge, MA: Harvard University Press.

Gotink, R. A., Meijboom, R., Vernooij, M. W., Smits, M., et al. (2016). 8-week mindfulness based stress reduction induces brain changes similar to traditional long-term meditation practice—A systematic review. *Brain and Cognition, 108,* 32–41.

Gottman, J. (1993). *Why marriages succeed or fail.* New York: Simon & Schuster.

Gouin, J.-P., Glaser, R., Malarkey, W. B., Beversdorf, D., & Kiecolt-Glaser, J. (2012). Chronic stress, daily stressors, and circulating inflammatory markers. *Health Psychology, 31,* 264–268.

Gould, S. J. (1994). Curveball. *New Yorker,* November 28.

Grazzani-Gavazzi, I., & Oatley, K. (1999). The experience of emotions of interdependence and independence following interpersonal errors in Italy and Anglophone Canada. *Cognition and Emotion, 13,* 49–63.

Green, R. E., et al. (2010). A draft sequence of the Neanderthal genome. *Science, 328,* 710–722.

Greene, G. (2005). *The third man* and *The fallen idol.* London: Vintage.

Gregory, R. L. (1997). *Eye and brain: The psychology of seeing, fifth edition.* Princeton, NJ: Princeton University Press.

Gribbin, J., & Cherfas, J. (2001). *The first chimpanzee: In search of human origins.* London: Penguin.

Grice, H. P. (1975). Logic and conversation. In P. Cole & J. L. Morgan (Eds.), *Syntax and semantics, 3. Speech acts.* New York: Academic Press.

Gruber, H. E., & Barrett, P. H. (1974). *Darwin on man: A psychological study of scientific creativity, together with Darwin's early and unpublished notebooks.* New York: Dutton.

Grünbaum, A. (2006). Is Sigmund Freud's psychoanalytic edifice relevant to the 21st century? *Psychoanalytic Psychology, 23,* 257–284.

Gu, J., Strauss, C., Bond, R., & Cavanagh, K. (2015). How do mindfulness-based cognitive therapy and mindfulness-based stress reduction improve mental health and wellbeing? A systematic review and meta-analysis of mediation studies. *Clinical Psychology Review, 37,* 1–12.

Hafiz. (circa 1380). "With that moon language" (D. Ladinsky, Trans.) *The gift: Poems by Hafiz, The great Sufi master* (p. 322). Harmondsworth: Penguin (current edition, 1999).

Haidt, J. (2001). The emotional dog and its rational tail: A social intuitionist approach to moral judgment. *Psychological Review, 108,* 814–834.

Haidt, J. (2007). The new synthesis in moral psychology. *Science, 316,* 998–1002.

Hall, G. S. (1912). Hermann L. F. von Helmholtz, in *Founders of modern psychology* (pp. 247–310). New York: Appleton.

Hamann, K., Warneken, F., & Tomasello, M. (2012). Children's developing commitments to joint goals. *Child Development, 83,* 137–145.

Hamilton, C. E. (2000). Continuity and discontinuity of attachment from infancy through adolescence. *Child Development, 71,* 690–694.

Haney, C., Banks, C., & Zimbardo, P. (1973). Interpersonal dynamics in a simulated prison. *International Journal of Criminology and Penology, 1,* 69–97.

Harlow, J. M. (1868). Recovery from the passage of an iron bar through the head. Reprinted in *History of Psychiatry* (1993), 4, 274–281.

Harris, P. L. (2000). *The work of the imagination.* Oxford: Blackwell.

Hartley, D. (1749). *Observations on man, his frame, his duty, and his expectations.* London: Hitch and Austen.

Haslam, S. A., Reicher, S. D., & Birney, M. E. (2016). Questioning authority: New perspectives on Milgram's "obedience" research and its implications for intergroup relations. *Current Opinion in Psychology, 11,* 6–9.

Hassabis, D., Spreng, R. N., Rusu, A. A., Robbins, C. A., Mar, R. A., & Schachter, D. L. (2014). Imagine all the people: How the brain creates and uses personality models to predict behavior. *Cerebral Cortex, 24,* 1979–1987.

Hatfield, E., & Rapson, R. (2006). Passionate love, sexual desire, and mate selection: Cross-cultural and historical perspectives. In P. Noller & J. C. Feeney (Eds.), *Close relationships: Functions, forms, and processes* (pp. 227–243). Hove: Psychology Press.

Havelock, E. A. (1978). *The Greek concept of justice: From its shadow in Homer to its substance in Plato.* Cambridge, MA: Harvard University Press.

Hawking, S. (2014). The development of full artificial intelligence could spell the end of the human race. BBC television show. http://www.bbc.com/news/technology-30290540james.

Hazan, C., & Shaver, P. (1987). Romantic love conceptualized as an attachment process. *Journal of Personality and Social Psychology, 52,* 511–524.

Hebb, D. O. (1949). *The organization of behavior: A neuropsychological theory.* New York: Wiley.

Helmholtz, H. v. (1866). *Treatise on physiological optics, Vol. 3* (J.P.C. Southall, Trans.). New York: Dover (current publication 1962).

Herculano-Houzel, S. (2016). *The human advantage: A new understanding of how the brain became remarkable.* Cambridge, MA: MIT Press.

Herrmann, E., Call, J., Hernandez-Lloreda, M. V., Hare, B., & Tomasello, M. (2007). Humans have evolved specialized skills of social cognition: The cultural intelligence hypothesis. *Science, 317*, 1360–1366.

Herrnstein, R. J., & Murray, C. (1994). *The Bell Curve: Intelligence and class structure in American life*. New York: Free Press.

Hickok, G. (2014). *The myth of mirror neurons: The real neuroscience of communication and cognition*. New York: Norton.

Hinton, G. E. (2007). Learning multiple layers of representation. *Trends in Cognitive Sciences, 11*, 428–434.

Hinton, G. E. (2015). Deep learning godfather says machines learn like toddlers. In A. M. Tremonti (Interviewer), CBC Radio, *The Current*, May 5.

Hinton, G. E., Krizhevsky, A., & Wang, S. D. (2011). Transforming autoencoders. International Conference on Artificial Neural Networks, Helsinki.

Hitchcock, A. (Director). (1945). *Spellbound* (Film). USA.

Hodges, A. (1983). *Alan Turing: The enigma of intelligence*. London: Unwin.

Hoffman, M. L. (2000). *Empathy and moral development: Implications for caring and justice*. New York: Cambridge University Press.

Holmes, J. (1993). *John Bowlby and attachment theory*. London: Routledge.

Homer. (762 BCE). *The Iliad* (ed. and trans. M. Hammond). Harmondsworth: Penguin (current edition 1987).

Horace. (19 BCE). Ars poetica (The art of poetry) (H. R. Fairclough, Trans.). In H. R. Fairclough (Ed.), *Horace: Satires, Epistles and Ars Poetica*. London: Heineman (current edition 1932).

Horney, K. (1942). *Self-analysis*. New York: Norton.

Hsu, F.-H. (2002). *Behind Deep Blue: Building the computer that defeated the world chess champion*. Princeton, NJ: Princeton University Press.

Hubel, D. H., & Wiesel, T. N. (1962). Receptive fields, binocular interaction and functional architecture in the cat's visual cortex. *Journal of Physiology, 160*, 106–154.

Huber, D., Henrich, G., Clarkin, J., & Klug, G. (2013). Psychoanalytic versus psychodynamic therapy for depression: A three-year follow-up study. *Psychiatry: Interpersonal and Biological Processes, 76*, 132–149.

Huber, D., Henrich, G., & Klug, G. (2013). Moderators of change in psychoanalytic, psychodynamic, and cognitive-behavioral therapy. *Journal the American Psychoanalytic Association, 61*, 585–589.

Hublin, J.-J., Ben-Ncer, A., Bailey, S. E., Freidline, S. E., et al. (2017). New fossils from Jebel Irhoud, Morocco and the pan-African origin of Homo sapiens. *Nature, 546*, 289–292.

Huizinga, J. (1955). *Homo Ludens: A study of the play-element in culture*. Boston: Beacon.

Hunt, L. (2007). *Inventing human rights*. New York: Norton.

Hunt, M. (2007). *The story of psychology*. New York: Anchor.

Huxley, A. (1932). *Brave new world*. London: Chatto & Windus.

Ibbotson, P., & Tomasello, M. (2016). Language in a new key. *Scientific American*, 71–75.

Jacobs, J. (1992). *Systems of survival: A dialogue on the moral foundations of commerce and politics*. New York: Random House.

Jahoda, M., Lazarsfeld, P. F., & Zeisel, H. (1971). *Marienthal: The sociography of an unemployed community*. Chicago: Aldine.

James, H. (1884). The art of fiction. *Longman's Magazine, September*, Reprinted in *The Portable Henry James* (1951) (Ed. M. D. Zabel). New York: Viking (pp. 1391–1418).

James, W. (1884). What is an emotion? *Mind, 9*, 188–205.

James, W. (1907). The energies of men. *Science, 25*, 321–332.

Jankowiak, W. R., & Fischer, E. F. (1992). A cross-cultural perspective on romantic love. *Ethnology, 31*, 149–155.

Jastrow, J. (1900). *Fact and fable in psychology*. New York: Houghton, Mifflin.

Jaynes, J. (1976). *The origin of consciousness in the breakdown of the bicameral mind*. London: Allen Lane.

Jenkins, J. M., & Astington, J. W. (2000). Theory of mind and social behavior: Causal models tested in a longitudinal study. *Merrill-Palmer Quarterly, 46*, 203–220.

Jenkins, J. M., McGowan, P., & Knafo-Noam, A. (2016). Parent-offspring transaction: Mechanisms and the value of within family designs. *Hormones and Behavior, 77*, 53–61.

Johnson-Laird, P. N. (1983). *Mental models: Towards a cognitive science of language, inference, and consciousness*. Cambridge: Cambridge University Press.

Johnson-Laird, P. N. (2006). *How we reason.* Oxford: Oxford University Press.

Jung, C. G. (1959). *The archetypes and the collective unconscious* (R.F.C. Hull, Trans.). London: Routledge & Kegan Paul.

Kahneman, D. (2011). *Thinking fast and slow.* Toronto: Doubleday Canada.

Kalakoski, V., & Saariluoma, P. (2001). Taxi drivers' exceptional memory of street names. *Memory and Cognition, 29,* 634–638.

Kamin, L. (1974). *The science and politics of IQ.* Potomac, MD: Erlbaum.

Kandel, E. R. (2012). *The age of insight: The quest to understand the unconscious in art, mind, and brain, from Vienna 1900 to the present.* New York: Random House.

Karg, K., Burmeister, M., Shedden, K., & Sen, S. (2011). The serotonin transporter promoter variant (5-HTTLPR), stress, and depression meta-analysis revisited: Evidence of genetic moderation. *Archives of General Psychiatry, 68,* 444–454.

Kawabata, H., & Zeki, S. (2004). Neural correlates of beauty. *Journal of Neurophysiology, 91,* 1699–1705.

Keats, J. (1816–20). "Ode on a Grecian urn," in *Selected poems and letters of Keats* (Ed. D. Bush). New York: Houghton Mifflin (current edition 1959), pp. 207–208.

Keith, J. M. (1988). Florence Nightingale: Statistician and consultant epidemiologist. *International Nursing Review, 35,* 147–150.

Kenny, D. A., Mohr, C. D., & Levesque, M. J. (2001). A social relations variance partitioning of dyadic behavior. *Psychological Bulletin, 127,* 128–141.

Kidd, D. C., & Castano, E. (2013). Reading literary fiction improves theory of mind. *Science, 342,* 377–380.

Kiecolt-Glaser, J. K. (2009). Psychoneuroimmunology: Psychology's gateway to the biomedical future. *Perspectives on Psychological Science, 4,* 367–369.

Kierkegaard, S. (1846). *Concluding unscientific postscript* (D. F. Swenson & W. Lowrie, Trans.). Princeton, NJ: Princeton University Press (current edition 1968).

King, L. A., Heintzelman, S. J., & Ward, S. J. (2016). Beyond the search for meaning: A contemporary science of the experience of meaning in life. *Current Directions in Psychological Science, 25,* 211–216.

Kirsch, I. (2009a). Antidepressants and the placebo response. *Epidemiology and Psychiatric Sciences, 18,* 318–322.

Kirsch, I. (2009b). *The emperor's new drugs: Exploding the antidepressant myth.* London: Bodley Head.

Klein, M. (1975). *Narrative of a child analysis: The conduct of the psychoanalysis of children as seen in the treatment of a ten-year-old boy.* London: Hogarth Press.

Koenigsberger, L. (1906). *Hermann von Helmholtz* (F. A. Welby, Trans.). Oxford: Clarendon Press.

Koestler, A. (1964). *The act of creation.* London: Hutchinson.

Kok, B. E., & Singer, T. (2016). Phenomenological fingerprints of four meditations: Differential state changes in affect, mind-wandering, meta-cognition, and interoception before and after daily practice across 9 months of training. *Mindfulness.* doi: http://dx.doi.org/10.1007/s12671-016-0594-9.

Kragel, P. A., & LaBar, K. S. (2016). Decoding the nature of emotion in the brain. *Trends in Cognitive Sciences, 20,* 444–455.

Kramer, P. D. (1993). *Listening to Prozac.* New York: Viking.

Kramer, P. D. (2016). *Ordinarily well: The case for antidepressants.* New York: Farrar, Strauss & Giroux.

Krebbs, A. (2011). The phenomenology of shared feeling. *Appraisal, 3,* 35–50.

Kreitman, N., Sainsbury, P., Morrissey, J., Towers, J., & Scrivener, J. (1961). The reliability of psychiatric assessment: An analysis. *British Journal of Psychiatry, 107,* 887–908.

Kristoff, N. (2016). Would you hide a Jew from the Nazis? *New York Times,* Sunday Review, p. 11.

Küfner, A.C.P., Back, M. D., Nestler, S., & Egloff, B. (2010). Tell me a story and I will tell you who you are! Lens model analyses of personality and creative writing. *Journal of Research in Personality, 44,* 427–435.

Ladinsky, D. (1999). *The gift: Poems by Hafiz, the great Sufi master.* Harmondsworth: Penguin.

Laing, R. D. (1960). *The divided self.* London: Tavistock (and Pelican paperback).

Larochelle, H., & Hinton, G. E. (2010). *Learning to combine foveal glimpses with a third-order Boltzmann machine.* Advances in Neural Information Processing, 23. Cambridge, MA: MIT Press.

Larocque, L., & Oatley, K. (2006). Joint plans, emotions, and relationships: A diary study of errors. *Journal of Cultural and Evolutionary Psychology, 3–4,* 246–265.

Lazarus, E. (1888). *The poems of Emma Lazarus.* New York: Houghton Mifflin.

Lazarus, E. (1903). "The new colossus." Liberty State Park, New York Harbor.

Leakey, R. E., & Lewin, R. (1991). *Origins.* London: Penguin.

LeCun, Y., Bengio, Y., & Hinton, G. E. (2015). Deep learning. *Nature, 521,* 436–444.

Lee, K. (2016). Nuralogix: Revealing what lies beneath. From http://www.nuralogix.com/home.html.

Leichsenring, F., & Rabung, S. (2008). Effectiveness of long-term psychodynamic psychotherapy. *Journal of the American Medical Association, 300,* 1551–1565.

Leichsenring, F., & Rabung, S. (2011). Long-term psychodynamic psychotherapy in complex mental disorders: Update of a meta-analysis. *British Journal of Psychiatry, 199,* 15–22.

Leslie, A. M. (1987). Pretence and representation: The origins of "theory of mind." *Psychological Review, 94,* 412–426.

Lewinski, P., den Uyl, T. M., & Butler, C. (2014). Automated facial coding: Validation of basic emotions and FACS AUs in FaceReader. *Journal of Neuroscience, Psychology, and Economics, 7,* 227–236.

Lewis, M. (2016). *The undoing project: A friendship that changed our minds.* New York: Norton.

Lewis-Kraus, G. (2016, December 18). Going neural. *New York Times Magazine,* 40–65.

Libet, B. (1985). Unconscious cerebral initiative and the role of conscious will in voluntary action. *Behavioral and Brain Sciences, 8,* 529–566.

Loftus, E. F., & Doyle, J. M. (1987). *Eyewitness testimony: Civil and criminal.* New York: Kluwer.

Lord, A. B. (2000). *The singer of tales.* Cambridge, MA: Harvard University Press.

Lorenz, K. (1937). Über die Bildung des Instinktbegriffes. *Die Naturwissenschaften, 25,* 289–331. (The conception of instinctive behavior. Translation in C. Schiller, Ed. & trans., *Instinctive behavior: Development of a modern concept.* London: Methuen, pp. 129–175.)

Lovejoy, C. O. (1981). The origin of man. *Science, 211,* 341–350.

Luria, A. R. (1976). *Cognitive development: Its cultural and social foundations.* Cambridge, MA: Harvard University Press.

Lutz, C. A. (1988). *Unnatural emotions: Everyday sentiments on a Micronesian atoll and their challenge to Western theory.* Chicago: University of Chicago Press.

MacFarquhar, L. (2003, March 31). The devil's accountant. *New Yorker, 79,* p. 64.

MacLean, P. D. (1993). Cerebral evolution of emotion. In M. Lewis & J. M. Haviland (Eds.), *Handbook of Emotions* (pp. 67–83). New York: Guilford.

Macmillan, M. (2001). John Martyn Harlow: "Obscure country physician?" *Journal of the History of the Neurosciences, 10,* 149–162.

Macnamara, B. N., Hambrick, D. N., & Moreau, D. (2016). How important is deliberate practice? Reply to Ericsson (2016). *Perspectives on Psychological Science, 11,* 355–358.

Macnamara, B. N., Moreau, D., & Hambrick, D. Z. (2016). The relationship between deliberate practice and performance in sports: A meta-analysis. *Perspectives on Psychological Science, 11,* 333–350.

Magai, C., & Haviland-Jones, J. (2002). *The hidden genius of emotion: Lifespan transformations of personality.* New York: Cambridge University Press.

Maguire, E. A., Spiers, H., Good, C. D., & al. (2003). Navigation expertise and the human hippocampus: A structural brain imaging analysis. *Hippocampus, 13,* 250–259.

Main, M. (1991). Metacognitive knowledge, metacognitive monitoring, and singular (coherent) vs. multiple (incoherent) models of attachment: Findings and directions for future research. In P. Marris, J. Stevenson-Hinde & C. Parkes (Eds.), *Attachment across the life cycle* (pp. 127–159). New York: Routledge.

Main, M., Kaplan, N., & Cassidy, J. (1985). Security in infancy, childhood and adulthood: A move to the level of representation. In I. Bretherton & E. Waters (Eds.), *Growing points of attachment theory and research. Monographs of the Society for Research in Child Development, 50* (1–2, Serial No. 209) (pp. 65–106).

Malatesta, C. Z., Culver, C., Tesman, J. R., & Shepard, B. (1989). The development of emotion expression during the first two years of life.

Monographs of the Society for Research in Child Development, 54 (1–2), 1–103.

Malcolm, J. (1982). *Psychoanalysis: The impossible profession.* London: Picador.

Mar, R. A., & Oatley, K. (2008). The function of fiction is the abstraction and simulation of social experience. *Perspectives on Psychological Science, 3,* 173–192.

Mar, R. A., Oatley, K., Hirsh, J., de la Paz, J., & Peterson, J. B. (2006). Bookworms versus nerds: Exposure to fiction versus non-fiction, divergent associations with social ability, and the simulation of fictional social worlds. *Journal of Research in Personality, 40,* 694–712.

Marr, D. (1982). *Vision.* San Francisco: Freeman.

Martinez-Conde, S., Otero-Milian, J., & Macknik, S. L. (2013). The impact of microsaccades on vision: Towards a unified theory of saccadic function. *Nature Reviews: Neuroscience, 14,* 83–96.

Marucha, P. T., Kiecolt-Glaser, J. K., & Favaghi, M. (1998). Mucosal wound healing is impaired by examination stress. *Psychosomatic Medicine, 60,* 362–365.

McCabe, D. P., & Castel, A. D. (2007). Seeing is believing: The effect of brain images on judgments of scientific reasoning. *Cognition, 107,* 342–352.

McCrae, R. R., & John, O. P. (1992). An introduction to the five-factor model and its applications. *Journal of Personality, 60*(2), 175–215.

Mead, M. (1928). *Coming of age in Samoa.* New York: Morrow.

Mellars, P. (2004). Neanderthals and the modern human colonization of Europe. *Nature, 432,* 461–465.

Mellars, P., & French, J. C. (2011). Tenfold population increase in Western Europe at the Neanderthal-to-modern human transition. *Science, 333,* 623–627.

Meltzoff, A. N., & Moore, M. K. (1977). Imitation of facial and manual gestures by human neonates. *Science, 198,* 75–78.

Mendelson, E. (2016, June 23). In the depths of the digital age. *New York Review of Books, 63,* 34–38.

Mesquita, B., & Frijda, N. H. (2011). An emotion perspective on emotion regulation. *Cognition and Emotion, 25,* 782–784.

Midgley, N. (2007). Anna Freud: The Hampstead War Nurseries and the role of direct observation of children for psychoanalysis. *International Journal of Psychoanalysis, 88,* 939–959.

Milgram, S. (1963). Behavioral study of obedience. *Journal of Abnormal and Social Psychology, 67,* 371–378.

Milgram, S. (1974). *Obedience to authority.* New York: Harper & Row.

Miller, G. A. (1956). The magical number seven, plus or minus two: Some limits on our capacity for processing information. *Psychological Review, 63,* 81–97.

Miller, G. A., Galanter, E., & Pribram, K. H. (1960). *Plans and the structure of behavior.* New York: Holt, Rinehart and Winston.

Mithen, S. (1996). *The prehistory of the mind: The cognitive origins of art and science.* London: Thames and Hudson.

Moore, M., Schermer, J. A., Paunonen, S. V., & Vdernon, P. A. (2010). Genetic and environmental influences on verbal and nonverbal measures of the Big Five. *Personality and Individual Differences, 48,* 884–888.

Moroney, T. A. (2011). The persistent cultural script of judicial dispassion. *California Law Review, 99,* 629–681.

Mumper, M. L., & Gerrig, R. J. (2017). Leisure reading and social cognition. *Psychology of Aesthetics, Creativity and the Arts, 11,* 109–120.

Munafò, M. R., Nosek, B. A., Bishop, D.V.M., Button, K., S., et al. (2017). A manifesto for reproducible science. *Nature Human Behaviour, 1.* doi: 10.1038/s41562-016-0021.

Neff, L. A., & Karney, B. R. (2005). To know you is to love you: The implications of global adoration and specific accuracy for marital relationships. *Journal of Personality and Social Psychology, 88,* 480–497.

Neisser, U. (1976). *Cognition and reality.* San Francisco: Freeman.

Nelson, K. (1989). *Narratives from the crib.* New York: Cambridge University Press.

Nelson, K. (2015). Making sense of private speech. *Cognitive Development, 36,* 171–179.

Nesse, R. (2010). Social selection and the origins of culture. In M. Schaller, A. Norenzayan, S. J. Heine, T. Yamagishi, & T. Kameda (Eds.), *Evolution, culture, and the human mind* (pp. 137–150). New York: Psychology Press.

Nickerson, R. (1999). How we know—and sometimes misjudge—what others know: Imputing one's own knowledge to others. *Psychological Bulletin, 125,* 737–759.

Nishida, T., Hasegawa, T., Hayaki, H. et al. (1992). Meat-sharing as a coalition strategy by an alpha male chimpanzee. In T. Nishida, W. C.

McGrew, P. Marler, et al. (Eds.), *Topics in primatology, Vol. 1. Human origins* (pp. 159–174). Tokyo: University of Tokyo Press.

Northoff, G., Heinzel, A., de Greck, M., Bermpohl, F., Dobrowolny, H., & Panksepp, J. (2006). Self-referential processing in our brain—A meta-analysis of imaging studies on the self. *NeuroImage*, 440–457.

Nussbaum, M. C. (1986). *The fragility of goodness: Luck and ethics in Greek tragedy and philosophy*. Cambridge: Cambridge University Press.

Oatley, K. (1990). Freud's psychology of intention: The case of Dora. *Mind and Language, 5*, 69–86.

Oatley, K. (2001). Shakespeare's invention of theater as simulation that runs on minds. *Empirical Studies of the Arts, 19*, 29–45.

Oatley, K. (2009). Communications to self and others: Emotional experience and its skills. *Emotion Review, 1*, 204–213.

Oatley, K. (2013a). How cues on the screen prompt emotions in the mind. In A. P. Shimamura (Ed.), *Psychocinematics: Exploring cognition at the movies*. New York: Oxford University Press.

Oatley, K. (2013b). Worlds of the possible: Abstraction, imagination, consciousness. *Pragmatics and Cognition, 21*, 448–468. doi: 10.1075/pc.21.3.02oat.

Oatley, K. (2016). Fiction: Simulation of social worlds. *Trends in Cognitive Sciences, 20* (8). doi: org/10.1016/j.tics.2016.06.002.

Oatley, K., & Djikic, M. (2017). The creativity of literary writing. In J. C. Kaufman, J. Baer, & V. Glaveneau (Eds.), *Cambridge handbook of creativity across different domains* (pp. 61–79). Cambridge: Cambridge University Press.

Oatley, K., & Djikic, M. (2017, June 8). Psychology of narrative art. *Review of General Psychology*, doi: http://dx.doi.org/10.1037/gpr0000113.

Oatley, K., & Duncan, E. (1994). The experience of emotions in everyday life. *Cognition and Emotion, 8*, 369–381.

Oatley, K., & Johnson-Laird, P. N. (2011). Basic emotions in social relationships, reasoning, and psychological illnesses. *Emotion Review, 3*, 424–433.

Oatley, K., & Johnson-Laird, P. N. (2014). Cognitive approaches to emotions. *Trends in Cognitive Sciences, 18*, 134–140.

Oatley, K., Sullivan, G. D., & Hogg, D. (1988). Drawing visual conclusions from analogy: A theory of preprocessing, cues and schemata in the perception of three-dimensional objects. *Journal of Intelligent Systems, 1*, 97–133.

Obama, B., & Robinson, M. (2015). President Obama and Marilynne Robinson: A conversation in Iowa. *New York Review of Books, 62*, 6–8.

Ocampo, B., & Kritikos, A. (2011). Interpreting actions: The goal behind mirror neuron function. *Brain Research Reviews, 67*, 260–267.

Olson, D. R. (1994). *The world on paper*. New York: Cambridge University Press.

Ormel, J., Bastiaansen, A., Riese, H., Bos, E. H., Servaas, M., et al. (2013). The biological and psychological basis of neuroticism: Current status and future directions. *Neuroscience and Biobehavioral Reviews, 37*, 59–72.

Orth-Gomer, K., Schneiderman, N., Wang, H. X., Waldin, C., Blom, M., & Jemberg, T. (2009). Stress reduction prolongs life in women with coronary disease: The Stockholm Women's Intervention Trial for Coronary Heart Disease (SWITCHD). *Circulation: Cardiovascular Quality and Outcomes, 2*, 25–32.

Orth-Gomer, K., Wamala, S. P., Horsten, M., et al. (2000). Marital stress worsens prognosis in women with coronary heart disease: The Stockholm Female Coronary Risk Study. *Journal of the American Medical Association, 284*, 3008–3014.

Page, D. (1955). *Sappho and Alcaeus: An introduction to the study of ancient Lesbian poetry*. Oxford: Oxford University Press.

Panero, M. E., Weisberg, D. S., Black, J., Goldstein, et al. (2016). Does reading a single passage of literary fiction really improve theory of mind? An attempt at replication. *Journal of Personality and Social Psychology, 111*(5), e46–e54.

Panksepp, J. (1998). *Affective neuroscience: The foundations of human and animal emotions*. Oxford: Oxford University Press.

Parssinen, T. M. (1974). Popular science and society: The phrenology movement in early Victorian Britain. *Journal of Social History, 8*, 1–20.

Patrick, C. (1935). Creative thought in poets. *Archives of Psychology* (R. Woodworth, ed.), 178, 35–73.

Pavlenko, A. (2005). *Emotions and multilingualism*. New York: Cambridge University Press.

Pavlov, I. P. (1927). *Conditioned reflexes* (G. V. Anrep, Trans.). New York: Reissued by Dover, 1960.

Pavlov I. P.: Nobel biography: http://www.nobelprize.org/nobel_prizes /medicine/laureates/1904/pavlov-bio.html.

Pennebaker, J. W., & Beall, S. K. (1986). Confronting a traumatic event: Towards an understanding of inhibition and disease. *Journal of Abnormal Psychology, 95,* 274–281.

Pennebaker, J. W., Kiecolt-Glaser, J. K., & Glaser, R. (1988). Disclosure of traumas and immune function: Health implications of psychotherapy. *Journal of Consulting and Clinical Psychology, 56,* 239–245.

Pennebaker, J. W., Zech, E., & Rimé, B. (2001). Disclosing and sharing emotion: Psychological, social, and health consequences. In M. S. Stroebe, R. O. Hansson, W. Stroebe, & H. Schut (Eds.), *Handbook of bereavement research: Consequences, coping, and care* (pp. 517–543). Washington, DC: American Psychological Association.

Perkins, D. N. (1981). *The mind's best work.* Cambridge, MA: Harvard University Press.

Perry, G. (2013). *Behind the shock machine: The untold story of the notorious Milgram psychology experiments.* New York: New Press.

Piaget, J., & Inhelder, B. (1969). *The psychology of the child.* London: Routledge and Kegan Paul.

Piccolino, M. (1998). Animal electricity and the birth of electrophysiology: The legacy of Luigi Galvani. *Brain Research Bulletin, 46,* 381–407.

Pickett, K. E., James, O. W., & Wilkinson, R. G. (2006). Income inequality and the prevalence of mental illness: A preliminary international analysis. *Journal of Epidemiology and Community Health, 60,* 646–647.

Pinker, S. (2011). *The better angels of our nature: Why violence has declined.* New York: Viking Penguin.

Plato. (375 BCE). *The republic.* Harmondsworth, Middlesex: Penguin (current edition 1955).

Plato. *Protagoras and Meno* (W.K.C. Guthrie, Trans.). Harmondsworth, Middlesex: Penguin.

Plomin, R., & Spinath, F. M. (2004). Intelligence: Genetics, genes, and genomics. *Journal of Personality and Social Psychology, 86,* 112–129.

Poincaré, H. (1908). Mathematical creation (translation by G. B. Halstead, of *Le raisonnement mathematique*, in *Science et methode*, Paris: Flammarion). In B. Ghiselin (Ed.), *The creative process.* Berkeley: University of California Press (1952).

Popper, K. R. (1945). *The open society and its enemies.* London: Routledge.

Popper, K. R. (1962). *Conjectures and refutations*. New York: Basic Books.

Povinelli, D. J., & O'Neill, D. K. (2000). Do chimpanzees use their gestures to instruct each other? In S. Baron-Cohen, H. Tager-Flusberg, & D. Cohen (Eds.), *Understanding other minds: Perspectives from developmental cognitive neuroscience* (pp. 459–487). Oxford: Oxford University Press.

Powell, B. (2002). *Writing and the origins of Greek literature*. Cambridge: Cambridge University Press.

Praszkier, R. (2016). Empathy, mirror neurons, and SYNC. *Mind and Society, 15*, 1–25.

Preston, S. D. (2013). The origins of altruism in offspring care. *Psychological Bulletin, 139*, 1305–1341.

Preston, S. D., Bechara, A., Damasio, H., et al. (2007). The neural substrates of cognitive empathy. *Social Neuroscience, 2*, 254–275.

Proust, M. (1913–1927). *À la recherche du temps perdu (In search of lost time)*. London: Penguin (Current edition 2003).

Proust, M. (1919). *À l'ombre des jeunes filles en fleur, Part II of À la recherche du temps perdu*. Paris: Gallimard (current edition 1988).

Prunier, G. (1995). *The Rwanda crisis: History of a genocide*. London: Hurst.

Ramón y Cajal, S. (1899). *Comparative study of the sensory areas of the human cortex*. Worcester, MA: Clark University.

Randerson, J. (2012). How many neurons make a human brain? Billions fewer than we thought. *Guardian* newspaper, blog notes & theories, February 28.

Rasbash, J., Jenkins, J. M., O'Connor, T. G., Tackett, J. L., & Reiss, D. (2011). A social relations model of observed family negativity and positivity using a genetically informative sample. *Journal of Personality and Social Psychology, 100*, 474–491.

Rawls, J. (1972). *A theory of justice*. Cambridge, MA: Harvard University Press.

Reed, C. (Director). (1949). *The third man* (Film). UK.

Reicher, S., & Haslam, S. A. (2006). Rethinking the psychology of tyranny: The BBC prison study. *British Journal of Social Psychology, 45*, 1–40.

Reicher, S. D., & Haslam, S. A. (2011). The shock of the old. *Psychologist, 24*, 650–652.

Reid, T. (1818). *Essays on the active powers of man (electronic resource)*. Philadelphia: Nicklin (current electronic edition, Early American Imprints, Series II: Shaw-Shoemaker, 1801–1819).

Richardson, S. (1740). *Pamela*. Oxford: Oxford University Press (current edition 2001).

Rimé, B. (2009). Emotion elicits social sharing of emotion: Theory and empirical review. *Emotion Review, 1,* 60–85.

Rimé, B., Mesquita, B., Philippot, P., & Boca, S. (1991). Beyond the emotional event: Six studies on the social sharing of emotions. *Cognition and Emotion, 5,* 435–465.

Risch, N., Herrell, R., Lehner, T., Liang, K., et al. (2009). Interaction between the serotonin transporter gene (5-HTTLPR), stressful life events, and risk of depression: A meta-analysis. *Journal of the American Medical Association, 310,* 2462–2471.

Rizzolatti, G., Fadiga, L., Gallese, V., & Fogassi, L. (1996). Premotor cortex and the recognition of motor action. *Cognitive Brain Research, 3,* 131–141.

Rizzolatti, G., Fogassi, L., & Gallese, V. (2001). Neurophysiological mechanisms underlying the understanding and imitation of action. *Nature Reviews: Neuroscience, 2,* 661–670.

Roberts, B. W., & Mroczek, D. (2008). Personality trait change in adulthood. *Current Directions in Psychological Science, 17,* 31–35.

Roediger, H. L. (1980). Memory metaphors in cognitive psychology. *Memory and Cognition, 8,* 231–246.

Rosenberg, D., & Bloom, H. (1990). *The book of J.* New York: Grove Weidenfeld.

Rutter, M. (1972). *Maternal deprivation reassessed.* Harmondsworth: Penguin.

Rumelhart, D. E., Hinton, G. E., & Williams, R. J. (1986). Learning representations by back-propagating errors. *Nature, 323,* 533–536.

Sandell, R., Blomberg, J., Lazar, A., Carlsson, J., Broberg, J., & Schubert, J. (2000). Varieties of long-term outcome among patients in psychoanalysis and long-term psychotherapy: A review of findings in the Stockholm Outcome of Psychoanalysis and Psychotherapy Project (STOPPP). *International Journal of Psychoanalysis, 81,* 921–942.

Sato, W., & Yoshikawa, S. (2007). Spontaneous facial mimicry in response to dynamic facial expressions. *Cognition, 104,* 1–18.

Scholz, J., Klein, M. C., Behrens, T. E., & Johansen-Berg, H. (2009). Training induces changes in white-matter architecture. *Nature Neuroscience, 12,* 1370–1371.

Schuster, M., Johnson, M., & Thorat, N. (2016). Zero-shot translation with Google's multilingual neural machine translation system. Retrieved from https://research.googleblog.com/2016/11/zero-shot-translation-with-googles.html.

Scribner, S., & Cole, M. (1981). *The psychology of literacy*. Cambridge, MA: Harvard University Press.

Scull, A. (2015). *Madness in civilization: A cultural history of insanity, from the Bible to Freud, from the madhouse to modern medicine*. Princeton, NJ: Princeton University Press.

Segal, Z. V., Williams, J.M.G., & Teasdale, J. D. (2002). *Mindfulness based cognitive therapy for depression: A new approach to preventing relapse*. New York: Guilford.

Seierstad, Å. (2015). *One of us: The story of Anders Breivic and the massacre in Norway* (S. Death, Trans.). London: Virago.

Selzam, S., Krapohl, E., von Stumm, S., O'Reilly, P. F., et al. (2017). Predicting educational achievement from DNA. *Molecular Psychiatry, 22*, 267–272.

Shakespeare, W. (1623). *Henry V*. In S. Greenblatt (Ed.), *The Norton Shakespeare* (pp. 1454–1523). New York: Norton (current edition 1997).

Shallice, T., & Burgess, P. W. (1991). Deficits in strategy application following frontal lobe damage in man. *Brain, 114*, 727–741.

Shariff, A. F., Greene, J. D., Karremans, J. C., Luguri, J. B., et al. (2014). Free will and punishment: A mechanistic view of human nature reduces retribution. *Psychological Science, 25*, 1563–1570.

Sheeran, P., & Webb, T. L. (2016). The intention-behavior gap. *Social and Personality Psychology Compass, 10*, 503–518.

Shelley, M. (1818). *Frankenstein, or Modern Prometheus*. London: Penguin (current edition 1985).

Sherif, M. (1956). Experiments in group conflict. *Scientific American, 195* (November), 54–58.

Sherif, M., & Sherif, C. W. (1953). *Groups in harmony and in tension*. New York: Harper & Row.

Sherman, N. (1997). *Making a necessity of virtue: Aristotle and Kant on virtue*. Cambridge: Cambridge University Press.

Shostrom, E.L.P. (Producer). (1966). *Three approaches to psychotherapy* (Film). Santa Ana, CA: Psychological Films.

Sibley, C., & Ahlquist, J. E. (1984). The phylogeny of the hominid primates, as indicated by DNA-RNA hybridization. *Journal of Molecular Evolution, 20*, 2–15.

Singer, T. (2015, 24 January). How to build a caring economy. Available online at https://agenda.weforum.org/people/tania-singer/bart.

Singer, T., Seymour, B., O'Doherty, J., Kaube, H., Dolan, R. J., & Frith, C. (2004). Empathy for pain involves the affective but not sensory components of pain. *Science, 303*, 1157–1162.

Skinner, B. F. (1938). *The behavior of organisms: An experimental analysis.* New York: Appleton-Century-Crofts.

Skinner, B. F. (1945). Baby in a box. *Ladies Home Journal* (October), 30–31, 135–136, 138.

Skinner, B. F. (1948). *Walden two.* New York: Macmillan.

Skinner, B.F. (1957). *Verbal behavior.* New York: Appleton-Century-Crofts.

Skinner, B. F. (1976). *Particulars of my life.* London: Cape.

Slater, L. (2004). *Opening Skinner's box: Great psychology experiments of the twentieth century.* New York: Norton.

Smillie, L. D. (2013). Extraversion and reward processing. *Current Directions in Psychological Science, 22*, 167–172.

Smit, Y., Huibers, M.J.H., Ioannidis, J.P.A., van Dyck, R., van Tilberg, W., & Artz, A. (2012). The effectiveness of long-term psychoanalytic psychotherapy: A meta-analysis of randomized controlled trials. *Clinical Psychology Review, 32*, 81–92.

Smith, A. (1759). *The theory of moral sentiments.* Oxford: Oxford University Press (current edition 1976).

Snell, B. (1953). *The discovery of the mind in Greek philosophy and literature.* New York: Dover (current edition 1982).

Snow, J. (1855). *On the mode of communication of cholera, second edition much enlarged.* London: Churchill.

Speer, N. K., Reynolds, J. R., Swallow, K., & Zacks, J. M. (2009). Reading stories activates neural representations of visual and motor experience. *Psychological Science, 20*, 989–999.

Spinoza, B. (1661–1675). *On the improvement of the understanding, The ethics, and Correspondence* (R.H.M. Elwes, Trans.). New York: Dover (current edition 1955).

Sprecher, S., Aron, A., Hatfield, E., et al. (1994). Love: American style, Russian style and Japanese style. *Personal Relationships, 1*, 349–369.

Stanovich, K. E. (2011). *Rationality and the reflective mind.* New York: Oxford University Press.

Starr, G. G. (2015). *Feeling beauty: The neuroscience of aesthetic experience.* Cambridge, MA: MIT Press.

Stern, W. (1914). *The psychological methods of testing intelligence.* Baltimore: Warwick & York.

Stock, B. (2007). *Ethics through literature: Ascetic and aesthetic reading in Western culture.* Lebanon, NH: University Press of New England.

Stock, B. (2016). *The integrated self: Augustine, the Bible, and ancient thought.* Philadelphia: University of Pennsylvania Press.

Stowe, H. B. (1852). *Uncle Tom's cabin or Life among the lowly.* Boston: John P. Jewitt.

Summerfield, J. J., Hassabis, D., & Maguire, E. A. (2010). Differential engagement of brain regions within a "core" network during scene construction. *Neuropsychologia, 48,* 1501–1509.

Szasz, T. S. (1960). The myth of mental illness. *American Psychologist, 15,* 113–118.

Taine, H. (1882). *De l'intelligence, Tome 2.* Paris: Hachette.

Tajfel, H., & Turner, J. C. (2010). An integrative theory of intergroup conflict. In T. Postmes & N. R. Branscombe (Eds.), *Rediscovering social identity* (pp. 173–190). New York: Psychology Press.

Tavris, C. (2013, 6 September). Book review: "Behind the shock machine," by Gina Perry. *Wall Street Journal.*

Taylor, C. (2016). *The language animal: The full shape of the human linguistic capacity.* Cambridge, MA: Harvard University Press.

Terman, L. M., & Merrill, M. A. (1937). *Measuring intelligence: A guide to the administration of the new revised Stanford-Binet tests of intelligence.* Boston: Houghton Mifflin.

Thomas, E. M. (1989). *The harmless people (revised edition).* New York: Random House.

Todes, D. P. (2014). *Ivan Pavlov: A Russian life in science.* New York: Oxford University Press.

Tolstoy, L. (1877). *Anna Karenina* (R. Pevear & L. Volokonsky, Trans.). London: Penguin (Translation, 2000).

Tomasello, M. (2008). *Origins of human communication.* Cambridge, MA: MIT Press.

Tomasello, M. (2011). Human culture in evolutionary perspective. In M. Gelfand, C. Chiu, & Y. Hong (Eds.), *Advances in Culture and Psychology* (Vol. 1, pp. 5–51). New York: Oxford University Press.

Tomasello, M. (2014). *A natural history of human thinking.* Cambridge MA: Harvard University Press.

Tomasello, M. (2016). *A natural history of human morality.* Cambridge, MA: Harvard University Press.

Tomasello, M., & Rakoczy, H. (2003). What makes human cognition unique? From individual to shared to collective intentionality. *Mind and Language, 18,* 121–147.

Tomkins, S. S. (1962,1963). *Affect, imagery, consciousness: Vol. 1. The positive affect; Vol. 2. The negative affects.* New York: Springer.

Turing, A. (1936). On computable numbers with an application to the *Entscheidungsproblem. Proceedings of the London Mathematical Society, Second series, 42,* 230–265.

Turing, A. (1950). Computing machinery and intelligence. *Mind, 59,* 433–460.

Turnbull, C. M. (1973). *The mountain people.* London: Jonathan Cape.

Tyldum, M. (Director). (2014). *The imitation game.* Film: USA & UK.

Ullén, F., Hambrick, D. Z., & Mosing, M. A. (2016). Rethinking expertise: A multifactorial gene-environment interaction model of expert performance. *Psychological Bulletin, 142,* 427–446.

van Bavel, J. (2016, May 27). Why do so many studies fail to replicate? *New York Times,* Sunday Review Section.

van Kleef, G. A. (2016). *The interpersonal dynamics of emotion: Towards an integrative theory of emotions as social information.* Cambridge: Cambridge University Press.

van Niel, C., Pachter, L. M., Wade, R., Felitti, V. J., & Stein, M. (2014). Adverse events in children: Predictors of adult physical and mental conditions. *Journal of Developmental and Behavioral Pediatrics, 35,* 549–551.

van Wyhe, J. (2004). *Phrenology and the origins of Victorian scientific naturalism.* Farnham: Ashgate.

Vanhaeren, M., d'Errico, F., Stronger, C., James, S. L., Todd, J. A., & Mienis, H. K. (2006). Middle paleolithic shell beads in Israel and Algeria. *Science, 312,* 1785.

Vessel, E. A., Starr, G. G., & Rubin, N. (2013). Art reaches within: Aesthetic experience, the self and the default mode network. *Frontiers in Neuroscience, 7,* 258. doi: org/10.3389/fnins.2013.00258.

Vittersø, J. (Ed.). (2016). *Handbook of eudaimonic well-being.* New York: Springer.

Vygotsky, L. S. (1930). Tool and symbol in child development. In M. Cole, V. John-Steiner, S. Scribner, & E. Souberman (Eds.), *Mind in society: The development of higher mental processes* (pp. 19–30). Cambridge, MA: Harvard University Press (1978).

Waldinger, R. J., & Schulz, M. S. (2016). The long reach of nurturing family environments: Links with midlife emotion-regulatory styles and late-life security in intimate relationships. *Psychological Science.* doi: 10.1177/0956797616661556.

Wallas, G. (1926). *The art of thought.* London: Cape.

Warneken, F., & Tomasello, M. (2009). Varieties of altruism in children and chimpanzees. *Trends in Cognitive Sciences, 13,* 397–402.

Waters, E., Hamilton, C. E., & Weinfield, N. S. (2000). The stability of attachment-security from infancy to adolescence and early adulthood: General introduction. *Child Development, 71,* 678–683.

Waters, E., Merrick, S., Treboux, D., Crowell, J., & Albersheim, L. (2000). Attachment security in infancy and early adulthood: A twenty-year longitudinal study. *Child Development, 71,* 684–689.

Watson, J. B. (1913). Psychology as the behaviorist views it. *Psychological Review, 20,* 158–178.

Watson, J. B. (1925). *Behaviorism.* New York: Norton.

Webb, T. L., & Sheeran, P. (2006). Does changing behavioral intentions engender behavior change? A meta-analysis of the experimental evidence. *Psychological Bulletin, 132,* 249–268.

Weinfield, N. S., Sroufe, A., & Egeland, B. (2000). Attachment from infancy to early adulthood in a high risk sample: Continuity, discontinuity, and their correlates. *Child Development, 71,* 695–702.

Weisfeld, G. E. (1980). Social dominance and human motivation. In D. R. Omark, F. F. Strayer, & D. G. Freedman (Eds.), *Dominance relations: An ethological view of human conflict and social interaction* (pp. 273–286). New York: Garland.

White, T. D., Asfaw, B., Beyene, Y., Haile-Selassie, Y., et al. (2009). Ardipithecus ramidus and the paleobiology of early hominids. *Science, 326,* 75–86.

Whitehead, A. N. (1979). *Process and reality.* New York: Free Press.

Williams, M. (1922). *The velveteen rabbit.* New York: Avon.

Williamson, M. (1995). *Sappho's immortal daughters.* Cambridge, MA: Harvard University Press.

Wilson, R. A., & Keil, F. C. (Eds.). (1999). *The MIT Encyclopedia of the cognitive sciences.* Cambridge, MA: MIT Press.

Wimmer, H., & Perner, J. (1983). Beliefs about beliefs: Representation and constraining function of wrong beliefs in young children's understanding of deception. *Cognition, 13,* 103–128.

Winnicott, D. (1953). Transitional objects and transitional phenomena; A study of the first "not-me" possession. *International Journal of Psychoanalysis, 34,* 89–97.

Winnicott, D. W. (1965). Ego distortion in terms of true and false self. In J. D. Sutherland (Ed.), *D. W. Winnicott: The maturational process and the facilitating environment: Studies in the theory of emotional development* (pp. 140–152). London: Hogarth Press.

Winnicott, D. W. (1971). *Playing and reality.* London: Tavistock.

Winograd, T. (1983). *Language as a cognitive process: Volume 1: Syntax.* Reading, MA: Addison-Wesley.

Wittgenstein, L. (1922). *Tractatus logico-philosophicus.* London: Routledge & Kegan-Paul.

Wolf, T. H. (1969). The emergence of Binet's conception and measurement of intelligence: A case history of the creative process. *Journal of the History of the Behavioral Sciences, 5,* 113–134.

Wolfe, T. (1975). The new journalism. In T. Wolfe & E. W. Johnson (Eds.), *The new journalism* (pp. 13–68). London: Picador.

Wolfe, T. (2016). *The kingdom of speech.* New York: Little Brown.

Wollstonecraft, M. (1792). *A vindication of the rights of women.* London: Dent, Everyman (current edition 1965).

Woolf, V. (1924). Mr Bennett and Mrs Brown *Collected essays. Vol. 1* (pp. 319–337). London: Chatto and Windus (this edition, 1966).

Yarmolinsky, A. (Ed.). (1973). *Letters of Anton Chekhov.* New York: Viking.

Yong, E. (2012, October 3). Nobel laureate challenges psychologists to clean up their act. *Nature News.*

Yoo, J. J., Hinds, O., Ofen, N., Thompson, T. W., et al. (2012). When the brain is prepared to learn: Enhancing human learning using real-time fMRI. *NeuroImage, 59,* 846–852.

Yudkin, D., Rothmund, T., Twardawski, M., Thalla, N., & Van Bavel, J. (2016). Reflexive intergroup bias in third-party punishment. *Journal of Experimental Psychology: General, 145,* 1448–1459.

Zanette, S., Gao, X., Brunet, M., Bartlett, M. S., & Lee, K. (2016). Automated decoding of facial expressions reveals marked differences in children when telling antisocial versus prosocial lies. *Journal of Experimental Child Psychology, 150,* 165–179.

Zangwill, O. L. (1980). Kenneth Craik: The man and his work. *British Journal of Psychology, 71,* 1–16.

Zayas, V., Mischel, W., Shoda, Y., & Aber, J. L. (2011). Roots of adult attachment: Maternal caregiving at 18 months predicts adult peer and partner attachment. *Social Psychological Personality Science, 2,* 289–297.

Zeldin, T. (1998). *Conversation.* London: Harvill Press.

Zeman, A., Milton, F., Smith, A., & Rylance, R. (2013). By heart: An fMRI study of brain activation by poetry and prose. *Journal of Consciousness Studies, 20,* 132–158.

Zillmann, D. (1996). The psychology of suspense in dramatic exposition. In P. Vorderer, H. J. Wulff, & M. Friedrichsen (Eds.), *Suspense: Conceptualizations, theoretical analyses, and empirical explorations* (pp. 199–231). Mahwah, NJ: Erlbaum.

Zimbardo, P. G. (2007). *The Lucifer effect: Understanding how good people turn evil.* New York: Random House.

NAME INDEX

Acevedo, Bianca, 157
Ainsworth, Mary, 201, 204–207
Alquist, Jon E., 302n10
Angell, Marcia, 140–141
Arbib, Michael A., 302n8
Arendt, Hannah, 254
Aristotle, 232, 290–291
Arnold, N. A., et al., 294n23
Asimov, Isaac, 118
Astington, Janet, 99–100
Auden, W. H., 7
Auerbach, Erich, 239
Augustine, 278
Azevedo, Frederico Augusto Casarsa
  de, 295n1

Bacon, Francis, 118
Banks, Curtis, 255
Barnes, Jennifer L., 306n37
Baron-Cohen, Simon, et al., 293n1
Barrett, Lisa, 46
Barrett, Paul H., 295n2, 302n1
Bartels, Andreas, 156–158
Barthes, Roland, 245
Bartlett, Frederic, 89, 90–95, 111, 214
Bartlett, Marian Stewart, 296n12
Bauer, Ida ("Dora"), 7–10, 148
Baum, Samuel, 296n14
Baumeister, Roy, 275, 282–283
Beall, Sandra, 150–51
Beckes, Lane, 170
Bergman Blix, Stina, 302n9

Bergson, Henri, 231
Bernays, Martha, 7
Binet, Alfred, 53–55, 56, 58–59, 126, 263
Bjork, Daniel W., 297n7
Black, Jessica E., 306n37
Blass, Thomas, 306n1
Blehar, Mary, 205
Bloom, Harold, 305n15
Bloom, Paul, 301n7
Boakes, Robert, 297n2
Boal, Augusto, 251
Boas, Franz, 91, 214–215
Boesch, Christophe, et al., 302n6
Boring, Edwin, 299n2
Bormann, Daniel, 306n37
Bowlby, John, 201, 202–206, 295n1
Bowler, James M., et al., 305n12
Bowman-Kruhm, Mary, 304n3
Brannigan, Augustine, 255
Bretherton, Inge, 303n7
Briggs, Jean, 213, 224
Brown, George, 138, 142–143
Browne, Dillon, 194
Browning, Christopher, 247, 256–
  257, 258, 306n7
Bryceson, Derek, 177
Buccino, Giovanni, 166–168
Buchanan, Tony W., 295
Burger, Jerry, 251
Burgess, Paul, 32
Burlingham, Dorothy Tiffany, 202,
  204, 303n2

SUBJECT INDEX

IMAGE CREDITS

Image credits for numbered images appear in captions; credits for unnumbered images are listed here.

Prologue: Photo by Keith Oatley.

Chapter 1: Photo by Keith Oatley.

Chapter 2: Santiago Ramón y Cajal, Microglia in the grey matter of the cerebral cortex, 1920; Chinese ink and graphite on paper; 69-5/16 x 6 5/32 in. http://wvasfm.org/post/life-and-art-unite-architectures-life. Courtesy of the Cajal Institute: "Cajal Legacy," Spanish National Research Council (or, CSIC), Madrid, Spain.

Chapter 3: Richmond, G. (1809–1896). Charles Darwin: Watercolor. https://commons.wikimedia.org/wiki/File:Charles_Darwin_by_G._Richmond.png.

Chapter 4: Wallace Wallin, J. A. (1911). A practical guide for administering the Binet-Simon Scale for measuring Intelligence. *Psychological Clinic*, 5 (1); https://commons.wikimedia.org/wiki/File:SimonBinet_Ugly_Face_Item_from_1911_journal.png.

Chapter 5: Pavlov Museum, Ryazan, Russia.Rklawton. CC-BY-SA-3.0 (http://creativecommons.org/licenses/by-sa/3.0/), via Wikimedia Commons.

Chapter 6: Nationaal Archief. Author: Hans Peters / Anefo; https://commons.wikimedia.org/wiki/File:Noam_Chomsky_(1977).jpg.

Chapter 7: Image by Jan van der Watering, front cover of Bartlett, F. C. (1932). *Remembering: A Study in Experimental and Social Psychology*. Cambridge: Cambridge University Press, 1967.

Chapter 8: Pilot ACE (Science Museum, London): WikiMedia Commons; https://commons.wikimedia.org/wiki/File:Pilot_ACE3.jpg Creative Commons Attribution-Share Alike 3.0 Unported license https://creativecommons.org/licenses/by-sa/3.0/deed.en.

Chapter 9: *People's Cyclopedia of Universal Knowledge* (1883), from https://commons.wikimedia.org/wiki/File:PhrenologyPix.jpg.

Chapter 10: Photo by Keith Oatley.

Chapter 11: Shutterstock: Stock photo ID: 588977807 © DedMityay/Shutterstock.com.

Chapter 12: Btarski, English Wikipedia, permission CC BY-SA; https://commons .wikimedia.org/wiki/File:Sensory_Homunculus.png.

Chapter 13: Creative Commons (CC Attribution 2.5, from Wikipedia Commons). Common chimpanzee in the Leipzig Zoo, Thomas Lersch, August 17, 2005. https://commons.wikimedia.org/wiki/File:Chimpanzee -Head.jpg.

Chapter 14: Photo by Keith Oatley.

Chapter 15: Front cover of *Child Care and the Growth of Love* by John Bowlby (Penguin Books, 1953). Copyright © Penguin Books Ltd, 1953.

Chapter 16: Smithsonian Institute via Flickr Commons; https://flic.kr/p/buYDDt Acc. 90–105; Science Service, Records, 1920s–1970s, Smithsonian Institution Archives.

Chapter 17: Susan Beattie, with permission.

Chapter 18: Photo by Isabelle Adam, Ontario Science Centre; https://www .flickr.com/photos/diamondgeyser/5727759849/in/photolist-9J9gsa, Creative Commons CC BY-NC-ND2.0.

Chapter 19: https://en.wikipedia.org/wiki/Royal_Pavilion#/media/File:Brighton _royal_pavilion_Qmin.jpg.

Chapter 20: Red-figure water vase with seated female figure with book roll, and three female figures. British Museum Number 1885,1213.18. © The Trustees of the British Museum. All rights reserved.

Epilogue: Photo by Keith Oatley.